W9-BSJ-338

Stranger at

SIMON & SCHUSTER

New York
London
Toronto
Sydney
Tokyo
Singapore ←--

the *Gate*

To be
Gay and
Christian
in
America

Mel White

SIMON & SCHUSTER
Rockefeller Center
1230 Avenue of the Americas
New York, New York 10020

Copyright © 1994 by Mel White

All rights reserved, including the right to reproduce this book or portions thereof in
any form whatsoever.

SIMON & SCHUSTER and colophon are registered trademarks of
Simon & Schuster Inc.

Designed by Hyun Joo Kim

Manufactured in the United States of America

1   3   5   7   9   10   8   6   4   2

Library of Congress Cataloging-in-Publication Data is available.

ISBN 0-671-88407-7

Contents

FOREWORD   5

CHAPTER ONE:
   In the Beginning—The Ghost of Silence   11

CHAPTER TWO:
   Adolescence—The Ghost of Fear   28

CHAPTER THREE:
   High School—The Ghost of Loneliness   45

CHAPTER FOUR:
   College—The Ghost of False Hope   63

CHAPTER FIVE:
1962–64, Learning to Tell the Truth   85

CHAPTER SIX:
1964–70, Learning About Friendship   100

CHAPTER SEVEN:
*1970–80, Taking the First Steps
Toward Integrity*   121

CHAPTER EIGHT:
1980–81, Facing Reality   141

CHAPTER NINE:
1981, Surviving Infatuation and Isolation   157

CHAPTER TEN:
1982–83, "It's Going to Be All Right, Dad!"   175

CHAPTER ELEVEN:
1984–90, Giving Up the Ghost!   192

CHAPTER TWELVE:
1990–91, One Last Year of Silence   222

CHAPTER THIRTEEN:
1991–93, A Ghost No More!   248

CHAPTER FOURTEEN:
1993–94, Time for Doing Justice!   265

APPENDIX: *Six Letters to the Religious Right*   289

Author's Notes, References, and Resources   318

Foreword

Mel White is a good person—kind, generous, funny, insightful, a man of faith and integrity. I ought to know. For twenty-five years I was married to him. I know what he went through trying to understand himself and what it means to be both gay and Christian. Whether you agree or disagree with Mel's perspective on the issue, I hope you will take his words seriously.

I ask you to do this, not because I want you to have sympathy for Mel, although I was with him during that great struggle to accept himself, and I do have sympathy. And not because I believe that Mel dealt with every situation well—like most of us when we have to do things that are painful and very difficult, we sometimes do them poorly.

I hope you'll take Mel's words seriously because what we learned together will be important to you and to your family as well. For example, after all those decades of trying, we discovered that no one can choose or change his or her sexual orientation.

Mel had no choice about being a homosexual. Believe me, if he had a choice, I know he would have chosen his marriage, his family, and his unique ministry; for Mel's values, like most of the gays and lesbians I know, are the same as mine and my heterosexual friends: love, respect, commitment, nurture, responsibility, honesty, and integrity.

I've also learned that Mel represents so many lesbians and gays in our culture including your sons and daughters, your friends, neighbors, and colleagues. Reading his story will help you better understand the homosexuals in your own life. And understanding them—seeing the face of Christ in their faces—will enrich your life and bring you closer to God and to each other.

It is sad that Mel and I could not share the richness of our marriage until "death us do part." But my life did not end with the break up of our marriage. It is still filled with fun, growth, beauty, joy, and much affection. Many supportive and interesting friends enrich my life. I even started my second career at age forty-seven, and today have the best job in the world as director of stewardship at All Saints Church in Pasadena, a place rich in worship, challenging to its members, and compassionate in its outreach ministry.

Mel and I remain friends. Together, we have raised two wonderful children who are thoughtful, caring, spiritually sensitive, and great fun. I also take special delight in our two-year-old granddaughter, Katie. She reminds me that we all share a responsibility to make this world a place that is nurturing and safe for all children, a world where no one is hated because of color, race, religion, or sexual orientation.

While Mel and I were married, we produced dozens of films and books together. Although he often disagreed with their politics, Mel also served as ghostwriter for Billy Graham, Pat Robertson, Jerry Falwell, Jim and Tammy Bakker, W. A. Criswell, Ollie North, and other leaders of the religious right. Because he shared their Christian faith and was eager to help shape their ministries, Mel tried to protect his clients by remaining behind the scenes during those trying times while dealing with his sexuality.

Mel has been very reluctant to confront publicly his old friends from the religious right. He liked these men and respected their sincerity, but the false charges they are making against gays and lesbians in America have led to so much suffering that he feels he has no choice.

I think you will be moved by the story of Mel's decision to "come out," and will at the same time understand why he is taking this public stand against his old friends and clients. I hope, too, that you will be convinced by the case Mel makes against the current homophobic rhetoric of the religious right.

I wish Mel great success in his new life and ministry. I, too, have many lesbian and gay friends. I have assisted in the blessing of their unions, been present at the baptism of their children, served with them in the ministry at All Saints Church, laughed and cried in their company.

We are all on this journey together, and we must ensure that the road is safe for everyone, including our homosexual brothers and sisters who for far too long have been unfairly condemned and rejected. Isn't it past time that we opened our hearts and our arms to welcome them home instead of seeing them as strangers still waiting at the gate?

—Lyla White

"I was a stranger and you took me not in . . ."

—Jesus

(Matthew 25:43)

Chapter 1

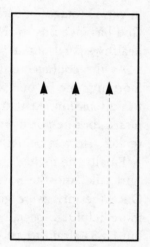

In the Beginning—

The Ghost of Silence

*A*t *a Christian summer camp in the Santa Cruz mountains when I was* twelve years old, a young pastor stood up to teach us something about "God's good gifts!" It was my first real summer camp, and the girls sat on one side of the room giggling and whispering in our direction and the boys sat on the other side pretending not to notice. When the new teacher turned and waited for silence, we expected another lesson from the Old or New Testament or another enthusiastic challenge to "witness" more faithfully to our friends.

"Masturbation is a gift from God," the young minister began. The giggling stopped and the room grew silent. I sat dumbfounded. The "m" word had never been spoken aloud in my presence, and I am certain that all the other boys, regardless of their experience, were also surprised to hear it.

"Some call it playing with yourself," the recent seminary graduate continued. Mouths dropped open and every eye in the room looked straight ahead. The silence was so complete you could have heard a seagull screech high above Monterey Bay three miles away. "Whatever you call it," the pastor continued, not even noticing that we were all in various stages of cardiac arrest, "it is a natural bodily function that God has given us to relieve sexual pressures when we have no other healthy sexual outlet."

As the courageous young man continued to speak that eventful morning, one by one we recovered from our shock and entered into the discussion. At first, our questions seemed awkward and embarrassed, but he put us immediately at ease with his casual, thoughtful replies. He was being honest with us and we were drinking it in.

Finally, he invited the girls to join his wife at the campfire area for "girl talk" and the boys to stay with him there in the meeting hall. Once the girls were gone, the discussion got even more frank and more helpful, especially to the other boys. I had questions of my own, but I was afraid to ask them.

I wanted to know, why didn't I feel the same way about girls that my friends all seemed to feel? Why did I want to tape pictures of boys and young men on my walls instead of pretty young women? Why did I want to hold hands with Steven and not with Joanne? Why did I get excited when I watched handsome European tourists in their brief, string bikinis dive from the wharf into Monterey Bay, or young fishermen stripped to the waist haul up their catch of lingcod and shark? Why did I think about boys when I lay on my bed at night and performed that previously unspeakable act?

"Any other questions?" the young pastor said one last time as I sat there staring at him, but with my thoughts 10 million miles away. "Maybe tomorrow you'll have a question," he said quietly, and I felt certain that he looked in my direction and smiled sympathetically as we ran from the room to the bunkhouse to get ready for lunch.

The minute we were inside that log-cabin-like, wood-frame building, the older boys slammed the doors, climbed up on the bunks, and began to chatter excitedly among themselves. "This is great," seemed to be the consensus. "Can you believe it?" was another universal response. "We've never talked about this stuff to anyone," a third person remarked.

I remember sitting on that saggy camp mattress, feeling their excitement, wishing that my questions would be raised as well, but by someone else, of course. "Maybe tomorrow . . . ," he had said. But I knew in my heart that a day wouldn't change anything. Hearing the "m" word had been startling enough, but any use then of the "h" word would have been unthinkable. I simply couldn't imagine sharing my feelings with anyone, not even that young pastor and his wife who seemed so determined to cross that deep chasm between our religious faith and anything that really mattered to our young lives.

Today, preachers and televangelists talk about homosexuality all the time, but I can't recall one sermon on homosexuality in all my early years of church and Sunday school attendance. In fact, I hardly remember anyone, including my loving parents, mentioning sex at all. When I was eleven or twelve, Dad—or was it Mom?—handed me a book about human sexuality (referring exclusively to heterosexuality, of course) with ink drawings of male and female genitalia that I still can't figure out today. Who looks like that? Nobody I know.

In those days of my childhood and adolescence, it was the silence that haunted me. Deep, dark, terrifying silence rose up from the ground like an icy wall, especially when someone dared to whisper the "h" word. In those days, I was dying to hear someone talk frankly about my secret feelings. Instead, silence haunted and harassed me. That terrible, aching silence took root in my young psyche and bore poisoned fruit: fear, ignorance, and self-hatred. My natural longings were a sin, or so I thought. That was the lesson their silence taught me. I was barely twelve, convinced that I was a sinner, condemned by God, lost for eternity. What other reason would call up such a silence? I was afraid to mention my fears even to my parents or my pastor. I didn't even dare to pray about them to God. The absolute silence surrounding the subject of homosexuality gradually engulfed me like a thick, winter fog.

Looking back now, I thank God for that silence. Imagine what young gays or lesbians face today in the churches of their childhood with televangelists calling gays "a plague upon the nation"; with pastors and Sunday school teachers calling our love "an abomination" and our feelings "straight from the devil"; with books, films, and videotapes shown in homes and churches viciously caricaturing and defaming gay and lesbian people and even declaring that in the ancient days of Moses "homosexuals were castrated, imprisoned, and executed for their sin," implying, sometimes stating outright, that it should be the same today.

Perhaps silence was a kinder enemy, but I still bear the scars of that terrible silence. When the other boys raced off to lunch that exciting day at camp, I stayed behind, lying on my bunk, begging God to heal me, to take away the feelings I could not understand, to make me like the rest of them once and for all. It was a prayer I had prayed hundreds of times before: I prayed it in my junior high gym when we showered together and I was terrified by my involuntary physical response to the other naked boys. I prayed it at the beach when I lay with my fellow surfers in the sand and was aroused by their bodies. I prayed it when I was alone in my room at night, cutting out ads from bodybuilding magazines and hiding them under my bed. Now, looking back, I realize that dealing with those sensual feelings should have been a natural part of my maturation as a young gay man, but in those days, there was only one option, heterosexuality. Silence surrounded and overwhelmed any other possibility.

I missed dinner that second night at camp. I couldn't let them see me; my eyes were too red from crying. I lay on my bunk and prayed over and over again, "Please, God, make me like the rest of them." Later that evening, when the evangelistic service began, I was in the front row. When the camp evangelist finally finished his sermon and the other children began to sing "Just as I am without one plea," I rushed to the rough, wooden altar railing, knelt before my fellow campers, and begged tearfully for God to forgive me once again. When the next morning finally came and we gathered excitedly in the chapel to hear that young pastor give his second lesson, we were stunned and saddened to learn that he "had been called home for an emergency."

In fact, I learned just weeks later that our courageous teacher and his wife had been sent home by the other ministers with strong warnings "to leave that kind of talk in the gutter where it belongs." To this day, I wonder if that young man survived the judgment and persecution of his peers. If, by any small chance, you are out there and reading these pages, know this: I will always remember you standing there before us talking frankly and courageously about things no one else would mention. I will always thank God for the courage it must have taken you to break through that curtain of silence that stunted our psychological and spiritual growth and, in many cases, ruined our lives. I often wonder, too, what you would have said if I had asked the questions that were plaguing me and what difference it might have made to at least one gay child trying desperately to find his way.

Who were these people who sent that young minister away just as he reached out to help us children answer the practical questions that were plaguing us? They were the forefathers of today's religious right. Actually, "the religious right," as we think of it today, is a fairly new phenomenon that I will date from 1979, when Jerry Falwell founded his "Moral Majority." Still, it wasn't the first time in our nation's history that an army of conservative Protestant Christians was called up for political, rather than spiritual, action.

Dr. Martin Luther King, a Baptist preacher, and tens of thousands of other African-American evangelical Christians, clergy and laity alike, were crucial to the success of the civil rights movement in the 1950s and 1960s. In 1925, William Jennings Bryan, a devout believer in the literal interpretation of Scripture, inspired an army of fundamentalists to fight "modernism" in his prosecution of a schoolteacher accused of teaching Darwinism. Carry Nation, another Bible-believing fundamentalist, inspired thousands of women to fight "the scourge of drink." Her crusade against alcohol lead to the ratification of the Prohibition Amendment to the U.S. Constitution in 1919. In the nineteenth century, the fervent, evangelistic preaching of Charles Finney helped mobilize both the abolitionist and the woman suffrage movements.

But when I was a boy, only the mainline denominations—Lutheran, Presbyterian, Methodist, Episcopalians, and the like—had demonstrated interest in influencing public policy. At that time, most conservative Christians associated with evangelical, fundamentalist, charismatic, and/or independent churches didn't believe in getting involved in political action. They were out to save the world spiritually, and it was to that end that they directed their energy and resources.

In those days, registering voters who shared their political views, picketing abortion clinics, or condemning homosexuals was of no real interest to conservative Christians. Now, all of that has changed. And though they are still very much committed to saving souls, they have joined with other religious conservatives, including those from main-line Protestant, Catholic, and Jewish traditions, on behalf of political action that will eventually "cleanse this nation of her sins."

And whether they are condemning homosexuality, as they are to-day, or silencing the talk about masturbation, as they did at my first youth camp, these fathers of the religious right base their views on their literal interpretation of select biblical passages that seem, on the surface, to support their particular biases, and on the ancient tradi-tions that have been built up around the misunderstanding and mis-use of those passages.

The young minister who tried to talk to us frankly about mastur-bation in my first youth camp in 1952 was very likely called up secretly before a tribunal of his fellow pastors. With the cabin door closed and a sentry posted to keep us children from hearing the proceedings, they probably opened their Bibles to Genesis, chapter 38, and read to the accused the story of Onan, a young man who was forced by law to marry his dead brother's wife so that his brother might have a legitimate heir. Not wanting to conceive a child who would not be his own, "Onan spilled his seed on the ground." And the thing he did "displeased the Lord: wherefore he slew him."

Upon that one biblical story, an antimasturbation tradition at least a thousand years old has been constructed. In A.D. 1054, Pope Leo IX issued the first official Roman Catholic teaching on masturbation, when he declared that "masturbators should not be admitted to sacred orders." Six centuries later, in 1679, a theologian named Caramuel attacked this antimasturbation tradition with these words: "Mastur-bation is not forbidden by the law of nature; therefore, if God had not forbidden it, it would be good and some times gravely obligatory." In response, Pope Innocent XI called Caramuel a heretic and reiterated that masturbation was "a scandalous and dangerous practice."

Poor Onan didn't want to father a baby that would not be his own, so he supposedly masturbated before sleeping with his deceased broth-er's wife. The passage didn't condemn masturbation. In fact, when you read the passage in its historic context, you realize the passage has nothing to do with masturbation at all. It condemned Onan for not doing his brotherly duty, for not producing a child to be his dead brother's heir; and yet century after century religious teachers ignored the historical context of that story and its true meaning to construct this false and misleading tradition that masturbation is so evil we shouldn't even talk about it to children.

In 1904, the Sacred Penitentiary of the Roman Catholic Church declared that masturbatory acts of a woman during the absence of her husband are "gravely illicit" and that any confessor who approves this practice should be "denounced to the Holy See." In 1929, when the Holy Office was asked if masturbation could be permitted for the purpose of obtaining semen "for the scientific detection and cure of a contagious disease," the theologians refused to allow it. And in 1952, the very same year of my first, fateful youth camp, Pius XII, in his encyclical "The Christian Education of Youth" made the following statement:

> We reject as erroneous the affirmation of those who
> regard lapses [occasional acts of masturbation] as in-
> evitable in the adolescent years, and therefore as not
> worthy of being taken into consideration, as if they
> were not grave faults. . . .

This year, 1993, even as I write, Pope John Paul II, in his encyclical "The Splendor of Sacred Truth" declares again that masturbation and homosexuality are grievous, mortal sins. Misusing biblical texts out of context to condemn, to silence, and to control is not something invented by the religious right; but in our time, the religious right, Catholic and Protestant alike, is falling back upon that ancient practice once again.

I was a victim of that misuse of Scripture in 1952 when that brave, young pastor was condemned and sent home for daring to tell the truth about masturbation; and I am a victim of that same misuse of Scriptures now, when Jerry Falwell, Pat Robertson, James Dobson or John Paul II, and the other leaders of the new religious right confuse, mislead, and condemn me with their antihomosexual rhetoric.

Don't misunderstand. In spite of all the problems they cause our community, I don't hate Jerry Falwell, Pat Robertson, or my other old clients and friends who lead today's religious right. In fact, I am a child of the conservative Christian forefathers and mothers of their movement. My spirit was conceived in the embrace of my conservative Christian parents and new-birthed at the wooden altar railing of their conservative Christian church. From infancy, I was shaped in their image by their Sunday schools and churches, at their youth groups and summer camps, in their Bible clubs and Youth for Christ rallies.

When the church doors opened, my family and I were there at Sunday school and Sunday-morning worship, at the Sunday-evening evangelistic service, at Wednesday-night prayer meeting, Thursday-night choir practice, and Friday-night potluck dinner and youth fellowship.

Mom or Dad prayed at every family meal and read to me and to my brothers, Marshall and Dennis, regularly from the illustrated version of Eggermeir's *Bible Story Book*. My hungry, young soul was nurtured, inspired, and given direction by the exciting, true-life tales of David and Goliath, Samson and Delilah, Jonah and the whale, and especially by the life, death, and resurrection of Jesus.

Often on Sunday nights, when the pastor or a visiting evangelist preached about giving our hearts to Christ and the congregation sang endless verses of "Just as I am without one plea, O, lamb of God, I come to thee," I was the first one to rush down the aisle and kneel at the altar to confess my sins and to feel God's forgiveness as friends and family knelt around me weeping.

In the early-morning hours before junior and senior high school, I walked the beaches near our home in Santa Cruz, California, and learned to pray. From childhood, I carried a three-ring notebook to record my daily spiritual pilgrimage and a well-underlined Bible from which I memorized and quoted long passages.

Even as a child, I witnessed (shared my faith) and passed out evangelistic tracts on the street corners and to our friends and neighbors. When Billy Graham preached at the Cow Palace in San Francisco, I sat in the front row, surrounded by several busloads of my high school classmates whom I talked into coming with me, tears streaming down my face, wanting more than anything in the world to be like Mr. Graham.

My spiritual heritage went back many years before Dr. Graham, however, and received its greatest influence not from any famous evangelist or pastor but from my own grandma Noni. She was the matriarch of our little clan, and she and Grandpa Melvin determined from the day of my birth to pass on their love for God to me. The memory of her Swedish pancakes and fresh loganberries floating in real maple syrup with piles of hot, crisp bacon on the side still causes my mouth to water and my stomach to growl with anticipation. And she prayed and witnessed to her faith with the same fervor that she cooked and canned and cared for us.

Melvin and Ruth "Noni" Rear were second-generation immigrants who came to America to escape from religious persecution by the Lutheran State Church in Sweden. From childhood, Noni studied the Bible with a kind of fiery passion, and when she felt God's call to preach, she didn't worry one moment about her acceptance by the male hierarchy, let alone their concerns about the ordination of women. She ordained herself and followed her dreams. She preached the Gospel of faith in Christ alone. For Noni, no church bishop, no local priest, no formal liturgy with "bells and smells," bowing and scraping, long prayers and even longer sermons, were needed to "make it right with God."

For twenty-five years, Noni used Grandpa Melvin's railroad pass on the Milwaukee Line to travel the rails of Minnesota holding tent revival meetings and planting little storefront churches in the hinterlands. As a teenager, my mother sang in Noni's Gospelaires Trio while Grandpa led the volunteers in setting up tents or renting little auditoriums, putting up the folding chairs in proper lines facing the pulpit and the rough, wooden mourner's bench, passing out the chorus sheets and hymnals, arranging for transportation to and from the meetings for the old and infirm, collecting the small offerings and using them to help create little storefront churches that would carry on the preaching and the teaching of God's "good news" long after he and Noni had moved on to another little town or village.

She never profited from those meetings. In fact, Noni sold the diamond wedding ring that Grandpa had given her to buy a piano for the church they started in St. Paul, Minnesota. "We minister by faith," Noni explained. "Melvin has a good job on the railroad. God has provided all we need up to this day. God will go on providing if we just go on trusting Him."

I wish with all my heart I could have heard my grandma preach in those days. Mom and Dad remember her meetings well. They tell me she was a crying preacher. "Salvation is free," Noni would say with tears streaming down her face. "They were real tears," Dad remembers, "tears of joy for her own salvation and tears of concern for the salvation of others."

"She would kneel and pray with each person who responded to her invitation to come forward to accept Christ at the wooden altar," my mother remembers. "And after the prayers were ended, one by one, the people would stand and hug your grandma and cry their own real tears of joy."

Melvin and Noni gave their lives to sharing the Gospel with everybody they met along life's way. And I do mean everybody. When I was just a little boy in Santa Cruz, my friends and I would spend Saturdays jumping off the railroad trestle high above the San Lorenzo River or playing skeeball at the Santa Cruz boardwalk or fishing for stone crabs off the pier. When we got hungry, we would wander over to Grandpa and Grandma's duplex on Branciforte Street. Noni would fix us piles of sandwiches and thin, snowflake-shaped, deep-fried rosetta cookies dipped in powdered sugar with milk, lead us in a long prayer of blessing, and then, as we ate, go around the table asking each child, "How are you with the Lord?"

I can still remember my friends on their first visits choking on their sugar cookies as they struggled to come up with the right answer to that strange question. Noni often embarrassed me and my friends with her spiritual preoccupation, but even a hard-boiled twelve-year-old atheist or agnostic could see the love in her eyes and hear the honest concern for his soul in her quiet, determined voice.

Grandma Noni saw herself as a witness to God's "good news." She loved Jesus and talked about him to anybody who would listen. Noni was certain that Jesus' death and resurrection had saved the whole world from a fate worse than death. "Just give God your heart," she would say to my playmates if they showed any interest in her invitation to being "born again." Then she would have them repeat after her a simple sinner's prayer. "God, thank you for your Son, Jesus. Please forgive me my sins and make me your child forever. Amen."

I can still remember my friends looking up from those prayers at Noni's knee with great big smiles on their faces and honest, preteen tears in their eyes. When the cookies were gone and the prayers had ended, Grandma would hug each boy good-bye before we ran back down Seabright Boulevard to the beach.

Praying with Noni was a kind of neighborhood tradition for my friends and me. But praying was never the end of it. Grandpa and Grandma followed through on every person "God gave" them. On

Sundays and Wednesday evenings, Grandpa would take his treasured, light green, 1948 mint-condition DeSoto from its spotless garage and drive the streets of Santa Cruz to pick up young and old people alike and to deliver them to and from every service at the little Church of God (affiliated with the "non-denominational" Church of God Fellowship, headquartered in Anderson, Indiana).

On weekends he would shop for the disabled pensioners in his care, drive them to the grocer, the doctor, the dentist, or the eyeglass maker, or over to Noni's for times of prayer and Bible study in their crowded living room. Those who were bedridden, Grandpa entertained with games of checkers or by quoting long, dramatic poems he had memorized from his precious *Leaves of Gold,* a collection of religious poetry.

I don't remember ever hearing Noni preach in that little church on the corner of Seabright and Broadway. By then she had retired to tend her garden of African violets, which she sold to raise money for the missionaries she and Grandpa supported in Africa. Grandpa's legs were crippled from the long years shoveling coal into the blazing furnaces of steam-engine trains. Noni cared for Grandpa, and together they spent much of their final years sharing their faith with me.

Grandpa bought me Bibles, Bible commentaries, and Bible atlases, all bound in red or blue leather with my name stamped on the covers in gold. Grandma cut out articles from Christian magazines and circled items I should notice, while Grandpa memorized and quoted back to me great passages that he wanted me to remember from the Old and New Testaments.

After my father phoned to tell me of Noni's death in 1982, I tried to sort out my feelings about her. She was our matriarch, for sure, a quiet, gentle woman made of tempered steel. I'm still not sure how she maintained power over my life, but she did it unfailingly. I don't remember loud or angry words. I don't remember threats or recriminations. But I do remember quiet questions, subtle asides, little judgments, warnings that cut me to the bone and left me bleeding, feeling guilty and angry.

She was a serene, gentle, almost ghostly presence who without loud words or angry gestures always remained in charge. Without once raising her voice or even threatening me, my beloved grandmother kept the fires of hell burning just beneath my feet. For Noni, the earth had a very thin crust, and only my obedience to God and to God's will as Noni saw it kept me from plunging through that thin crust into my eternal damnation. According to Noni (and to most of my friends and family), I had one task in life and one task only, to guarantee my soul's salvation by saving other sinners from plunging through that crust as well.

From childhood, I memorized her favorite biblical texts. "All have sinned and fallen short of the glory of God." "The wages of sin is death but the gift of God is eternal life through Jesus Christ His Son." "If we confess our sins, He is faithful and just to forgive our sins and to cleanse us from all unrighteousness." "He that believeth not is condemned [to hell] already."

I numbered those and other supporting passages in my Bible in their order of use so that I could lead my classmates through God's "plan of salvation." When I "led someone to Christ," Noni wept with joy and announced the good news to our Wednesday-evening prayer service. During my school days, I earned a lot of trophies, but Noni wasn't interested in hearing about the speech contests or debates I won, or the academic honors or the music awards or the athletic letters I received. "But have you witnessed today," she would say to me when I tried to share my own good news. To Noni, the only trophies that counted were those souls I had "rescued." In her words, again quoting Scripture, all those "worldly honors" were just "chaff which the wind driveth away."

Noni also practiced what she preached. She enforced the same demanding standards on her life that she applied to mine. One afternoon when I sat in her kitchen trying to figure out how she made her Swedish pancakes so thin and delicate without burning them, she took off her apron and sat down beside me. I can still see her sitting there in that pleasant, fragrant kitchen with the little wooden plaque on the wall behind her that spelled out "Give us this day our daily bread" in Swedish. I was just a child, but for reasons I still don't understand, she told me a story that day that confused and frightened me.

According to Noni, she loved Grandpa Melvin very much, but early in their marriage she had to make the difficult choice between loving him and using her full time and energy for "the work of the Kingdom."

From that day, Noni said, she had given up sex with Grandpa to serve Jesus. It had been "hard on Melvin," she confessed, but in time, "he had learned to live with it." "Jesus is coming soon," Noni warned me again. "Don't be distracted by anything."

I still wonder what price Grandpa paid for Noni's "sacrifice." Long before he died, Grandpa's crippled legs would barely hold him, even with a cane. I can still see him sitting alone in the living room in his favorite La-Z-Boy recliner, reading his Bible or memorizing his poems. On an after-school visit, when I entered the room, he would grin and hold out a hand in greeting. I would take his hand in mine and almost invariably his eyes would fill with tears. Grandpa seldom spoke. He just smiled up at me, teary-eyed and grinning, obviously proud but strangely silent. In fact, I can't remember a word Grandpa ever said to me. Noni's voice seemed to echo around us from the kitchen.

For Noni, and for so many other conservative Christians from my past, there was a war waging between our bodies and our spirits. Sex was purely for the purpose of procreation. Other than that, even between husband and wife, sex was seen as a tool of the devil to distract us from our spiritual duties and lead us into lust, sin, and death. As the Apostle Paul wrote to the church in Corinth, Greece, "I beat my body and make it my slave so that after I have preached to others, I myself will not be disqualified for the prize" (I Corinthians 9:27).

Noni used this text to warn us, even as children, about the power of our sexual drives to destroy our lives and send our souls plunging into darkness. If Saint Paul, himself, was afraid of God's wrath for some small, sexual indiscretion, then what would God do to me if I "gave in" to playing with myself, let alone to the longings of my homosexual orientation that I had felt from earliest childhood. If God would use a lewd or lustful lapse to condemn to hell the founder of the first-century Christian church, the greatest Christian missionary in history, the author of at least thirteen New Testament books, what would God do to me?

"Be ye perfect," Noni quoted to me often, "even as your Father in heaven is perfect." The followers of John Calvin might not know for certain whom God has chosen for salvation, but at least salvation is out of their hands. For those of us non-Calvinists who grew up in

Arminian or "holiness" denominations, our salvation was up to us. With one false move, we could end up on that swift descent to hell.

Every night I prayed desperately for God to forgive me my day's sins, fearing that if I died in the night, I would be cast by God and His angels into outer darkness. My only hope was to heed Noni's warning to "be perfect as my Father in heaven is perfect." In spite of all the good gifts they gave me, Noni and my extended conservative Christian family made my childhood and adolescence a time of confusion, guilt, and fear. However, just this year, I learned something about Noni's own miserable years of childhood that helped me understand her passion to be perfect that she passed on to me.

Before Noni was born to Swedish immigrants living on a farm in Minnesota, her parents had another child, also named Ruth. That first Ruth was "the apple of my father's eye," Noni had said, and the large Nelson family often gathered at the end of the day to play with Ruth and to admire her special qualities. Apparently, Ruth was a perfect child, beautiful, sensitive, and above all, obedient.

Railroad tracks passed through the backyard of the Nelsons' property. Ruth's mother was always careful, always sure the child was safely in the house when they heard the sounds of an approaching train. But one terrible afternoon, little Ruth chased a kitten onto the tracks just as a train passed by. The child was struck and died instantly, and the family, especially Ruth's father, was paralyzed with grief.

After a time of mourning, they decided that "what God had taken away, He would supply again." So, they conceived another Ruth to take their perfect daughter's place. My grandmother, Noni, was that child. Apparently, she spent her life, too, trying to be the perfect child for her poor, grieving parents. Knowing that sad story helped me better understand and more easily forgive the awesome demands that Noni placed on me.

The intensity and the sincerity of her faith drove my grandmother and helped shape me. Like a coach, Noni pushed me hard on the field. Like a teacher, she grilled, reviewed, and assigned. Like a general, she barked out her commands. Like a warden, she kept me in line. Noni was tough and unbending. She set high standards and assumed that I would meet them. And though she proved her love to me, she had her own quiet ways to set me straight if I ever dared to wander from her plan. Noni may be dead, but she is still present in my life, pruning back, weeding out, coaching, teaching, ordering me about, keeping me in line in death as she did in life.

My spirit was shaped by Noni and by Grandpa, by my paternal grandparents, James and Effie White, who prayed for me with equal fervor, by my loving, generous, deeply spiritual parents, and by our pastors, Sunday school teachers, evangelists, and songwriters, all of them forefathers and foremothers of today's religious right.

From them all, I learned to trust the Bible in all the important "matters of faith and practice." From them, I learned that the spinning globe on which we travel is not a result of random chance, but the handiwork of our loving Creator. From them, I learned that God created us to be free and then worked tirelessly through prophets, martyrs, saints, and especially the life, death, and resurrection of Jesus to rescue us from the consequences of our own bad choices. From them, I learned that God loves us beyond our wildest hopes and dreams and that we, in turn, are called to love one another. From them, I also heard the stories of Christian martyrs and saints through the ages. And I determined that whatever it cost me, I would remain true to God's voice in my heart.

Conservative Christians shaped the very core of my faith and passed on to me my love for Jesus, the Bible, and the church. So, in my determination to oppose the evil that some conservative Christians do today under the banners of the new religious right, I will not forget the good they did for me. But all through those wonderful days of childhood and early adolescence, a heavy layer of clouds floated between me and the heavens. In spite of their many gifts to me, those same conservative Christians remained silent about the secret longings of my heart. And though I was surrounded by their loving presence, that same silence left me feeling increasingly isolated and lonely. In the days of my gay childhood, there was no one who even tried to help clear up my growing confusion, guilt, and fear.

Then, when I was just thirteen, I went to a Boy Scout camp in the high Sierra. To earn a merit badge in Indian lore, we put on loincloths, painted our faces and chests with Indian symbols, and danced around the campfire to the beat of animal-skin drums and ancient Hopi chants.

As I remember it, two or three dozen boys, maybe more, were dancing that night, most of them feeling embarrassed and bored by the "stupid" requirement. But I had never danced before. In those days, conservative Christian leaders taught us children that dancing was evil and could lead to premarital sex. As the old joke goes, "Do you know why Southern Baptists don't believe in premarital sex? Because it might lead to dancing."

That night I stripped to a loincloth, painted my face, and began to dance. At first I was inhibited by my new freedom, then excited and liberated by it. As the drums beat and the boys danced around the blazing fire, I watched another Scout, a boy named Darrel, moving in a slow, elegant rhythm, his head back and his arms lifted toward the crescent moon. His body glistened with sweat and his eyes sparkled.

Darrel's dance was different from the rest. Something about him seemed familiar. When he looked at me across the campfire and smiled, I felt a sensation in my stomach that I had never felt before. We were kindred spirits. Something mysterious, compelling, intimate, sensual, drew us together like magnets.

I was caught totally off guard when that same young Scout from San Diego, California, moved through the dancing boys in my direction. Without missing a step, Darrel wrapped his left arm around my right arm, and suddenly, like Zorba the Greek and his uptight English friend, we were dancing and whirling and chanting together.

When the drums ended, we said good-night and returned to our different tents. In the morning, we exchanged silent smiles over breakfast, but neither of us had the courage to speak. After one last assembly, we broke camp, loaded into separate vans, and started the long drive down the mountain. I saw Darrel one last time through the window of his van. He smiled, waved at me, and was gone.

When the rolls of film I had taken at the Scout camp were finally developed and shipped back to Contrera's Photo Studio in Santa Cruz, I picked them up, ran all the way to West Cliff Drive, and sat on my favorite beach overlooking seal rock. There, isolated and alone, I finally dared to open the envelope and examine the photos, hoping against hope to find Darrel's handsome face in the crowd. When I did find him smiling up at me from one lone photo surrounded by boys in bathing suits on the banks of the Merced River, I trembled with excitement.

From that moment, I was determined to find Darrel, to see his smile and dance with him again. I tried to look him up in a San Diego phone book, but I didn't even know his last name. My scout master hadn't kept a record of the Scouts who camped with us. I called San Diego

Junior High School and told the principal's secretary some lie about needing to find him, but she told me that the school records were private and that last names could not be released.

I ended up in total despair, praying for Darrel, writing him letters in my diary, dreaming that one day we would find each other once again. All that summer, I looked for him in every crowd of tourists on the beach, at the boardwalk, or walking in the redwoods at Cowell's Park. Once I chased a car filled with strangers down Pacific Avenue thinking Darrel was in the backseat only to discover to my embarrassment after waving the car down that it wasn't him at all. I never saw Darrel again, but I carried his picture in my wallet until the image faded and the sad and haunting memory finally dimmed.

For months following the Scout camp I thought of Darrel with a painful ache in my heart. Like virtually every other thirteen-year-old, I had fallen in love for the very first time, only my love was as Oscar Wilde called it, "the love that dare not speak its name." When my friends talked about the girls they had crushes on, I thought about Darrel and felt embarrassed and ashamed. Nothing was worth the risk of being called "fairy" by my classmates. And though I loved and trusted my father and my mother, I couldn't even tell them of the awful pain I carried. I didn't think they could or would understand how I felt after my first and only dance with Darrel.

During those adolescent years, my church, my school, my family, and my friends were all silent about the subject that concerned me most, and for me, their silence was the worst form of condemnation. What could be so bad that you can't even talk about it with your friends and family without fear of ridicule or abuse? Their silence convinced me that my feelings for Darrel were sinful in the extreme and that the puppy love I felt for him was condemned by the very Creator who had planted it in my heart.

In fact, that first adolescent crush on Darrel was one of God's great gifts to me. During the two decades of silence and fear that followed, the happy memory of that night often returned. In his spontaneous, courageous, defiant act, Darrel broke through the wall of silent condemnation, risked the laughter and the taunts of our fellow Scouts, took my arm in his, and led me in my first real dance. And at that moment, the Spirit of my loving Creator briefly broke the tortured silence of my early adolescent years.

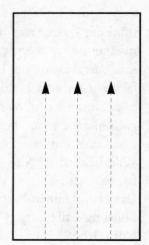

Adolescence—

The Ghost of Fear

*F*eeling lost, lonely, and afraid, I spent my childhood and adolescence living in a closet. Strangely enough, no one in Santa Cruz, California—not my parents, my teachers, my classmates, not even my counselor—suspected that I lived all those years feeling almost totally alone and doomed to hell. Elected student-body president, decked out with more awards on my letter sweater than almost anyone else on campus, I was Mission Hill Junior High's most happy fellow, tall, blond, and gifted, elected by teachers and students "Mr. Mission Hill," the young man most likely to succeed.

At least that's how I seemed on the outside, but inside, I was miserable and for only one reason: I was gay. I don't know when or why it happened. (The best of the behavioral scientists are still not sure.) I didn't even know what to call it then. But from the beginning, I had only same-sex desires and fantasies. I didn't plan it. I didn't choose it. I didn't desire it. And no one forced it on me. I wasn't recruited, raped, or abused. No one is to blame.

The truth is, from the beginning up to this day, homosexual thoughts and desires have been as much a part of my life as was my heart beating or my lungs taking in air. I can't scapegoat anyone for my sexual orientation. I realize all that now. After more than four decades of struggle, I know for certain that my sexuality was a part of God's creative plan. But in those early years, I thought for certain that my secret longings were a sign that my Creator had abandoned me.

Simultaneously with my first homosexual needs and desires came that terrible fear. My earliest memories are of a child who through childhood and adolescence never stopped feeling afraid and condemned because he liked boys instead of girls. Why that seemed so evil in those days of sexual silence is still unclear to me since discussion about sex of any kind was strictly taboo. I was gay, and the few antigay comments I had heard had me believing that gay was evil. I don't know who set loose in me the feelings of homophobia (fear of all things homosexual) and homohatred (hatred of all things homosexual). I'm not sure where this great, haunting specter of misinformation came from, but I am sure that it tortured and almost ruined my adolescent years.

I can't blame Noni. She never mentioned homosexuality. And I certainly can't blame my father, either. Like Noni, Dad loved me. He wasn't great at talking about it, but that's easy to forgive. Besides, without demanding anything in return, he gave me every possible opportunity a child could dream. And though I never raised the homosexual issue with my father until I was grown and had a family of my own, that silence was as much my fault as it was his. Then, I didn't think talking about it would have helped either one of us anyway, but I'm not sure. Maybe it's always better to try.

Dad was an Arkansas farm boy who ran away from farming while still in his teens. Somehow, he ended up as the assistant manager of a dime store in Minneapolis, Minnesota, where he met and married Mom. Determined to be a pastor, he entered Anderson College, a conservative Christian school in Indiana, but his education was interrupted by the stork bearing me, and his first attempts at pastoring, at a church in Redwood City and an impoverished little congregation in Watsonville, California, left him unsatisfied, eager to find a better life for himself, and his family.

Soon after I was born, Dad and Mom moved to Santa Cruz, where he bought and traded property, became a successful builder, ran for city council, and was appointed mayor during my senior year in high school. After spending a lifetime feeling inferior about his unfinished education, Dad graduated from a local college in 1969. He was a fighter and he passed on that spirit to me.

Even as a child, however, I was something of a mystery to my father, probably because I was such a mystery to myself. He loved power tools and guns, old Cadillacs, pickup trucks, and campers. I didn't. He liked to build houses, hunt deer, and tinker with engines, and he would have enjoyed having me working and playing at his side, but while he was out in the shop painting, plumbing, or rewiring, I was lying on the living room floor, listening on the radio to Milton Cross narrate Texaco's "Saturday Morning at the Opera." While Dad rebuilt a carburetor or refitted an old army jeep for camping, I tinkered with poetry, prose, and dramatic dialogue. He loved his noisy electric saw or his powerful electric sander. My favorite tools were *Webster's Collegiate Dictionary* and *Roget's Thesaurus*.

Dad tolerated graciously (but with a little sadness) my complete disinterest in joining him at those things he liked most. Inadvertently, from the beginning, we both seemed caught up in two different but parallel worlds. As a result, though we saw each other almost every day, we seldom had long, "meaningful" conversations about anything. We were both too busy running in different directions, but we liked and even admired each other across the distance.

And in spite of our differences, we both still have happy memories of the times we did spend together, hunting and deep-sea fishing, camping in Yosemite, praying and studying the Bible together as a family, working side by side to help rebuild Camp Monte Cristo, bulldozing a sea of mud from the streets of Santa Cruz after the terrible flood of 1955, showering naked in the rainwater pouring off my grandpa's farmhouse in Arkansas, shooting empty shell casings off the farm's old fence post with a twenty-two rifle, or trying to ride the waves on giant inflated pillows off the beach at Santa Cruz. My father was a strong, caring, generous person who never even once yelled, hit, or abused me. My sexual orientation, or my fear of it, can't be blamed on Dad.

And I can't blame my mother, either. Mom was a speech therapist and the volunteer choir director at our little, evangelical church. She was Noni's only child, committed to the Christian faith with her own unquestioning passion. Like Noni, Mom was tough and even controlling in her own quiet way. As a child, when I grew restless at church, Mom rubbed my back and smiled, but she never once let me miss a meeting. When I didn't feel like practicing the piano, she sat beside me on the bench until the lesson was learned. If there was a Christian camp or convention, rally, or retreat for teenagers, Mom saw that I attended. She hosted beach and slumber parties for our youth fellowship group. And almost every meal she called the family to prayer.

Mom loved music (but not opera) and books (nonfiction only, I'm afraid) and laughter (but no dirty jokes) and swimming (she still swims laps in her seventies) and people (kept the house filled with them), and especially, Mom loved God. "Son," she would ask me (as she asks me now), "is your heart right with the Lord?"

Still, with all her Christian fervor, she was a good and loving mother who danced around the kitchen when the music played, who loved to walk the beach and talk about my dreams, who could make a box of English toffee last forever, who canned and preserved fruits and vegetables from her garden, who bought me my first trombone and sat in the bleachers grinning with pride while our high school band marched up and down the field, and who sat in the balcony of the Santa Cruz Plunge and bribed me with chocolate bars until I dove off a real diving board.

I can't blame my sexual orientation or my deep, fearful silence about it on my parents or on our life together as a family. With my two brothers (and later with our foster sister, Judy, one of several children Mom and Dad took in) we had a rich and exciting family life. We worked, played, and worshiped together. Our home was a safe, wonderful, and deeply spiritual place complete with the smell of homemade cinnamon rolls baking in the oven and oak logs burning in the fireplace.

I can't blame my childhood pastors, either. Though I attended a small, conservative Protestant church, most of my pastors were part-time seminary students who took the Bible seriously and used its original languages, cultures, and historical contexts to make its lessons clear to me. I don't remember ever hearing a sermon or a Wednesday-night Bible study deriding "the sins of homosexuality."

I can't even blame Mr. B., my junior high gym coach, for my early fear and guilt. Although I think he liked me, I do remember Coach getting angry when I brought a note from home excusing me from gymnastics. "Listen, you little fairy," he said, tearing up the note, "you'll do somersaults the full length of the gym and you'll do them now." When Coach got angry, he called everybody a "little fairy." I don't remember taking it personally or even taking it seriously. And though I obeyed his rough command, I did get even. At the end of that long, blue mat he was waiting, and as I rose to accept his congratulations, I also threw up all over his clean, white tennis shoes.

And I certainly can't blame my fellow students. Nobody called me queer, fag, or fairy (except Coach B.), at least not that I remember. I'm sure there were "homo" jokes in circulation, but no one aimed the jokes at me. Once Henry W. beat me up after class for something I said, but he apologized later and we became friends. At our twenty-fifth high school reunion, we laughed about his one swift punch and my black eye, but I'm sure the knockout or its effects on my fragile psyche wasn't the blow that landed me in my closet of fear and denial.

And I can't blame the older gay men in our town, either. If they were there, and they must have been, they never even introduced themselves, let alone molested, recruited, or frightened me. My scout-masters, my winter-camp ski instructor, my youth director, my pastors, and my counselors never once committed any kind of sexual indiscretion in my presence. If they had, believe me, this book would tell the story.

I honestly don't know where my homophobia and self-hatred came from. No one that I remember talked much about homosexuality in those days, neither to condemn nor to support it. I'm sure I'd read or heard those ancient passages calling men who slept with other men an "abomination," but I wasn't sleeping with other boys. I just dreamed of it, and those dreams that I had known since earliest adolescence seemed so evil and so damning that I locked myself and my dreams away in a closet of silence and self-torture for the next twenty-five years.

In the closet, I learned two things necessary for the survival of a typical gay adolescent. First, pretend that you like girls. And second, don't let anyone know that you really like boys. I wasn't pretending in order to deceive or mislead; I didn't want to be drawn to boys. So, I pretended to like girls because it was "the right thing to do." For me, pretending was doing right.

It wasn't so difficult in elementary and early junior high school when my hormones were more or less in check. Avoiding girls and hanging out with the guys was just part of the package. But during those four years in high school, I had to be on guard against my natural feelings every hour of every day, even when I slept.

In high school as in junior high gym, when I stood in the showers with other naked boys, or with my teammates in the locker room, I lived in constant fear of being stimulated and having an untimely erection. When I was invited to spend the night with a classmate or a friend, I dreaded being forced to sleep with him in the same bed. While the other boy slept, I lay awake all night, longing to touch and to be touched, to hold and to be held. On ski trips to Yosemite or summer camps at Monte Cristo, I lay awake surrounded by sleeping boys, tormented by my desire and tortured by my guilt.

And though I was tortured by them, now I know that my longings were normal for a young gay man. Even when my hormones were raging, I didn't molest or misuse anyone. I didn't even know about oral or anal sex in those early days. Haunted by my own homophobia, I couldn't imagine how wonderful and how natural it could be for me to make love to another gay man. I just wanted someone to hold my hand or touch my face or hold me in his arms.

Unfortunately, in a homophobic culture, there is almost no opportunity for gay and lesbian young people to hold hands, to touch faces, or to dance cheek to cheek, let alone to discover, celebrate, and come to terms with their natural passions. It is one more way society punishes what it doesn't understand. Now, looking back, I am amazed and impressed with my restraint and with the restraint of my fellow gay and lesbian adolescents.

I remember one instance in particular. Johnny B. could have been a *GQ* model with his blond crew-cut hair, his lithe swimmer's body, and a smile that I still remember thirty-five years later. We met at a state track meet in 1957 as juniors in high school. We both ran the mile. Milers spend much of the meet warming up, walking the infield, watching the field events, and talking about that moment the starter's gun fires and the four long, painful trips around the four-hundred-and-forty-yard track begins.

The first time I saw Johnny, he was lying across the empty bleachers on his back in the sun wearing just his track shoes, his silky red racing shorts, and a pair of dark sunglasses. I looked away immediately. Gay teenagers learn quickly to look away when they are stimulated by another boy. When the other guys were watching our pretty female classmates and commenting gleefully among themselves, I smiled and pretended to notice. But when my eyes focused on a young man's muscular biceps or well-shaped butt, I couldn't point or smile, let alone share my intimate feelings. Instead, I immediately forced myself to look in the other direction and to think of other things.

Sometimes it was impossible to escape. When an encounter couldn't be avoided, I learned another trick. When a boy, like Johnny B., whose features matched my particular sensual grid spoke or smiled at me, I usually grinned a phony grin, hit him playfully on the shoulder, and said something inane, like "What about those Yankees?" I read the sports page like I crammed for an English test, having just enough statistics ready, enough play-by-play accounts in mind, to keep a conversation going long enough to escape the room.

At the track meet that day three and a half decades ago, Johnny seemed to be dozing in the sunlight so I stole a long, stimulating glance at his beautiful body and handsome face. Suddenly, he sat up, took off his glasses, and smiled at me. "Aren't you Jim White," he said, calling me by the more macho name I had chosen for my junior and senior high years. My mother named me James after my paternal grandfather and Melville after my maternal grandfather, Melvin, and the writer Herman Melville.

I froze in place, afraid that I had been "outed" by my innocent glance. I don't know what I feared exactly. Would he call me queer? Would he tell the coach and my teammates that he had caught me staring? The closet was a place of constant fear—fear that I would be discovered, fear that I would shame myself, my family, my church, fear that someone would pin a scarlet Q on my letter sweater and that I would have to wear that letter of shame and derision for the rest of my high school years.

"Yes, I'm Jim White," I said quietly, trying to hide my fear.

"We met at Monte Cristo last summer," Johnny said, jumping up and walking toward me. "You spoke the last Sunday morning. I played the piano, remember? You were great."

Indeed, Johnny and I had met the summer before, at a church youth camp. Immediately I remembered him. The first time I had seen him, Johnny was playing jazz piano after a service in the camp's chapel. He played like Ray Charles with his head back and his eyes closed. For an ecstatic moment I watched him playing, obviously lost in his music, swaying with the changing rhythms, smiling to himself that smile that left me weak and unnerved. Immediately all the warning bells had begun to ring in my head.

Gay kids are just like their heterosexual counterparts. We aren't stimulated by every boy who passes any more than nongay boys are stimulated by every girl. But now and then someone wanders into view who meets all those mysterious criteria that make our heart beat faster and our mouth dry with excitement. In that youth-camp chapel, even from a distance I had known that Johnny B. was "dangerous," so I turned quickly and walked away.

My own fear and misinformation about homosexuality had a terrible hold on me during those important high school days. Instead of allowing my natural feelings to be expressed with another boy, instead of experimenting with gay puppy love and infatuation, instead of experiencing courtship, dating, acceptance, and rejection with my own kind, instead of going through all those wonderful, sensual maturation tasks that my heterosexual friends were going through, I fled the very scene of battle before I even knew whether it was an enemy or a friend I faced.

At camp that summer, when I saw Johnny the next afternoon coming to swim at the Monte Cristo pool in his tight bathing suit, I left the water and walked quickly up the hill to my bunk. And on that last Sunday, when I delivered the final camp devotion, if I had seen him sitting in the crowd smiling up at me, I would have turned away quickly in order to keep my focus. Yes, indeed, I did remember Johnny.

"Nice to meet you, Johnny." I quickly added, "Gotta warm up," and turned to walk away.

"Let's warm up together," he replied, draping his arm around my shoulder and walking beside me toward the pole-vault pit. I couldn't believe it was happening, right out there in front of God and everybody. My teammates were everywhere. I knew they would see Johnny's arm draped over my shoulder. I thought they would think the worst; so I tried to pull away. But Johnny just kept walking and smiling, his arm draped casually around my neck. And no one even seemed to notice.

Stripped to our thin clads, doing our stretching exercises side by side in the sun, talking about our mutual interests—music, track, our Youth for Christ Bible clubs—I felt excited and energized. By the time we finished our warm-ups and headed for our different coaches to plan our strategies for the longest, hardest race of the day, I was walking on air. Just before we stepped to the mark, I looked down the line of runners and saw Johnny looking back at me, smiling.

I ran the mile in four minutes and twenty-eight seconds that day, my personal best, the third man to cross the finish line in the all-region meet. I beat Johnny by ten long seconds, but when I stood on the cinder track and received my first (and only) bronze medal, he was in the front row clapping, cheering, and smiling that deadly smile. Only this time, his arm was draped around a beautiful girl and she was wearing a man-sized athletic letter jacket with Johnny's name on the sleeve.

On our walk to the showers, Johnny introduced his girlfriend to me. I have forgotten her name, but I have not forgotten that sense of jealousy and loss I felt when I saw them standing together. It was so difficult to recover from moments like that. Healing was slow and the ache stayed with me for a long time. It's another reason I learned to turn away when I saw muscular biceps or a handsome face. Those rare moments when I felt intimate contact with another young man always seemed to end in disappointment and confusion.

During my early high school yars, I learned a new word that I associated with my feelings for Johnny. Of course, I didn't know what the word meant exactly, but during my high school years I had heard adults speak occasionally about a "sodomite" in the neighborhood. When the subject of sodomy had been raised in my hearing, it always seemed to be something so evil they talked of it in whispers. The references were veiled in mystery, but the implications were growing more clear. Apparently, sodomites were men who liked to have sex with other men. Clearly they were "evil" and "condemned to hell." And those who condemned these poor sodomites seemed to base their anger and hatred on the ancient story of Sodom.

Because I longed to sleep with other boys, I was terrified of that four-thousand-year-old account, so during my senior year I determined to find out for myself what the Bible really taught about sodomy and Sodomites. In the evenings and sometimes on a Saturday or a Sunday afternoon, I locked myself into my little apartment in the back of our family home in Santa Cruz, surrounded by every Bible translation, Bible dictionary, Bible atlas, and Bible commentary I could find. I told no one the subject of my painful, self-imposed search. I discovered the original story of Sodom in Genesis, chapter 19, and began by reading it over and over again, begging God to help me understand its meaning.

According to the ancient text, Abraham's brother, Lot, had moved to the city of Sodom, one of five ancient cities that now lie buried beneath the shallow waters of the southern tip of the Dead Sea. Lot was sitting at the city gate when he saw two angels approaching. Thinking them men of nobility, he bowed to the ground and invited the two strangers to spend the night at his house.

That same evening, before the strangers went to bed, all the males of Sodom, old and young, and the people from every quarter, surrounded the house and demanded that Lot bring his visitors outside so that the crowd "might know them." Lot pleaded with them on his guests' behalf. He even offered to give up his two virgin daughters to pacify the angry crowd. When the original Sodomites threatened to break down the door, the angels finally acted, blinding the leaders of the crowd and warning Lot and his family to leave the city before God destroyed it in the morning. That next day, Lot's wife turned into a pillar of salt because she disobeyed the angels' warning to not look back upon this wicked, burning city.

The story was as frightening as it was unclear. At night, I lay in my bed, reading and rereading it, praying for God to help me understand. What were the Sodomites up to that last night before they died in a hailstorm of fire and brimstone? What had they done to deserve such angry contempt from their Creator?

The King James version said that the men and boys of Sodom simply wanted "to know" the strangers. Surely, God wouldn't destroy a city because its men wanted to get acquainted with a couple of tourists, even if they were from heaven. One scholar explained that demanding "to know" them in the middle of the night was one more example of the people's refusal to provide hospitality to the strangers in their midst. "To know" them in that case was a kind of abuse.

I circled the verb *to know* and went searching for its translation in other English Bibles. One version said the Sodomites wanted "to have intercourse with" the strangers. Another suggested "rape." It didn't even make sense that all the men and boys in such a large city, even in a strange, foreign city, would be homosexual, let alone gather in the middle of the night to rape two strangers. Besides, if the story were about gang rape, it certainly didn't apply to me. The whole idea of rape, heterosexual or homosexual, was ugly and intolerable.

What was happening here? Why were the people of Sodom destroyed? I began to look up every other reference to Sodom in the Old and New Testaments. The prophet Isaiah claimed that Sodom was destroyed for lack of doing justice (Isaiah 1:10; 3:9). Jeremiah, my favorite prophet, accused the Sodomites of adultery, lying, and the unwillingness to repent (Jeremiah 23:14). Ezekiel said that God was angry at Sodom because the people were proud and overly prosperous and that they refused to aid the poor and needy (Ezekiel 16:49).

Each prophet added a piece to the puzzle. A clearer picture of Sodom's sin began to form. The Sodomites were greedy, self-centered, and inhospitable. They were not interested in doing justice or in helping the poor. Any sexual encounter the people might have had in mind was to demean and dehumanize the strangers. God had already condemned the city in an earlier conversation with Abraham. The angels had been sent to give the city one last chance, and when the people refused to provide genuine hospitality to God's messengers, it was the last straw. Not one prophet mentioned homosexual intercourse or even homosexual rape, let alone homosexual orientation or intimacy among the reasons for God's wrath.

After spending weeks in the Old Testament, I turned to the New Testament. The Apostle Paul didn't refer to Sodom in any one of his thirteen letters. The Apostle Peter did mention it, simply as an example of what happens to those who live ungodly lives. The story is mentioned again in the tiny book of Jude, but none of these references lead me to believe that the sins of Sodom were homosexual intercourse or homosexual rape.

Finally, I turned to the Gospels. Jesus spoke of Sodom when he sent out His disciples to do God's work in the world. "Whoever will not receive you," Jesus said, "nor hear your words, when you depart, shake off the dust of your feet. Verily I say unto you, It shall be more tolerable for the land of Sodom . . . in the day of judgment than for that city" (Matthew 10:15).

Jesus' own reference to the sins of Sodom was perfectly clear. Every town that refused to welcome His disciples with appropriate hospitality, every village or city that was unwilling to treat them and their message with respect, would be judged as the people of Sodom were judged. To be inhospitable, greedy, self-centered, unconcerned for the needs of others, even strangers, led directly to God's wrath. To be hospitable to strangers was to do justice and to show mercy, traits at the center of God's will for all people. Like the prophets, Jesus didn't even mention homosexuality or homosexual acts when He spoke of that doomed city. It was obvious, even to this high school senior who hadn't yet learned Greek or Hebrew, that the original Sodomites weren't homosexuals at all.

After weeks of study, I emerged from my little space, more confused than ever. If the story of Sodom is really about wicked, greedy, self-centered people who refused hospitality to strangers and even threatened to abuse them or to rape them as a sign of contempt, what did the story have to do with people like me? Should I see myself as a Sodomite for wanting to dance with Darrel? Should I be afraid that God would rain down fire and brimstone on my head because I want to hold Johnny in my arms?

Now, I know the answer. As with the subject of masturbation, and the story of Onan, conservative Christians were using the misinterpretation of that biblical text and the ancient homophobic tradition based upon it to enforce their own secular agenda with Biblical authority. Even the name they gave us, Sodomite, was derived from an Old Testament story that proved to have absolutely nothing to do with homosexuality or homosexuals.

Isn't it ironic that this misinterpretation of the ancient story has become ingrained in our culture to the extent that the laws in twenty-four states condemning homosexual intimacy are still called "sodomy laws"? Even the U.S. Supreme Court helps perpetuate the myth that sodomy has anything to do with homosexuality. Somehow the ancient biblical misinterpretation got rooted in our culture, and no one seems able to dig it up and tell the truth.

Is it too much to say that those who condemn gay or lesbian people and chase us into our closets or out of our churches are the true Sodomites, for they refuse to obey God with acts of justice and hospitality? I wish I had been as aware of their misreading of the Scriptures then as I am now. Because I allowed their misuse of the Bible to outweigh my own study of those passages, I went on living in fear that I might be wrong, terrified that one day someone would point his finger and sneer that word at me. "So-do-mite!"

In those days, I had never even heard of homosexual orientation. No one had ever explained to me that my sexuality, too, was a gift from God or that I needed to accept and live out that gift with gratitude and integrity. I didn't even dream that there were other gay young men just like me living in their own miserable closets. I thought I was a sinner who just hadn't disciplined my mind or body long or hard enough. I thought if I prayed and fasted, if I witnessed to my faith and "led enough people to Christ," if I got elected president of the student body or was appointed drum major, or won a Bank of America scholarship to college, maybe then I would please God enough to be sure that my soul wasn't lost in hell for all eternity. Even though I carried this "dirty little secret," maybe I could achieve enough to be acceptable to God in the end.

Peter W. was one of the young men I introduced to the Christian faith. He was only five feet six inches tall when we met at S.C. High, but he was built like Michelangelo's sculpture of young King David. At least that's the way I saw him. He was the center on our high school's junior varsity football squad. When the Cardinals played, I was there to cheer my favorite player. Even when I was student body president, almost daily I wandered out to the football field to watch the junior varsity practice. "You have a real team spirit," the JV coach told me one day. In fact, I was there to watch Peter in his sexy scarlet and white uniform that was padded in all the right places.

One day Peter wandered into our YFC Bible Club meeting and stayed after to help me fold chairs and take down posters. He didn't know much about the Christian faith, but he was willing and eager to learn. We went on long walks together and talked about God. I taught him to pray. But from the beginning, I knew that I was drawn to Peter for more reasons than his soul.

Peter loved to surf, and though I was terrified of the giant breakers, I bought myself a forty-pound balsa surfboard and paddled with him out to Steamer Lane. I almost died of fright trying to surf the world-class waves of Santa Cruz. Actually, I spent most of my time trying to keep that heavy surfboard from cracking my skull and the riptides from pulling me out to sea. But I was willing to risk life and limb just to be near this handsome boy with his curly hair, his kid-brother grin, and his perfectly sculpted body.

After returning fairly late one Saturday night from a Youth for Christ rally in San Jose, Peter stayed over to attend church with our family the next morning. We stayed together in my small apartment in a separate shoplike building at the rear of our home. Peter stripped to his shorts, climbed into my bed, and almost immediately went to sleep. I put on my pajamas and lay down beside him. It had become more and more apparent to me that Peter was interested in girls. Still, after all those months I had slept alone in that bed, thinking about him, wanting to touch him, to hold him, to have him touch and hold me, it was incredibly exciting to have him there, sleeping beside me.

Quietly, afraid I would awaken him, I got up on one elbow to look at him. I traced the length of his body with my eyes. My heart raced with excitement and with fear. I lay awake half the night on my elbow looking down at the young man at my side or lying in the semidarkness, listening to him breathe, fearing that in my sleep I would throw my arm involuntarily across his shoulder and awaken to his anger or his disgust.

Like Johnny, Peter turned out to be a heterosexual. Nevertheless, as our friendship grew, I spent many nights with Peter, lying awake, watching him sleep, longing to hold him. And though they were long, miserable nights, I learned to discipline my adolescent desires while I was lying there. Those were my training days, my boot camp for the lifetime war that all gays and lesbians have to fight.

From childhood I was thrown together in intimate settings with the very objects of my desire. In the closet, out of necessity, I learned how to control myself and to deny my needs. Somehow, I managed to keep my emotions in check by brute strength. We gays and lesbians are a tough and self-disciplined crowd. We have to be. We learn it in the closets of our childhood.

Today, in a few understanding locales across this country, there are places gay and lesbian teenagers can meet. There are a handful of organizations (such as Project Ten) that sponsor alternative proms, picnics, and parties where gay and lesbian young people can date and develop and mature just like their heterosexual friends. There are even wise and loving parents (like those in P-FLAG, Parents, Families, and Friends of Lesbians and Gays), who support their gay sons or lesbian daughters, who accept them as they are, who refuse to allow their beloved children to be trapped in a closet of fear, guilt, and anger.

But wherever you find these courageous centers of love, acceptance, and understanding, you will usually find people from the religious right with their loud and hateful accusations, carrying picket signs, writing petitions to school boards, passing antigay legislation, telling lies about this "threat to family values," driving all of God's gay and lesbian children deeper into their dark, lonely closets.

One ugly, closet memory from my high school years stands out above the rest. I was seventeen, a high school senior. At the time, my father was the mayor of Santa Cruz and I was president of the Santa Cruz High School student body. Visitors, young and old, streamed through our home on Seaside Drive. One of my dad's associates in city government, a man whose face I still remember but whose name not even my father can recall, was an official with urban renewal or the Chamber of Commerce.

Mom liked the young man and took pity on him because he didn't have a wife or family. Often, he ate Sunday dinner with us, and after he helped us clear the table and wash the dishes, he would ask me to play the piano or he would walk to the nearby beach with me and my younger brothers, Marshall, twelve, and Dennis, seven. He was genuinely interested in each of us, quizzing me about track or student government, asking my brothers about their stamp collections or their new miniature racing cars.

One weekend morning, I picked up our home-delivered copy of the *Santa Cruz Sentinel News* and saw the young man's picture staring back at me. The headline made me gasp: "Local Official Murdered in New York City." I read the ugly, mysterious story with growing fear. The details themselves were bad enough, but something was written between the lines that left me weak with wonder.

The nude body of our family friend had been found handcuffed, strangled, and bludgeoned to death in a cheap hotel regularly "frequented by male prostitutes." Earlier, an eyewitness had seen the young man from Santa Cruz "drinking in a homosexual bar." Police were searching for a suspect with a reputation for "sadomasochism."

I folded the paper and rushed to my room. My imagination went berserk. I had never heard of "male prostitutes" or "homosexual bars," let alone of men with a reputation for "sadomasochism." I hid the paper under my bed and went for a long walk on the beach, praying desperately for the young man's soul, and, of course, for my own. He was such a gentle, caring man. As I walked, I tried to answer the questions being raised in my mind by my misunderstanding of homosexuality.

Do all homosexuals end up nude, strangled, and bludgeoned to death? Would the same thing happen to me if I ever dared to act on my growing needs for intimacy with another person of my own sex? Was God using this tragic death to warn me and keep me from that path?

Neither my father nor my mother ever spoke of the young man's death, and I was too embarrassed and afraid to ask the questions that were haunting me. If only *someone* had asked them. Now I know what those unasked and unanswered questions did to my already fearful little soul. Not only did they drive me deeper into the closet, but they set loose a whole new reign of terror in my life.

Today, I think I understand the real tragedy behind the young man's death. In all probability, he, too, had felt the same forbidden passion that I felt from my childhood. He, too, must have lived his early years in a dark and lonely closet just like mine. The young man must have been afraid to reach out to another gay man in our conservative little town. If he had allowed himself to fall in love in Santa Cruz, to live with his partner, to be seen with him in restaurants, in church, or walking on the beach, he could have lost his job, his apartment, his good name.

So, instead of taking that terrible risk, he took another. One night in the anonymous streets of New York City, he could stand the loneliness no longer. In a rough gay bar in the East Village he finally gave in to his lifelong desire for human intimacy that met his real needs. In exchange for one desperate moment of love, he reached out to the wrong man and lost his life.

For years I blamed the unknown "male prostitute" for my friend's untimely death. Now I see things differently. Very likely, both men, my young friend and his killer, were victims of fear and misunderstanding. I have no proof of this, but I believe that each man was driven to his behavior by the ignorance about homosexuality that still hangs like a dark cloud over the homes, the schools, and the churches of this country. And it is my old friends on the religious right who use that ignorance and the fear that goes with it to raise money and to mobilize their constituents when they should be answering the real questions that terrorize gay and lesbian people and keep them isolated in their fearful closets.

For the last few months I have searched through the back files of the *Santa Cruz Sentinel News* trying to find the young man's name. For all practical purposes he just disappeared the night he was murdered in Greenwich Village. But his face and his story linger sadly in my memory. And when I think of him, I think about myself and how easily his story might have been mine.

If anybody reading of this incident knows the young man's name and where he might be buried, I would like to know. I want to bring roses to his grave. I want to sit there alone and weep for his abbreviated life and for all the lives that have been wasted because we go on believing all the lies about gay and lesbian people when the truth would set us free.

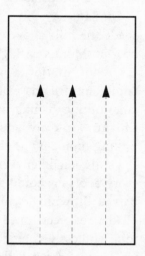

Chapter 3

High School—

The Ghost of Loneliness

*I*n 1953, I first met Lyla Lee Loehr in Miss Hilda Van's seventh-grade homeroom at Mission Hill Junior High School in Santa Cruz, California. We were friends and neighbors through all those junior and senior high years. In 1958, during our last year in high school, we dated for the first time. In 1962, we were married.

If you want to understand us now, you have to see us in high school, at seventeen; me, a gay child, from a conservative Christian family, determined to "do right" as I understood it, swimming through a riptide of confusing sexual and spiritual currents, eager to please God and God's people, but seeing sin and death in every shadow; and Lyla, bright, beautiful, eager, untouched by religion yet deeply spiritual, fascinated by my idiosyncrasies, excited by my questions and determined to understand.

During our entire junior and senior high school years, Lyla and I lived just six or seven blocks apart, but in all that time, our two families never made contact. Lyla's father, Lyle, was a fireman at the main station near City Hall where my dad was city councilman, then mayor, and ultimately director of the city's urban renewal program.

On Saturdays, Lyle hunted deer among the ancient redwoods that shade the hills above our home or fished for salmon from his fishing boat on Monterey Bay's bright, blue Pacific scallop. On Sundays, Lyla's mom, Marjorie, barbecued fresh venison or salmon steaks for family and friends who gathered in their backyard to play cards and talk hunting, fishing, and city politics over cigars and bottles of Italian Chianti; while my family spent our weekends (and almost every other waking moment) at church.

I still remember seeing thirteen-year-old Lyla in the library reading every book she could get her hands on from Nancy Drew to Elizabeth Barrett Browning, while the rest of our classmates were out playing kickball at recess or eating bag lunches in the cafeteria. She was short, thin, endlessly energetic, and California cute in spite of the reading glasses that magnified her sparkling blue eyes. In junior high school, Lyla had absolutely no interest in the Bible study group I started on Monday afternoons and exactly the same amount of interest in me.

During our senior year in high school, we were both elected to the student council. Lyla was commissioner of social affairs. I was student-body president. We met daily during sixth period with the other student leaders in a statewide educational experiment to conduct school business and to study political science and the art of governance. By then, Lyla had dropped her reading glasses and, with a little help from Light and Bright, had become a drop-dead gorgeous blond, petite, tough, determined, smart, and very ambivalent about me.

No wonder. By my senior year, I was a case study in sexual sublimation. I had dated a string of Christian girls and confused them thoroughly. Motivated, at least in part, by my growing confusion, I had proven myself "the best little boy in the world" by getting elected president of our high school student body, of our Church of God Youth Fellowship group, and of our Youth for Christ club at Santa Cruz High, and by being student conductor of the concert and pep bands, a not-too-embarrassing miler on the track team, a winner of endless speech and essay-writing contests, a recipient of the International Order of Odd Fellows six-week United Nations tour, the class salutatorian, etcetera ad nauseam.

I couldn't accomplish enough to satisfy the demons that were pursuing me. Because I continued liking boys instead of girls (in spite of my unceasing prayers for "deliverance"), I was convinced that God had abandoned me or was in the final stages of making that decision. It was my desperate hope that with the very next achievement I could win back God's blessing and confidence. At that very moment, Lyla stumbled unwittingly into my life and somehow managed to rescue me.

I remember the exact place our lives first really connected. She was standing at one end of the long student-council conference table and I was standing at the other. She was feeling angry and I was feeling stupid. She was shouting. I was pretending calm. As commissioner of social affairs, Lyla was responsible for the junior-senior prom. It was a Santa Cruz High School tradition that the student body president would lead the first dance, but my church didn't believe in dancing. So I had recommended that the vice president, Lon Bell, take my place.

"I don't care if you dance or don't dance," Lyla said loudly, her words echoing around the room. "But you will attend the prom. It is your duty." She followed that first shot with a barrage of angry, articulate criticism that totally won my heart. In those days, most people didn't bother to confront me. It would be like attacking motherhood or apple pie. Besides, I argued like Noni, politely self-righteous, gently domineering, and impossible to dissuade. Lyla's patience had ended. She was thinking seriously of starting a movement to have me impeached and ended her speech with hints in that direction.

I caved in quickly. Lyla was right. It was my duty. Besides, I had secretly wanted to attend the school dances, but my parents and my friends at church would have been stunned and disappointed at the "moral outrage." I don't know when in recent history fundamentalist churches turned against dancing, but when they did turn, it was with a vengeance.

During my junior high years I had watched my classmates dancing to the music of Dinah Shore and Perry Como, the Everly Brothers, and Elvis Presley at the lunchtime sock hops in the cafeteria. I still remember how I longed to join the dance. But I was afraid that my "Christian witness" would be damaged if I joined in such "sinful frivolity." Besides, I wanted to hold the boys, not the girls, in my arms, and you can imagine what kind of all-school scandal that would have caused.

Actually, I don't look back on those antidancing days with any great sense of loss or regret. The alternative events that our churches sponsored to replace the high school dances—banquets, slumber parties, concerts, and even trips to Monterey or San Francisco—didn't keep most of my Christian friends from all those "vices" that our parents feared. After the last prayer was prayed or the last song sung, religious kids just got in their cars, drove to West Cliff Drive, and did exactly what the other kids from school were doing.

Besides, we evangelicals also had roller-skating at the Moon Light Roller Palladium on Seabright Avenue. There, Christian heterosexual teenagers learned to do it all on wheels at twenty-five miles an hour while navigating in sensual, side-by-side embrace through runaway children, senior citizens, and the first-time skaters sprawled spread-eagle on that dusty wooden floor.

The jocks, the cheerleaders, and the rest of our high school in-crowd wouldn't be caught dead on skates, but Christian kids had no choice. Roller-skating in pairs was as close to dancing as we could get. And always, at the center of the rink, spinning, jumping, and figure-eighting alone, was Karen K., a quiet senior classmate with red, short-cropped hair and freckles, a lithe, muscular body, and a sad but determined face. While the other female figure skaters practiced in tights and stiff tutus, Karen wore faded jeans and a boy's T-shirt with the sleeves rolled up.

When the tall kid with the whistle ordered the girls to one side of the rink and the boys to the other, and the music began to play, and the boys chose their partners, Karen would be left standing alone with a resigned look in her eyes. So, I always chose Karen. She didn't have any more passion for holding me in her arms than I had passion for holding her, but Karen loved to skate and obviously appreciated being rescued from that cruel little sexist ritual.

And though she pretended to let me lead as we skated together around the rink at her breakneck speed (with Karen skating backward and me holding on for dear life), at times she somehow managed without even slowing down to keep us from serious injury by catching me and holding me up until I got my skates untangled and aimed in the right direction once again.

When the whistle was finally blown and "Everybody skate" was called, Karen would squeeze my hand, look embarrassed, and say, "Thanks, Jim." Already, she knew something about both of us that would take me years to learn, but she never spoke of it. Karen just smiled sadly and skated away from me back to the center of the ring to dance with her invisible partner and wait until that day when she, too, would finally be allowed to be paired with the skater of her choice.

There was at least one real downside to this well-meaning but ridiculous rule against dancing, and I still regret it. We who obeyed the rule felt cut off, isolated, set apart from our classmates at a time in our lives when we desperately needed to fit in. And that isolation only added to the loneliness of those difficult adolescent years. And we gay and lesbian folk, who already felt about as left out as you can feel, wandered between both worlds, looking in at happy couples dancing or not dancing, wondering if there ever would be a place or a time for us.

At dinner that night after the student council debate with Lyla, I asked my mom and dad how they would feel about my attending the junior-senior prom: "Not to dance, of course, but to fulfill my responsibility as student body president."

They were both calm and understanding, but it must have been another traumatic moment in our life together because I can still remember the two of them sitting in the living room looking surprised and obviously concerned, especially my mother. "It's your decision," she finally said, breaking the awkward silence, "but remember, *if* you go, we'll be home praying for you."

I grew up really believing that God was on my parents' side and that any of my intuitions, desires, or feelings that didn't conform to theirs had to be straight from hell. Mom and Dad sincerely desired "God's best" for me, but I don't remember their ever having any doubts about what "God's best" might be, let alone sharing those doubts with me. No matter how much I achieved in those days, no matter how bright or articulate, wise or experienced I became, if my opinions differed from theirs, mine were automatically wrong in their sight and, so their comments implied, wrong in the sight of God as well.

If going to dances could lead to hell, is it any wonder that I didn't even think about bringing up the issue of homosexuality? By then, I had memorized the Old Testament lines from Leviticus that say a man who sleeps with another man is an abomination and should be killed. (Of course a little earlier in the same text, anyone "who touches the skin of a dead pig" is also called an abomination. There goes "Monday Night Football.") It may seem funny now, but it certainly wasn't funny then. Although I thought that God still loved me, I wasn't certain how far God's love would go if I ever "gave in" to my "evil passions."

And to be honest, there was already at least one clear sign of "giving in." Walking up the shaded pathway that led through a stand of redwoods on our high school campus, I had my first "passionate" gay encounter. Gordon H. was a member of our thin-clad track team. He ran the 880 and often practiced with us milers. Gordon was a handsome, quiet kid who wore tan khaki pants instead of jeans, button-down, long-sleeve shirts rolled up fashionably to the elbow instead of T-shirts, a sweater draped casually across his shoulder, and penny loafers without socks. He didn't speak much in class or even on the campus, but when he did risk venturing his opinion, it usually ended the conversation. We knew in our hearts that he was smarter and better informed than the rest of us.

Gordon didn't socialize much, but I often found him sitting alone nearby, sketching in a little pad or writing poetry. Now and then I caught him looking in my direction; but when I smiled or motioned for him to join us, Gordon always looked away as though he had been caught in some kind of indiscretion. After a while, when we gathered for a student assembly or to eat lunch on the cement steps of the new school quad, I found myself searching for Gordon as he seemed to be searching for me.

When our eyes did meet, I felt strangely excited, as though an electric circuit breaker had been switched on the moment we made contact. My body chemistry responded to Gordon's glance unlike it responded to anyone else's on campus. My heart beat more rapidly. My palms sweat. And though I fought it with all the gloom and guilt I could muster, I found myself being sexually aroused every time I saw him, even at a distance.

At sixteen, I was terrified and guilt-ridden by my feelings. What a shame. Now I know that what happened to me when Gordon smiled was the same natural, God-given, sensual process that sparked my heterosexual classmates to life. They could at least think about celebrating their passion. I hid and hated mine.

Gordon and I first touched late one afternoon after a track meet on the path that led from our high school gym to Laurel Street where I began my long walk home. I had watched him run the 880, and he had stayed until I had finished the mile. We walked back to the gym without speaking, undressed, and stepped into the showers, which, for some unknown reason, were empty at the time. Warning bells rang in my brain. I stood in a cold stream of water, chatting awkwardly about any number of unrelated subjects, hoping that my body wouldn't betray my secret, scared all the while that Gordon would read my mind.

I dressed hurriedly, grabbed my pack, and headed up the redwood-shaded pathway, thinking I had escaped, yet longing for Gordon to come after me, embarrassed and afraid to look back down the trail. "Wait up, Jim," I heard him say quietly. I waited. We walked slowly up the trail together. I felt his arm rub momentarily against mine. Then his left hand brushed against my right. He seemed to be testing me as we walked. This time, I didn't pull away.

I tried to start a conversation but the words died in my throat. Suddenly I felt Gordon's hand on my back. He turned me gently toward a break in the trees, and I went trembling into those dark, waiting shadows, not knowing what I might find, certain that whatever awaited me there would lead to my destruction.

When we were completely hidden from view, I turned to face Gordon. He looked as nervous and as unsure as I was feeling, but he took my book bag out of my hand, lowered it to the ground, took me in his arms, and kissed me. I could have died and gone to heaven on the spot. Roman candles went off in my brain and my heart nearly burst from excitement. For a moment we hugged awkwardly, then, in spite of my desires, I began to pull away.

Even though I felt at home in my body for the very first time, even though Gordon's embrace was natural, good, and right, even though I know now that God was laughing with delight at my new found pleasure, my adolescent guilt and fear levels skyrocketed off the top of the charts.

Apparently, Gordon could see the growing terror in my eyes. "Lighten up, Jim," he said quietly, grinning his all-knowing little grin and taking my hands in his. I grew defensive and pulled away. The ancient words of Leviticus echoed once again in my brain: "Any man who lies down with another man is an abomination." With all my heart I wanted to stay in Gordon's embrace, and with all my heart I wanted to run away. Gordon saw my panic, picked up my book bag, handed it back to me, and without saying a word, we both walked out of the shadows and up the pathway home.

If my parents were afraid for me to attend the prom, imagine what they would have thought of Gordon's kiss. They implied that going to the prom was my choice. It may have been, but their implication was clear: make that choice and risk losing your soul. "We'll be home praying for you" implied for all the world that I wasn't just going to dance. I was about to risk a walk across a thin wire stretched precariously across the pit of hell. If teenage heterosexuality presented such risky choices, I thought my interest in Gordon was directly from the Devil.

Unfortunately, this unfair and unwise predicament is still common for tens of thousands of gay and lesbian youth in "Bible-believing" Christian homes and churches. We are trapped between two uncompromising forces: our parents' or our pastor's determination to follow a "traditional values" standard based on a literal interpretation of select biblical passages and our natural, God-given needs and passions. We are plainly warned by the authority figures in our young lives that our souls will be lost if we do "give in," and though we struggle valiantly, we know in our hearts that it won't be long until "resistance" is impossible.

Feeling trapped, spiritually lost and lonely, we spend more and more time in our closets, afraid even to raise the questions that plague us. Eventually, that intense loneliness takes its toll. There seems to be no way out. Now I know for certain that there is a way out, that Christian faith and sexuality (whether gay or nongay) can be integrated happily; but when you are young and terrified by your impossible choices, you sometimes think it's better to die. I remember those nights alone when I toyed with walking into the surf or driving my jeep off a mountain road just to end the loneliness. Better to get it over with, we think quite wrongly. Thank God, I didn't give in to those thoughts of death when there was so much life ahead for me.

In spite of my parents' not-so-subtle warnings of potential spiritual disaster, I decided to "do my duty" as student body president. On that fateful junior-senior prom night in 1958, I walked into our decorated high school gymnasium like a stranger in a strange new land, feeling both liberation and terror. Lyla and her volunteers had transformed that dismal, sweaty place into a scene of wonder and magic. Overhead, a spinning, mirrored globe splashed the colorful, cardboard streets of Paris with moving prisms of light. Crepe streamers arched downward from the globe creating a giant rainbow tent above our heads.

I hardly recognized my fellow students in their white dinner jackets and formal gowns. Needless to say, the girls were beautiful, but the sight of Gordon H. in his black tie and fitted jacket left me feeling strangely unnerved. Now, I can celebrate those moments when I am stimulated by a beautiful man, but then I stood in the shadows wearing my best Sunday suit feeling awkward, guilty, and terribly out of place.

Immediately, I planned my route of escape. I would watch the first dance—it was, as Lyla had shouted, my presidential duty. Then, I promised myself, I would flee the scene and drive my jeep to the sanctuary of Cowell's beach. At that desperate, lonely moment, David G., a jazz trumpeter wearing a French beret and standing under a Parisian streetlamp, played a kind of ragtime fanfare signaling the first dance to begin. And suddenly, out of the crowd, Lyla walked toward me, smiling and holding out her hand.

I couldn't believe my eyes. Right in front of God and everybody, she was asking me to dance. It was one thing to disobey the teachings of my parents and the church, but it was another thing to make a fool of myself. I didn't know my left foot from my right. I often danced around the living room when I was home alone listening to the Boston Pops or to a live broadcast of Stan Kenton's band, but I didn't know the bugaloo or the mashed potato from a two-step or a waltz.

"Don't worry," Lyla said as she put her left hand on my shoulder and moved me toward the center of the floor. "I'll hold you up." With only that brief warning, the music began to play. Under the colorful crepe canopy splashed in moving lights and protected from close scrutiny by the merciful semidarkness, Lyla taught me how to dance. There was mischief sparkling in her playful blue eyes as she led me like a prized captive across the floor. I knew I had been tricked, but somehow it didn't matter. For that moment, I wasn't a Christian or gay. I was just Jim White, one of the guys with a pretty girl in his arms, and it felt wonderful.

When the dance was over, I stood alone for a moment, basking in the adrenaline rush of that first and only dance, watching my classmates, including Gordon, in couples, moving gracefully to the music.

I could feel that little black cloud of loneliness moving back into place just inches above my head when, once again, Lyla appeared, this time carrying two glasses of punch and grinning like Lewis Carroll's Cheshire cat.

"Wasn't so bad, was it!" she said with an amazing mix of genuine friendship and sweet revenge.

"No," I answered honestly. "It was great."

The next thing I knew Lyla's date danced her away from me and I was alone again. That night on the beach I somehow came to the conclusion that Lyla must be a part of God's mysterious plan for my life. In those days, as today, I believed that our loving Creator takes a daily interest in the difficult choices that we make. When Lyla appeared from that crowd and took me in her arms, I thought here, at last, was the answer to my prayers. I may have had more sensual interest in her handsome date, but her eager, determined spirit took me captive even as she guided me to the center of the floor.

If I had rushed home to tell my parents about that encounter with Lyla, their first response would have been to ask, "Does she love the Lord?" If I had answered "No" or even "I'm not certain," in all probability they would have looked sad, taken out their Bibles, or quoted from memory this handy little verse: "Be ye not unequally yoked together with unbelievers."

I wasn't asking Lyla to marry me (or to "yoke up with me" as the Bible not so romantically describes the marital relationship). I wasn't even falling in love. I had just danced my first dance and wanted to tell my parents about it, but I was afraid that once again their attitude would have been made quite clear. Fall in love with "a heathen" and there will be hell to pay.

So, rather than telling my parents about Lyla, I set out to "lead her to the Lord." This all sounds so Machiavellian as I read it back. In fact, I really did (and do) love Jesus. Telling people about Him then was as easy as telling people about Him now. Only then, I had an agenda for every person I told. Now, I don't. Now I know that other people's spiritual choices are their business and the business of God's loving Spirit. My job is to tell my story honestly. Happily, the rest is in God's hands.

But in those awful teenage years, I was convinced that the "salvation" of practically everyone I met was more or less my responsibility.

What a terrible load to place on the back of anyone, let alone a gay kid who was already buried under guilt. But in those days, our pastor, our Sunday-school teachers and youth directors, and our evangelical parents were determined to make us all into missionaries, carrying the Gospel onto our high school campuses and sharing Christ with our "unsaved" friends.

The visiting Sunday-night or weekend evangelists from that period often told us the story of Dwight L. Moody, a fundamentalist preacher whom God called to preach to the people of Chicago. Unfortunately, he hesitated just long enough for Mrs. O'Leary's cow to kick over that famous lantern and set a fire that burned down the city with terrible loss of human life.

"Those souls were lost," the evangelists used to tell us impressionable kids, "because Dwight L. Moody didn't obey God in time. And," they added, their voices trembling with emotion, "if you don't share *your* faith in time, *your* friends, too, may end up in hell with those poor lost souls from Chicago."

In 1958, the most popular Christian film in circulation was *Silent Witness,* the story of a young Christian teenager whom God supposedly called to witness to the school's star quarterback. To make a long and dreadfully melodramatic story short, the poor kid didn't stammer out his "witness" before his football hero was killed in a head-on collision.

At least that's how I remember the terrible story, and believe me, I remember it well. My pastor and youth worker, my Sunday-school teachers and camp counselors, must have shown it to us a dozen or more times before my senior year. And each time, when the film ended and the lights came on, we were asked to bow our heads and pray that God would use us "to reach our friends in time."

During that long, painful senior year I couldn't stop worrying about Gordon's soul. My guilt-ridden little teenage mind was certain that our moment together in the shadows would lead to his spiritual destruction. And no matter how hard I prayed, I longed to go back into the shadows with him again.

Once, I called Gordon and tried to explain that I wasn't "one of those homosexuals," and that I was "sorry" if I caused him "any confusion." He didn't reply. I invited Gordon to our Bible Club. He attended one or two meetings, but quickly lost interest. We never talked again about that moment in the redwoods, and in spite of my growing desires to the contrary, I made certain that we never found ourselves alone again.

In those days, I thought that being an effective "Christian witness" was the only thing that mattered. I was wrong. I still believe in talking openly with our friends and families about questions of faith. I still believe that our loving Creator is powerfully present when people get together to share honestly the stories of their spiritual journeys. I still believe that the Spirit of Jesus walks among us to heal broken hearts and mend wounded lives. But I get angry when I think back about those days when well-meaning but ignorant Christian leaders used guilt and pressure techniques to get us teenagers to "share" our faith with our classmates "whose souls might be lost" if we failed.

If we felt isolated and lonely before that guilt campaign, imagine how we felt after it. I was almost afraid to get close to a fellow student at Santa Cruz High for fear that his or her soul would end up my responsibility. For me, and for other sensitive evangelical kids like me, no conversation could be wasted. Whatever the reason for getting together with our friends, there was also the oppressive missionary agenda to deal with.

When I boarded the school bus to drive with my classmates to a distant city to run a race, to cheer a team, or to perform with the concert band or choir, I thought that at least part of that trip should be spent witnessing to classmates. I don't remember going to the cafeteria or sitting in the bleachers at a football game or drinking Cokes and eating burgers at a drive-in or lying on the sand at the beach or walking through the halls or standing at my locker when I didn't feel guilty until I mentioned God, the church, or our Bible Club.

It's a wonder my fellow students didn't tie up this overzealous missionary and throw me into a pot of boiling water. In fact, my classmates were not only tolerant, they often accepted my invitation to attend church or youth fellowship or Bible Club or a YFC rally. And every now and then, one of them would respond to the evangelist's appeal and "give his or her young heart to God."

So, in light of this evangelical preoccupation to share the faith with everyone, it was only natural that my first date with Lyla would also have a spiritual agenda. I was amazed when she accepted my invitation to attend a Saturday-night Youth for Christ rally in San Jose,

California. When I drove into her driveway that night with a station-wagon-load of classmates, she looked surprised but took it in stride. "I've never dated a whole carload before," she said, sliding in beside me.

And though it definitely was an acquired taste, the Saturday-night YFC rally was never dull or predictable, what with bands and choirs, guest musicians, a dramatic film, and a fiery preacher. Surrounded by several thousand Christian teenagers singing and praying, stamping their feet and waving their arms, Lyla sat beside me without saying a word.

It was easy to see by the look in her beautiful eyes that my date was in shock. How was I to know that this was only the second time in her life that Lyla had even attended a religious meeting, let alone a massive evangelistic rally? And that one Easter service that she had attended four years earlier in the stately Congregational church on High Street didn't compare in any way to the noisy, enthusiastic Youth for Christ event.

When the meeting ended, I was afraid that Lyla would ask me to drive her home and never risk wasting another Saturday night on me. After the closing prayer, I can still remember walking beside her slowly up the aisle through the mob of kids that had filled to overflowing San Jose's Memorial Auditorium. Lyla didn't say a word.

When we finally got to the exit and stood side by side on the curb, I asked her casually, "Well, how did you like it?" Lyla looked up at me and smiled. She didn't say a word, but her warm smile and sparkling eyes seemed to be saying, "If that's what you like to do on Saturday nights, I'm game for anything." In the awkward silence that followed, she took my hand in hers. I stood there waiting for the light to change, feeling her hand in mine, knowing that my entourage of Christian friends were standing behind us, amazed at this sudden development.

When the stoplight flashed to green, Lyla and I sprinted together hand in hand across the street and through the crowded parking lot with my entourage running along behind. My faithful little band had driven to San Jose singing choruses and telling stories, but on the long drive home down Highway 17, everyone sat in stunned silence and disbelief. I suppose they were as confused by Lyla's unself-conscious act of intimacy as I was.

"Isn't that Lyla Lee Loehr, the social affairs secretary who plans the school dances? Didn't Jim invite her to the rally to lead her to the

Lord? How come he's holding *her* hand? Who converted whom tonight? Has he lost his mind just before his soul goes down the drain?
Where will all this end?"

Maybe my little group of evangelical friends were just tired after the
long, exciting rally. Maybe they weren't asking any of those loaded
questions. Maybe I was the only one asking them. I can tell you this.
My brain went into overload when Lyla reached out to hold my hand.
I know now that she was just being her spontaneous, reassuring,
whimsical, loving self; but then I felt excited, bewildered, and even
terrified by the implications of her action. Once again I dared to
wonder if Lyla wasn't a part of God's plan to "save me from the pit of
hell."

While we rode across the Santa Cruz mountains that night, Lyla
and I chatted quietly in the front seat about student government,
about growing up in Santa Cruz, about our friends and families, and
even about Jesus. I felt as though I was discovering a kind of teenage
soul mate, free of all the religious clichés but genuinely interested in
all those spiritual questions that were at the center of my life.

Lyla spoke her mind freely. When I tried to propagandize her, she
hunkered down and called my bluff. When I spoke honestly from my
experience, she asked penetrating questions and listened carefully to
my replies. We came from two very different worlds, but we were
rapidly building bridges to reach each other across the chasm.

After my friends had been delivered to their respective houses, Lyla
and I parked for a moment in the driveway of her family home on
Ladera Drive. I can still see her sitting in the semidarkness facing me
across the wide front seat of my father's 1958 Mercury station wagon.
Her legs were curled comfortably beneath her and she leaned toward
me, gesturing excitedly with every new idea. We talked until our jaws
hurt and then sat silently in the moonlight.

Even though my conservative Christian church had a ban on attending theaters that was as rigidly enforced as their ban on dancing,
I knew from the few romantic films that I had seen that walking Lyla
to the door and giving her a good-night kiss was the appropriate
end-of-first-date behavior. I couldn't do it. In the first place, I was
haunted by the crazy notion that until she was a "real" Christian, I
didn't dare kiss her. And in the second place, kissing girls was not my
thing in the first place.

Somehow, I ended the evening efficiently and drove the last few blocks home grinning and humming to myself. I wasn't even tempted to head for the beach and walk in lonely silence. I didn't feel quite so lonely anymore. Of course spiritual and sexual questions were lurking in the shadows of my seventeen-year-old brain, but something about Lyla eased my fears and made me feel confident.

Several Sunday evenings later, Lyla accepted my invitation to visit our humble little cement-block evangelical church on the corner of Seabright and Broadway. She wore a silky, red flapper dress that night with matching red Capezio sandals. I'll never forget the surprised looks this beautiful young stranger, hair streaked blond by the sun, received from the members of our congregation as I led Lyla to a seat near the front.

I played the slightly out of tune piano for the singing that night while Lyla sat alone on that hard wooden pew trying unsuccessfully to sing the unfamiliar hymns and gospel songs led by my mother and her small volunteer choir. Lyla listened with sincere interest to our young pastor as he read his text and preached his sermon. She watched with fascination as the altar call was given and several people knelt before us to receive Christ as Savior and to be welcomed into the fellowship of our congregation. She looked on with growing shock when the healing service began and everyone in the church but Lyla gathered around a crippled man laid out on the front pew for the pastor to anoint him with oil and the people to lay their hands on him to pray the prayer of faith.

And after the service, when my mother had politely hugged Lyla and my father had smiled and shaken her hand, I tried to answer her battery of questions about God and the church and our congregation as we drove slowly along West Cliff Drive. "Why did those people go forward to kneel at the altar?" she wondered.

"To ask God to forgive their sins."

"What happens if you don't feel like you're a sinner?"

"We've all sinned and come short of the glory of God," I answered, quoting a verse from Saint Paul, but smiling secretly to myself that she was asking questions most people dared not ask.

In front of her home that night, Lyla finally asked the question I had been waiting to hear. "How can I become a Christian?" she said softly.

I knew she hadn't asked the question just to please me. "Ask Jesus to come into your heart."

Almost immediately, without even bowing her head, Lyla prayed a prayer that was so honest, so simple and sincere, that my eyes filled with tears.

I know we were both just seventeen. I know, too, that we were playing parts in a spiritual ritual passed down to me by Noni and a whole line of conservative Christians who shaped my childhood. But Lyla's decision to follow Jesus was not an emotional capitulation to the pleading of an evangelist or the endless melodramatic verses of an invitation hymn. She didn't see herself as a sinner being "saved by grace," but a seeker of truth taking her first step toward her loving Creator. Neither of us knew where those first steps would take Lyla on her journey of faith, but we both knew it was a genuine beginning.

After her short, moving prayer, I hugged Lyla awkwardly. For a moment, she clung to me. I could feel her heart beating against my chest. And though she had just eliminated the first big spiritual "obstacle" to our relationship, the second sexual "obstacle" would not be overcome so easily. As I held Lyla briefly in my arms, it would have been a perfect time for our first kiss. It never even crossed my mind.

Neither Lyla nor I remember kissing once during our senior year. We often walked hand in hand or arm in arm along the beach or through the redwoods in Cowell Park; but we never "made out" in the backseat of a car or held each other passionately and kissed on the sofa in her living room. Other young men in our class responded to Lyla in more natural ways. And no wonder. She was (and is to this day) bright, beautiful, and sensual to the core.

I loved every minute we spent together, but I didn't kiss Lyla that year, even after her kid sister, Sharon, took me aside and asked me point-blank, "What's wrong with you, Jim?" I drove Lyla into the mountains to pray at sunrise. I escorted her to endless rounds of rallies, services, and church meetings, parties, concerts, games, and plays. We read together from C. S. Lewis, Alfred Tennyson, and Elizabeth Barrett Browning. We took carloads of kids to Billy Graham rallies and Elton Trueblood meetings. She sat in the front row of my speech contests and debates and cheered me when I ran the mile or the 120-yard high hurdles. We spent endless days and long, wonderful nights talking, arguing, reading, praying, and working together, but we didn't kiss.

Thirty-five years later, Lyla remembers thinking it strange for me to be so passionate about ideas and yet to have so little sexual passion. In fact, I was burning up with sexual passion and from the guilt that invariably followed each involuntary thought or sensual fantasy. Though it often crossed my mind, I just couldn't run around campus planting kisses on the lips of the school quarterback or the jazz trombonist in the concert band. I was afraid of getting decked by a quick right to my extended jaw.

Lyla almost got her first kiss in front of two thousand students. As student body president, I was chosen to drive the convertible carrying our homecoming queen onto the football field at halftime during the biggest game of the year. After introducing her to the enthusiastic crowd, it was my much envied opportunity (one totally wasted on me) to kiss her and lead her to her throne. Lyla was elected a princess in the court and missed being queen by only a few votes. Ironically, my one heterosexual kiss that year was delivered to the upturned face of a near stranger while Lyla looked on, smiling graciously.

Lyla never knew about the other kiss. I didn't dare talk about that "evil" moment in the shadows with Gordon even to this loving, accepting, understanding person with whom I shared my intimate thoughts. And I never spoke of it to Gordon either. After that intimate moment between us, he was off-limits. I didn't ignore him. I just made sure we never ended up alone. It is still one of my great regrets.

In 1968, at our tenth-year class reunion, Lyla and I were shocked to learn that Gordon H. was dead. Not one of our classmates seemed to know exactly how or why he had died. Someone had heard that one day not long after graduating from an Eastern university, Gordon stepped off a subway platform into the path of an approaching train. Was it an accident? No one seemed to know for certain. When I heard the news, I found an excuse to leave the crowded hotel ballroom, hid myself in an empty stall in the men's room, and cried like a baby.

Twenty-five years later, in 1993, on the morning after our thirty-fifth class reunion, I drove alone to the Santa Cruz High School campus, and after wandering through the administration building and in and out of those old, familiar classrooms, I walked down the hill to see the gym, the running track, and the quiet, shaded trail through the redwoods.

Although the rest of the state was sweltering in the summer sun, a layer of cool, dark fog blanketed my hometown. The large wooden gym and shower room had been torn down, but the path ascending through the redwoods was still in place, almost overgrown now with wild blackberries and tall, green ferns.

I stood at the base of that steep, narrow pathway, feeling melancholy descend like the cool, dark fog of summer. The hands on the clock in my brain whirled backward. I was sixteen again, remembering the old loneliness and the fear of those long-ago adolescent days. Then, drawn by a dark, happy memory, I turned and started up the trail. My heart raced with excitement exactly as it had that day in the shower room when Gordon and I found ourselves alone at last. Once again, I was praying that he would follow me, terrified that my prayers would be answered.

Suddenly, I was not alone. I could feel Gordon's arm rub against mine. Once again, the fingers on his left hand caressed in passing the fingers on my right. When we reached that first large redwood tree, I could feel his hand on my shoulder, guiding me into the shadows. But when I turned to face him, Gordon was gone. Only his memory lingered to haunt me.

"Gordon," I whispered, hoping that somewhere he could hear and forgive me. "I did love you then, you know."

For a moment I stood alone in the shadows, hating the memories, regretting the losses, wishing I had not missed my adolescent years. Then, at that very moment, I sensed Gordon's presence. He was grinning his wise, knowing grin that once made my stomach tighten and my heart beat fast. "Lighten up, Jim," I heard him say again, and though his words still made me feel defensive, I couldn't help but grin back at him through my tears.

I stood there for a long time in the silence, remembering Gordon, feeling his presence, trying to work out those unfinished tasks. Then, hidden by the giant, ancient trees, I embraced him one long, last time and walked alone back down the narrow, shaded pathway.

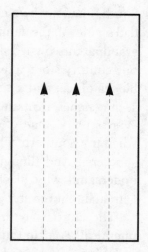

Chapter 4

College—The Ghost of

False Hope

$\mathcal{M}$*artin Luther King was arrested in Montgomery, Alabama, on Sep-*tember 5, 1958, the day Lyla and I enrolled at Warner Pacific College in Portland, Oregon. I still remember hearing the radio news report of Dr. King's arrest while driving the seven hundred miles from Santa Cruz. Riding with me in our 1958 Mercury station wagon were the three most powerful women in my life: my best friend, Lyla, my mother, Faythe, and my grandmother Noni. After hearing the news report, I told them the story of my week with Martin and Coretta King and wondered to myself if I would ever have the courage to join him in his fight for justice.

During that senior summer, the American Friends Service Committee invited a handful of high school student leaders from across the country to spend a week with Dr. and Mrs. King at Asilomar, a rather plush conference center near trendy Carmel-by-the-Sea on Monterey Bay. We walked the sand dunes and sat around the fireplace listening to this Baptist preacher who loved Christ's church, but who finally dared to move beyond its "acceptable" limits and by his courage changed the world.

When Dr. King described the conditions of black Americans in the South, I had my own childhood memories of family reunions with my dad's side of the family in the Ozark Mountains of Arkansas. My grandparents owned a little farm outside Dalton, a tiny village with one country store, a five-cent Coke machine with drinks kept cold by blocks of ice, and a single gas pump. While driving to Dalton, I had seen benches, drinking fountains, and waiting rooms plainly marked, WHITES ONLY. One of our family reunions ended in a terrible fight when my Southern cousins insisted on calling their slingshots "nigger shooters." And though my grandma tried to explain it, I could not understand why black Christians were not welcome in the white Christian church my grandparents attended.

"The church at times has preserved that which is immoral and unethical," Martin Luther King reminded us. "Called to combat social evils, it has remained silent behind stained-glass windows. . . . How often the church has been an echo rather than a voice, a taillight behind the Supreme Court rather than a headlight guiding men progressively and decisively to higher levels of understanding."

I was stunned by Dr. King's words. I had never before heard anyone criticize the church. The idea of Christians combating social evil was a whole new idea to me. My conservative Christian pastors and Sunday-school teachers saw Jesus as interested purely in "saving souls." Those evil forces in this life that threatened to cripple the human spirit—poverty, hunger, disease, discrimination, injustice, inequality (let alone homophobia)—were not really our business. True, we sent medical missionaries to Africa to heal bodies, but practicing medicine was just another way of gaining entry to a foreign nation for the real reason of winning souls.

"The Christian gospel is a two-way road," Martin told us. "On the one hand it seeks to change the souls of men and thereby unite them with God; on the other hand it seeks to change the conditions of men so that the soul will have a chance after it is changed."

I knew all about winning souls. It was my passion, the reason I entered our denomination's Warner Pacific (Bible) College instead of using my scholarship to attend Stanford University. Just twelve months before those long walks on the beach with Martin Luther King, in July of 1957, I watched television and cheered another of my heroes, Billy Graham, as he preached to the largest crowd in Yankee Stadium's history, 100,000 people. According to the official record, Billy's New York campaign recorded 35,228 "decisions for Christ" plus an unknown number "saved" by watching the meetings on television.

I hadn't yet made the connection between winning souls and doing justice. Just four weeks after watching Billy's New York Crusade, Arkansas governor Orval Faubus, also a Christian and a staunch opponent of racial integration, defied federal law and ordered state militia to Little Rock to stop nine African-American students from entering the all-white high school. It never occurred to me that the governor's fellow Christians should rise up in opposition to his arrogant acts of racial injustice.

"In spite of the noble affirmations of Christianity," Martin explained, "the church has often lagged in its concern for social justice and too often has been content to mouth pious irrelevancies and sanctimonious trivialities. It has often been so absorbed in a future good 'over yonder' that it forgot the present evils 'down here.'"

From my earliest childhood, conservative Christians had indoctrinated me about "winning souls," but in all the millions of words I had heard from the preachers and teachers of my past, I don't remember one single call to "do justice." Maybe I heard it and missed it. Maybe in Dr. King's life I was seeing for the first time what "doing justice" looked like. Whatever happened, in that week on the sand dunes, Martin Luther King told me the story of Jesus in a way I had never heard it before.

"Jesus did not seek to overcome evil with evil," Martin assured us. "He overcame evil with good. Although crucified by hate, he responded with aggressive love."

When Martin used the story of Rosa Parks as an example of "aggressive Christian love," I was deeply moved. According to Martin, on December 1, 1955, when Rosa Parks defied the state law of Alabama and refused to give up her seat in the front of a bus, she was demonstrating with her life the aggressive love of Jesus.

"Too often . . . men have responded to Christ emotionally," Dr.

King said, "but they have not responded to his teachings morally. The notion of a personal Savior who has died for us has a great deal of appeal, but too often Christians tend to see the Resurrected Christ and ignore the man Jesus, turning His face to Jerusalem and deliberately accepting crucifixion rather than deny God's will and give in to the pressures of the scribes and Pharisees to take back much of what He had taught concerning all men as sons of God."

For me, arriving on the Mt. Tabor campus of Warner Pacific College was "turning my face to Jerusalem." I wanted more than anything in the world to serve Jesus and His church with my whole heart, mind, and body. I knew my heart and mind were pointed in the right direction, but that first night in that little dorm room with my handsome, new roommate, I was terrified again to learn that my body just didn't want to go with the program.

That men's dormitory, with shared rooms, shared showers, and shared halls filled with young men in various stages of undress was a real challenge. Still, not once in those four, long years was any one of them, even the most vulnerable, in any kind of danger from me. I hated when my body responded naturally to the beautiful young men in that place. I felt guilty that I was attracted to them in spite of my discipline and determination to the contrary. I was constantly afraid that they would see the conflict in my eyes. I lay awake at night, praying that God would take away my unwanted, unworthy passion. And in the daytime, I worked to prove myself a good person in spite of it.

During the next four years, I proved myself a model student. I sang in the college choir and oratorio association. I studied pipe organ under Lauren Sykes, the president of the American Guild of Organists. I lead a large church choir and preached and taught in churches around the state. I produced a weekly television program, "The World of Youth," for Portland Youth for Christ. I started a film company and made 16mm motion pictures for educational and religious release. I started Bible clubs in high schools. I coached Bible quiz teams. I was elected president of the Warner Pacific College student body, president of the Council of Portland College and University Student Bodies, and president of my denomination's International Youth Fellowship Association.

If there had been a weather satellite in the skies above Portland, my path would have looked something like a tropical hurricane gathering speed and fury with each new passing day. During my junior year, I roomed with Paul Gessler, at six foot seven inches the tallest man on campus. He used to lie on his stretch version of a dormitory bed and watch me fly in and out on my various "urgent missions."

"Why don't you relax now and then," "Tall" Paul used to say in sincere but irritating tones. "The world already had one Messiah. Don't you think He was enough?" I remember smiling politely, pausing just long enough to try to explain my current crises, then rushing, in Paul's words, "pell-Mel" from the room.

Looking back now, Paul, I wish I had heard you. I wish I had accepted your invitation to join you and Agnes and your friends in the student center to sit around the fireplace, drink coffee, talk late, and listen to the classics, especially your favorite, Ravel's *Bolero,* on the stereo. But I had "souls to save," my own at the top of the list; so I missed the friendship we might have had as I missed so many others.

My achievements weren't all pathologically motivated, to be sure. It is a real danger here to oversimplify and explain everything as a desperate attempt to escape the cloud of misinformation and fear about homosexuality that shadowed me throughout those college days. Actually, I enjoyed my far-too-busy life, at least most of it, but the person everyone else saw when they saw me was certainly not the person I knew myself to be.

In those days I thought I was a heterosexual struggling against an odious, sinful, straight-from-the-devil sexual preoccupation with men. I thought God was testing me and that if I ever gave in to those evil homosexual passions, God, the church, my parents, even Lyla, would abandon me. In large part, that ever-present fear kept me moving at breakneck speed.

To understand those days a little better, you need to hum along as I sing one verse of the Warner Pacific College school song: "Nestled on Mt. Tabor's bosom. Glorious Hood in view. Caressed by Willamette's zephyrs, stands Pacific true. Loyal to the Holy Bible and the Spirit's Voice. Hail to thee, beloved Pacific. Sons of men, rejoice."

The song may seem a bit overwritten. (Do mountains have bosoms?) And it is certainly sexist by anyone's standards, but thirty-five years ago, we sang it at assemblies and athletic events without even blushing. Actually, the campus was (and still is) "nestled" on the side of Mt. Tabor, a mountain park in the heart of east Portland with sparkling blue reservoirs and scenic paths wending their way through massive evergreens, rhododendron bushes, and acres of lush, carefully tended landscape.

And the song is correct. On a clear day, you can see snow-crowned Mt. Hood, an active volcano still belching sulfur, thrusting itself into the blue Oregon sky just fifty miles east of the city. Having our humble college campus on the edge of that great mountain park was another of God's loving gifts to me. Whenever my guilt or fears threatened to overwhelm me, I rushed from my dorm room, walked north across the college grounds, passed our Quonset-hut chapel, and hurried up the steep flight of steps that carried me into the safe shadows of Mt. Tabor's wooded trails.

There was another reason I escaped to that quiet hillside park. And believe it or not, this, too, was a gift from God to me. Often, at the end of the day, I would see other young men walking alone on the more secluded trails. When we chanced to meet in those safe shadows, they would look directly into my eyes, stare for a searching second, then smile awkwardly and hurry away. Although we never touched or even talked, just their presence was comforting; it made me realize that I was not alone in the world.

I learned quickly how to turn from their longing looks just before they saw the mutual desire in my eyes. But even as these young gay men moved on to smile and stare at other young gay men, my heart pounded with desire and disappointment. In that excited, agitated state, I would rush back to campus and write a whole paper or produce another weekly television show on the adrenaline rush I was feeling.

Several times on isolated trails I spotted men embracing and kissing in the shadows. My heterosexual college classmates who also stumbled onto these intimate scenes were shocked and horrified by what they saw. But I remembered Gordon holding me in the redwoods and the painful years that I had waited in my lonely closet for that brief but wonderful embrace. I didn't feel shock or horror when I saw men embracing in the shadows. I just felt more loneliness, more frustration, and, as always, more guilt.

The spirit of homophobia drove us into the shadows and then condemned us when we were found embracing there. Now, courageous and determined young gays and lesbians hug, kiss, and act up "outrageously" in gay marches or demonstrations, free at last of their closets, happily flaunting, even playfully caricaturing, their love to show that never again will they be forced back into the shadows. But in those days, the shadows were all we had.

Not once in four years did I even smile back at all the young men I passed on the trails or even on our campus. In fact, other male classmates "struggling with their sexuality" often asked me to counsel them. We talked, prayed, and struggled together in private when we should have been laughing, dating, holding hands, and thanking God for our unique gift.

During my junior year, Jeffrey S., a first tenor in our Youth for Christ men's choir, approached me backstage during a Saturday-night YFC rally in Portland's Civic Auditorium. Dr. Winfield C. Arn was the host of those huge, weekly rallies attended by as many as five thousand young people. I was the emcee and song leader who held it all together.

Jeffrey was a sophomore at Cascade College, Warner Pacific's sister Christian school with a similar specialty in religious studies. Jeff and I were both nineteen, but given my position as emcee of the rallies, he assumed I was the older and thus the wiser guy. And because Lyla was often with me, he never even imagined that I, too, was tied up in emotional knots over my sexual orientation.

From his childhood, Jeffrey had been taught that masturbation was a sin. Because he masturbated occasionally, Jeff was convinced that he was a lost sinner, doomed to spend eternity in hell. I quickly assured Jeffrey that he had been misinformed. Quoting that courageous young pastor from my childhood, I tried unsuccessfully to convince him that masturbation is "another of God's loving gifts to help us relieve sexual pressure when there is no better way." When Jeff didn't seem convinced, I told him that even if I was wrong and masturbation proved to be a sin, God forgives all sins and loves us as we are.

During the next year we talked and prayed together on several occasions. Though Jeffrey never got up the courage to discuss homosexuality, it seemed fairly apparent that he, too, was struggling to overcome his sexual orientation. Maybe his guilt over masturbation was the primary concern. Either way, the silence, the misinformation, the threat of divine wrath hanging over Jeffrey's life, took a terrible toll on this sensitive young man.

On the surface, Jeffrey was another of those "best little boys in the world." He was a gifted singer, a star tennis player, and he often performed in dramatic skits on our World of Youth weekly television series. But just beneath the surface, Jeffrey was doubled over in emotional anguish. No one had any idea how depressed Jeffrey was becoming. I was not trained to notice. Eventually, he dropped out of the YFC choir. He missed so many television rehearsals that we had to cut him from our cast. Finally, we just lost sight of Jeffrey altogether. Because I liked and missed him, I called Jeff's home several times and left messages with his parents. Jeffrey never returned my calls.

One Saturday night at least a year later, Jeffrey's father approached me after the YFC rally. He asked to talk to me in private. Even as I led him backstage, I sensed that something terrible had happened to Jeffrey. We sat in silence for a long time in an empty dressing room before he could find the energy to share the awful news with me.

"Jeffrey," he said, "is in the state hospital at Salem."

He paused again and began to weep bitterly. I don't remember ever before hearing a grown man cry with such force. His body shook. Between heart-wrenching sobs he said, "I'm sorry," to himself or to Jeffrey or to God over and over again. Finally, he got control enough to blurt out the tragic news.

"Jeffrey cut off his testicles with a razor blade!" he cried. "We don't know why. He almost killed himself, and we still can't understand it. I'm his father and he's a stranger to me. He always spoke highly of you. Can you help his mother and me understand what we did wrong?"

I knew that Jeffrey's father was an evangelical pastor who often traveled to distant cities to conduct evangelistic crusades. I met his mother only once. She was quiet, sincere, and, according to Jeffrey, strict with him and with his two sisters because their father was often gone.

I had little comfort to give that poor, anguished man. What could I say? There was no way for me to know what really happened on that desperate night when Jeffrey emasculated himself. Nor could I know what happened in Jeffrey's life during the weeks, months, and years before that led him to that tragic act.

When Jeffrey's father was finally gone, I wandered out into the empty auditorium and sat in the semidarkness remembering Jeffrey up on that same stage singing with the men's choir, dressed in their matching white slacks and red-stripped shirts with black suspenders and yellow straw hats, clowning on cue, gesturing in sync, blending his first-tenor falsetto in perfect harmony with the others, making the audience laugh and applaud. Sitting there alone, remembering, I could only cry.

Months later, I called Jeffrey's parents and asked if I could visit their son in the sanitarium where he was recovering. They seemed pleased and even grateful. After getting several clearances, I was escorted through security to Jeffrey's little room. He was sitting in a corner on the floor. His face was pale, his body thin and fragile. When the attendant opened Jeffrey's door, he looked up at me for a moment with blank, lifeless eyes. There was no sign of recognition. I tried to engage him in a simple conversation. He never even looked up at me again. Living all those years in his lonely closet, feeling isolated from family, from friends, and even from his loving Creator, Jeffrey finally gave in to guilt and despair.

The agony of my own closet days in college was eased by a number of influences: the presence of God's loving spirit on those long walks on Mt. Tabor; a schedule so full that I had no time to brood; loving WPC faculty members such as Milo and Maurinda Chapman, Wilma Perry, Tom Smith, Lauren Sykes, and others who invited me into their homes for dinner, who took me skiing or hiking, and who let me invade their privacy and fill up their spare hours with my endless doubts and questions; and Lyla Lee Loehr, who loved me through it all.

If I called Lyla in the middle of exam week to take a long walk with me, she would leave her studies, grab my hand, and lead me through Portland's rose gardens overlooking the city or along the path above the Columbia River at the base of Multnomah Falls. I walked too fast. She walked too slow. Maybe that's why Lyla was always holding my hand, trying to keep up or trying to slow me down.

If I needed someone to cohost a TV program or to pull together an emergency cast of extras or to write a last-minute narration or to make phone calls or write letters or run errands, Lyla always said, "Yes!" And when I just needed to talk, Lyla was there, day or night, always eager, always interested and interesting, always opinionated, always tough and resilient and brimming over with love.

Our favorite hideaway was Rose's Deli on Twenty-first Street where we often shared one of Rose's one-pound, homemade cinnamon rolls dripping in melted sugar and consumed with hunks of fresh, salted butter. To celebrate a triumph or to raise our spirits before a term paper or final exam, we took our friends to Farrell's first ice cream parlor and cheered when The Zoo was delivered on the shoulders of two grown men carrying their million-calorie, ten-pound load of homemade mocha, chocolate, and vanilla ice cream covered with sliced bananas, canned cherries, and hot fudge, caramel, and coconut syrups.

We first kissed in the front seat of a little red Sunbeam that my parents had loaned me. (Sunbeam? Are there Sunbeams now?) After going through so much together, it seemed only natural to take Lyla's hand, to hold her in my arms, and to kiss her. She was beautiful and kind and smart and sensual, and she loved me more than anyone had ever loved me before.

I suppose I should have told her that I was gay, but in those days, I didn't know it. All through high school, college, grad school, and the first years of teaching, I really believed that homosexuality was a disease that could be cured, a bent that could be straightened, an obsession that could be overcome, a deviation that could be healed, a case of retarded adolescence that could be outgrown.

No one bothered to explain to me the difference between sexual "orientation" and sexual "preference." Perhaps no one knew it then, at least no one in my life. Now, I understand my mistake. Today, scientists explain that sexual *orientation* is involuntary, something that happens to two gametes at conception, or to a fetus in the womb or to an infant in the first few years of childhood. If our heart beats fast and our mouth grows dry with excitement when we look at an attractive person of our same sex, instead of the opposite sex, that's the way it is and always will be for us. A few folk in the middle of the sexual-orientation scale are stimulated in both directions. They may have a choice. But most of us don't. Like the color of our eyes or the size of our hands or the shape of our feet, our sexual orientation cannot be changed no matter how much we would like to change it. It can be stifled, sublimated, beaten down, condemned, and hated, but it cannot be changed.

In those painful college days, when people talked about sexual "preference," they assumed quite wrongly that we had a choice. Now, thirty years later, in spite of all the scientific and personal evidence to the contrary, that same dangerous, misleading assumption goes on taking its terrible toll. Like so many conservative Christians, then and now, I really believed that I could choose the object of my sexual desire as I could choose a cinnamon roll at Rose's Deli or The Zoo at Farrell's Ice Cream Parlor. So, I spent those college years trying to change my sexual orientation to something I "preferred."

When I walked with Lyla along the Columbia River or kissed her in the shadows of Multnomah Falls, I believed that I could change my "preference" from homosexual to heterosexual by an act of pure will, aided by God, by daily discipline, and by the beautiful, young woman at my side. "All you really need to get over this homosexual thing is a good woman," or so I heard. And after hearing it so many times and from so many different sources, I believed it. Sadly, I was wrong. My sexual orientation, like everybody else's, is forever, and to ignore or to deny that fact can be a fatal mistake.

Toward the end of my senior year at Warner Pacific College, Johnny B., the handsome young athlete and jazz pianist from my high school days, called from the Portland International Airport wondering if he could spend the day with me on campus. I still had a photo of Johnny tucked into the back pages of my study Bible. For years, he had been the object of many of my fears and fantasies. His call made me feel excited and scared at the same time.

I had a serious crush on this intelligent, attractive, energetic young man. Just being near him made my palms clammy and my heart beat fast. There was something mysterious and powerful about the way he affected me, and it would be a treat to spend the day in his company. However, my high school crush on Johnny had been a painful experience. Somehow, I had managed to conquer my runaway feelings about him, and I didn't want to go through all that again. Not understanding that my crush had been a normal gay response to a young man who fit perfectly my sensual grid, I thought my feelings were wrong, even satanic. So when I thought about spending the day alone with Johnny, I felt ambivalent at best.

Instead of driving directly to the airport, I called Lyla in her room at the women's dorm and asked if she would like to spend the day with us. We weren't even dating then, but once again Lyla was eager to help and glad to be invited. She jumped into the car, eyes sparkling. I truly loved this bright, beautiful woman. She was the best and closest friend I'd ever had. I just couldn't get my sexual feelings to go along with the program. But having her around always made me feel safe and comfortable.

We drove to the airport and found Johnny waiting on the curb. Even from a distance, I could spot him in the crowd. His college days had been good to Johnny. He had continued his interest in amateur athletics, and his body was in perfect shape. He was still tanned from the summer and his biceps and chest filled out his T-shirt like I had always wanted to fill out mine.

When Johnny hugged me at the airport, my skin tingled and my body shivered with excitement. And when he reached out to Lyla and picked her up off the ground in his arms, I felt jealous, not of him, but of her. I could see that when Johnny hugged a beautiful woman, he felt the same rush that I felt when he hugged me.

The whole experience left me feeling dazed and anxious. With the involuntary sensual excitement I felt that day came another wave of guilt and fear. Why is it happening again? Why do I feel this way in the arms of a man when I should feel this way in the arms of a woman? Is it a sign that God is giving up on me and that evil is winning in my life?

Somehow we made it through breakfast at Rose's, the morning worship service at the Holiday Park Church, and a quick drive around Mt. Tabor and the Warner Pacific campus. En route, Johnny spotted a theater marquee advertising *West Side Story*, Leonard Bernstein and Stephen Sondheim's latest Broadway musical filmed in Technicolor and 70mm Panavision. Spontaneously, we parked, got into line, and entered the theater. I sat between Lyla and Johnny, holding her hand, feeling his arm against mine, loving her, desiring him.

For a small-town boy from Santa Cruz who didn't go to many movies in his childhood, watching and hearing the story of Romeo and Juliet played out again in the wild streets of New York City left me deeply moved. When Natalie Wood held her fatally wounded lover in her arms and sang, "There's a place for us, a time and place for us. Hold my hand and we're almost there," I was embarrassed by my tears.

When I rented the film twenty years later to show it to our family, it all seemed a bit melodramatic, even silly to our children. "What's the root of the word *melodramatic*, Dad," one of them asked me, grinning. "Mel," I replied, rewinding the tape and wondering to myself why in 1962 *West Side Story* had moved me so.

Whatever it was, after dropping Johnny off at the airport, I asked

Lyla if she would like to ride with me out the Columbia River road to see the lights on Multnomah Falls. We weren't even dating in those days. Weeks before we had broken up again for the umpteenth time. Lyla had gone through that traumatic, unhappy process so many times during those four uneasy years at college. After seeing each other regularly for several months, I would take her to a restaurant or to a park and tell her that she should find someone else, that I wasn't "ready" for a serious relationship or that I wasn't "sure that God is in it." Other male students were grateful for the chance to date Lyla. She accepted their invitations but knew in her heart that she still loved me.

Whatever excuses I may have used to break up with Lyla during those dreadful days, they weren't the whole truth. I was terrified that my homosexual longings would ruin a heterosexual relationship. I loved Lyla. I didn't want to deceive or to mislead her. Maybe it was true that all I needed was a good woman, but in my heart, I was afraid that even a great woman such as Lyla could not change my sexual orientation or take away my growing need for intimacy with another man. But I was willing to try anything "to please God" and "to end this awful struggle."

Sitting in the theater watching Natalie Wood hold that fallen young man in her arms, I thought of Lyla and how much I loved and needed her. When we were together, I felt safe. When I saw her walk across campus with a male classmate, I felt jealous, sad, and terribly alone. As we drove along the Columbia Gorge, I determined to end this vacillation forever.

As we sat in the car watching the illuminated falls, I was probably still humming that sad little tune from *West Side Story*. "There's a place for us, a time and a place for us . . ." In the darkness Lyla took my hand. "Hold my hand and we're halfway there . . ." I knew that with Lyla, I could do anything. Without her, I felt lost.

"What would you say," I whispered suddenly without even thinking about the question in advance, "if I asked you to marry me?"

Lyla didn't even pause. "First, I'd say, is it what God wants?"

"I think so," I said honestly, believing with all my heart that God had been in our friendship from the beginning.

"Second, I'd say, is it really what you want?"

"I do." I felt waves of certainty and uncertainty at the very same time.

"Then, third," she said, grinning up at me, "I'd say, yes!"

At that very moment, a policeman walked up from behind us, flashed his light on Lyla through my open window, and asked, "Are you all right?"

"Sure," I answered, surprised and scared by his sudden appearance.

"Not you," he replied gruffly. "Her."

Lyla leaned forward, smiled broadly, and flashed her baby blue eyes at the policeman. "I'm all right," she said happily. "He just asked me to marry him."

"Then I've come too late," the officer said as he walked away grinning. "I've come too late."

For a long time, Lyla and I held each other in the darkness. We knew one thing for certain. We loved each other. What we couldn't anticipate then were the terrible tests our love would face in the years ahead.

During the years we spent at Warner Pacific College (1958 to 1962), courageous white students from more "liberal" Christian schools and seminaries spent their summers in the South registering voters, rebuilding homes and churches, providing food and medical supplies, marching, picketing, and participating in pray-ins, sit-ins, and teach-ins. They had deep spiritual convictions against racial bigotry and discrimination, so they put their lives on the line, riding south in buses, trains, and cars to work with Martin Luther King to end segregation and begin a new era of justice.

Like me, they found Martin's dream to be contagious. But unlike me, they had the courage to risk their lives to help see that dream come true. These young freedom riders were jeered, threatened, pelted with rocks and bottles, chased by mobs, bitten by police dogs, knocked down by clubs and high-pressure hoses, arrested, jailed, driven off the road by racists in pickup trucks with racks of loaded guns, even tortured, killed, and buried in makeshift graves.

For the most part, conservative Christian students, including me, just stood by and watched. I wanted to march with Martin and the brave white students who were risking their lives alongside his for the cause, but I hesitated. There were endless excuses: tuition to earn, tests to pass, and papers to write. Besides, Christian activism looked so radical. It wasn't a convenient time. The struggle seemed far away. Worse, I wasn't sure that it was God's will for me to register voters, to kneel and pray in a segregated restaurant, or to stand with my brothers and sisters against police dogs and fire hoses when I could be out "winning souls."

Consequently, instead of marching arm in arm with Martin, with my African-American brothers and sisters in the South, and with those courageous white students who joined them, I studied the Bible at Warner Pacific College and worked with Youth for Christ winning souls and coaching Bible quiz teams. And in the process, I let that pivotal moment in history pass me by.

On the morning of June 4, 1962, a front-page story in the *Oregonian* announced the Supreme Court's decision to overturn the convictions of four young freedom riders who had been arrested, convicted, and imprisoned in the South. I still remember cheering their good news. That same morning of their release, I left Warner Pacific College on a choir tour to sing and preach the Gospel to young people across the U.S. and Canada and to recruit new students for my alma mater.

That tour in the summer of 1962 was about as close as I got to being a freedom rider during my college days. I still wonder how the direction of my life might have changed if I had joined Martin for those last few years of his crusade.

Wearing her new engagement ring, Lyla hugged me and waved good-bye as our choir began its long, hot, eight-week odyssey in a school bus jam-packed with sound gear, personal luggage, and boxes of student recruitment materials.

The routine was simple. Every morning we drove to a new village, town, or city. Every afternoon we unpacked our speakers, plugged in our mikes, unfolded our little propaganda table, and piled the brochures in neat little stacks. Every evening we changed into our matching slacks and blazers, dimmed the houselights, welcomed the people, sang and preached our hearts out, gathered in the fellowship hall to counsel converts and recruit new students, rode home in pairs to lie down in guest rooms and on foldout sofas, and then sleep fitfully. Every morning we joined the host family for breakfast, met at the church for prayers with the pastor and his wife, packed the bus, and began the whole routine again.

Within a short time, the days became painfully predictable. The endless, flat highways between towns would be hot and boring. The churches would be packed with enthusiastic young people. The piano would be out of tune. The offering would be small. But the piles of fried chicken and the wedges of homemade peach or apple pie would make up for all the rest, at least until we grew tired of fried chicken. I still can't bring myself to eat it (and now I live in Texas). What we couldn't anticipate was the personal nightmare that two of us would experience during those long, painful weeks on the road.

One of our choir's tenors, Ted D., was a twenty-year-old junior majoring in speech and communications. When we first met, two years earlier, Ted was an attractive, enthusiastic freshmen from a small town in Iowa. He won my heart when he volunteered to help me with the grunt work for our weekly YFC television program.

We rushed about together in those busy days, choking down burgers and swilling shakes on the run, improvising furiously backstage at the rally or television station, finding emergency extras for crowd scenes and getting them fitted and into place just in time. For three summers running, Ted also assisted with the "cast of thousands" I had assembled for the spectacular July Fourth pageant and fireworks display performed seven nights each year to overflow crowds at the Alpenrose Dairy arena.

Often, after an early-evening choir practice, Ted and I would climb the steps behind the chapel up to the moonlit paths of Mt. Tabor and stroll in the semidarkness talking about music or studies or the next day's business. It never once dawned on me that Ted was falling in love. He knew the unwritten rules. Homosexuality was "of the devil." If he had any feelings about me, he hid them skillfully. We all learned to fake it in those days, but Ted was one of the best. He even fooled me.

On campus, surrounded by fellow students, staff, and professors, there was always a way to hide our fantasies, sublimate our crushes, and escape our temptations. But on that summer tour, Ted and I were often assigned to be roommates. On a few happy occasions, wealthy hosts provided two guest rooms, one for each of us. But most families only had one guest room, and in that room there was usually only one regular-sized bed.

During those first nights lying side by side with me in the same narrow bed, Ted never slept. Apparently, he was suffering from the same kind of infatuation that I had known with Peter and with Johnny, lying awake all night, turned-on and terrified. Fortunately, when we changed partners, Ted got some sleep, but he still pitched, tossed, and rolled, longing to hold and to be held. After seven or eight weeks of intense frustration, Ted grew desperate. He was exhausted and stressed to the limits. He couldn't sleep when we were together and he couldn't sleep when we were apart.

Finally, in a very small town in North Dakota, I awakened after midnight to the quiet sounds of scratching on my window. Somehow, Ted had managed to find his way through the strange, darkened streets from the home he had been assigned to the bedroom of the house where I lay sleeping. Until just before sunrise, I sat in the darkened living room listening to Ted pour out his story of homosexual guilt and confusion and his painful, unrequited feelings for me.

By the time I hugged him and hurried him away, Ted had risked revealing to me his "deepest, darkest secrets." I tried to minimize his fears and downplay his embarrassment, but I confessed nothing. My engagement to Lyla had just been announced. There was every reason to believe that I was straight as an arrow. Whether Ted believed it or not, he didn't say. The next night we found ourselves together in another narrow bed.

"Let's read for a while," I suggested, taking out a prayer book and turning to the evening vespers pages. We read from the Psalms. We quoted favorite scriptures. We talked for more than an hour. We prayed long, sincere prayers. And then, when I thought us both tired enough, I turned out the lights, rolled over on my side facing the wall, and almost immediately went to sleep.

I awakened shortly after to find Ted cuddled up against me with his arm draped over my shoulder. I didn't draw away. It seemed innocent enough. Maybe draping his arm around me would help Ted sleep. Besides, I liked it. Ted wasn't particularly my type, but he was young, attractive, sensitive, and we were two thousand miles from home. I had already determined to set a "good example" for Ted, but as I lay there debating to myself, it seemed apparent that leaving his arm draped casually over my shoulder was certainly not going to "lead him on" or "set his feet down the road to hell."

Without realizing it, by leaving Ted's arm in place, I was sending the first of a series of mixed messages that thoroughly confused my troubled roommate. Within the hour, I was awakened again. This time Ted's body was pressed tightly up against mine. I could feel his warm breath on the back of my neck. He was holding me in a kind of desperate embrace.

"Ted," I said, sitting up and swinging my legs over the side of the bed, "I'll just sleep in the armchair for a while. You keep the bed."

As I gathered up one of the blankets and moved to the old, leather recliner, Ted buried his face in the pillow.

"I'm sorry," he whispered. "I'm so embarrassed. I won't do it again. Please, don't sleep over there."

Again, we talked for half the night. Ted told me about the junior and senior high classmates whom he had secretly loved. He told me about being caught by a neighbor hugging another junior high boy in the park near his home. They were both reported to their parents, who subsequently punished them.

"My father made me promise I would never speak to my friend again," Ted recalled sadly. He remembered feeling embarrassed about that brief hug for the next two or three years.

During his senior year in high school, Ted had fallen deeply in love with another gay boy a year younger. For several weekends they had managed to sleep over at Ted's home. They spent the nights holding each other and exploring each other's body. But on the third weekend, Ted's father suddenly appeared at the open door, flipped on the lights, and found the two boys embracing. Four years later, Ted still blushed when he spoke of the terrible embarrassment he felt.

His father hardly spoke to Ted after that. His mother took him to a Christian counselor every Saturday afternoon for many months. The counselor was kind and understanding but insisted that homosexuality was a sin. Ted prayed for forgiveness at the counselor's desk and spent dozens of weeks in "therapy" studying the biblical passages by Moses and Paul that are used to condemn gay and lesbian people. Ted was never allowed to camp out, sleep over, or spend unchaperoned time with other young men again until he went away to college. During his freshman year, Ted fell in love with me.

By the time Ted finished this second, long confessional, we were both exhausted. We catnapped during the next day's drive and managed somehow to get through our evening concert. That same night, we were guests in a parishioner's summer home on a Minnesota lake; and once again, Ted and I ended up in the same bed. I knew it was a mistake, but I was too embarrassed to go to our host to change rooms or to the other guys to change partners.

That night, we began a restless routine that led us to even higher levels of exhaustion and frustration. Each time Ted tried to embrace me, though I wanted and needed his embrace, I got out of bed and slept on the floor. When he got down on the floor beside me, I climbed back into bed. Every other night, for the next three or four weeks, we were thrown together, and every other night I repeated my ridiculous routine: out of bed, onto the floor, back into bed, onto the floor again, a routine interrupted several times each night by long, heart-wrenching conversations, pleas, bargains, tears, and even threats.

I was young, naive, misinformed, bound up by my own denial, driven by natural, God-given impulses I didn't understand, trying to do what was "right" and at the same time feeling more and more drawn to Ted. I couldn't see it at the time, but during all those hot, restless, overstimulated summer nights together, I was rejecting him with one-half of my heart and reaching out to him with the other.

While denying it even to myself, I was revealing to Ted my own secret, aching need for intimacy with a man. In spite of my denials, I think he continued his nightly "seductions" probably because he sensed that I wanted him to continue. And, he was right. I hate to admit it, even to myself, but my mixed messages were at least partially the cause for Ted's desperate, driven acts during our last Sunday afternoon together.

Two nights before our tour was scheduled to end, in a town of just five hundred souls in Alberta, Canada, Ted found me reading alone in the pastor's study. I was sitting in a leather chair, my back toward the open door. Somehow, he had managed to climb the stairs and enter the room silently. Suddenly, I sensed someone standing in the room behind me. I turned to discover Ted staring at me from the doorway. He was obviously disturbed. His face was gray and his whole body was trembling slightly. Ted's left hand was leaning against the doorjamb. His right hand was holding something behind his back.

I spoke quietly, calmly, inviting him to pull up a chair and talk. He didn't respond. He just stood there looking down at me with his tired, angry eyes. As I watched, Ted dropped his right hand slowly to his side. He was clutching an ax. I don't know if he really meant to do me any harm, but I do know that he was angry and hurt, and I think we both knew there was some justification to his anger.

The summer had been a nightmare for both of us. Inadvertently, I had led Ted on while at the same time rejecting him. As a result, he had become more and more depressed. During the last few weeks, I had called a counselor at Warner Pacific and another member of our administration seeking guidance. Neither one had responded with any helpful advice, but somehow Ted had found out that I had called. He was certain that I had betrayed him by telling them his secret. He was probably terrified about what might happen when he returned to campus, or worse, when he went home to see his parents. In those last hours, his mood spiraled downward. He stood there in the silence, gripped by fear and terrible anger.

Suddenly, he began to weep. As I stood to comfort him, he turned quickly away from me, ran down the stairs and into the empty street. I rushed after him, shouting his name, hoping the pastor or one of the parishioners wouldn't see us, thinking I would find him and calm him down in time for the evening concert.

I could hear Ted sobbing even as he ran. The street was wide and empty of traffic. A huge grain elevator towered over the handful of stores all closed on Sunday. I lost him at the edge of town. And though we searched for hours, we never did find him. Two days later, we learned that Ted had hitchhiked to a nearby town and caught a train bound for New York City.

For thirty-one years I searched for Ted. Once, on a visit to Portland, I saw him walking in a city park. He stopped and turned toward me when I called out his name. I rushed up, hoping to embrace him, to beg his forgiveness for the inept way I had handled everything that summer, to find out how life had been for him since that terrible day in Canada when he had run away. But when Ted saw me standing there, he smiled sadly and turned away.

"Ted," I said, walking along beside him, "let me at least tell you this. During the tour, I wanted to make love to you, too."

For a long, searching moment he just stood there, staring at me silently. Finally, he said quietly, "That helps some." Then, without saying another word, he hugged me awkwardly and walked away.

Once we knew for certain that Ted had been found alive and well, the choir headed home to Portland. The last days of that long summer tour were even more miserable than the rest. With all that we had been through, I missed Ted with a growing melancholy. Already, I was beginning to wonder why I had insisted on rejecting him when I longed to be in his embrace. Of course, I couldn't explain to the others what had really happened. I was too embarrassed, too confused, too caught up in my denial to be honest about those terrible weeks. Still, I felt lonely without Ted, and though I was scheduled to leave almost immediately on a working tour of Europe and the Middle East, I didn't want to go alone.

After dinner, we walked from our cheap hotel to a nearby theater where once again *West Side Story* was playing. Once again, I was deeply moved by the tragic story of Romeo and Juliet set in the gang-ridden streets of New York City. Once again, my eyes teared up when Natalie Wood held her dying lover in her arms and sang, "There's a place for us, a time and place for us." Haunted now by the recent memories of those long, confusing nights with Ted, and by the terrible sight of him running and sobbing alone through the empty streets, once again I thought of Lyla.

She was spending the summer at her mother's home in Upland, California. Lyla's parents divorced shortly after her younger sister, Sharon, graduated from Santa Cruz High School. Lyla's mother had married an administrator in the California Juvenile Authority System. They had recently been transferred to southern California.

"Will you marry me?" I shouted over the static-plagued, long-distance connection from Canada to the U.S.

"I already answered that one," she shouted back, laughing.

"I mean next week. Seven days from now."

After only a short pause she shouted her reply. "Of course!"

In just nine days, I was scheduled to fly to New York City, catch the *Queen Elizabeth* for Europe, and begin a sixteen-country Volkswagen drive from London to Jerusalem with Dr. Milo Chapman and his wife, Maurinda. I would be carrying film and sound equipment to interview youth in all sixteen countries for a YFC television special.

"Can you be ready to leave for Europe and the Middle East, just twenty-four hours after the wedding?" I shouted to Lyla.

"Yes," she shouted back without a moment's hesitation.

Within twenty-four hours the wedding invitations were printed, addressed, and mailed. Lyla and her wonderful mother, Marjorie Smith, drove to Los Angeles to get one-day service on Lyla's first passport. Marge and Lyla shopped for a beautiful wedding dress. In just five days, Lyla borrowed matching dresses for her bridesmaids, ordered flowers, reserved and decorated the church, bought clothes for the trip to Europe and the Middle East, got blood tests and vaccinations, and met me at the Greyhound bus station with a kiss and an armload of flowers.

"I love you," Lyla said as she cuddled up beside me in the car.

"I love you, too," I answered, longing to tell her everything but terrified into silence by the secret that was haunting me. I wanted to be honest, but I was too afraid. She was a woman. I was a man. It was the way God intended things to be. We loved each other and we were convinced that our love would take care of everything. Looking back now on the thirty-one years that followed I am amazed at how right we were and how wrong.

Chapter *5*

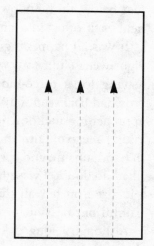

1962–64,

Learning to

Tell the Truth

O*n that last day before our wedding, September 6, 1962, I rushed* around Santa Cruz, confirming airline and cruise-ship tickets, fitting my rental tuxedo, buying gifts for my best man, Ed Scrivner, and my other last-minute wedding attendants, memorizing, or trying to memorize, the lyrics to "I'll Walk Beside You Through the World Tonight," the song my mother convinced me to sing to Lyla during the short wedding service we had planned, and picking up our simple gold wedding bands inscribed with *Te Adoro* (I love you), Spanish words, I am embarrassed to admit, from the sound track of *West Side Story*.

Noni made Swedish pancakes for the wedding rehearsal breakfast. Her eyes filled with tears as she prayed God's blessing on our marriage. Noni loved Lyla and was convinced that she would make the perfect wife for a preacher. Neither she nor Grampa ever doubted that was my calling. During the rehearsal as we practiced our vows, Noni sat in the back of the little cement-block church listening carefully to every word we said, praying for God's guidance in our lives and crying happy tears.

When the rehearsal ended and the sanctuary emptied at last, Lyla and I sneaked into the nursery, lay on the floor in the semidarkness just below the window where parents spied on their children, and held each other in a kind of frenzied embrace.

It was all happening so fast. I had just returned from that ill-fated eight-week choir tour with Ted. In just two days, Lyla and I would be leaving for a three-month drive from London to Jerusalem in the crowded backseat of a Volkswagen Bug. Our adrenaline flow was fast approaching meltdown. We were both excited and afraid. We were taking a leap of faith and beginning a once-in-a-lifetime journey, hand in hand, unsure and certain at the very same time. I loved Lyla, of that I had no doubt. I was glad to feel safe in her arms again, and that night I focused on her all the feelings I had barely bottled up during the painful but passionate weeks on tour.

Although I longed for an intimate relationship with a man, when the wedding vows were made that next day and the service finally ended, it was a woman standing at my side. It wasn't Darrel or Gordon or Ted who wore my wedding ring or kissed me before the applauding crowd of family and friends, it was Lyla. It was to her that I pledged my lifelong love and loyalty. Now, looking back, was that a cruel trick I played? Was it a terrible mistake for both of us? Was I really in love with someone else and not in love with Lyla?

The answer is a resounding "No!" to all three questions. I loved Lyla in those days as I love her now. How could I ever call the next twenty-five years a mistake when we had such a loving, productive life together as a couple, a relationship that produced our two wonderful children? And it certainly wasn't a cruel trick I played on Lyla, marrying her as a kind of cover for my homosexuality. I married Lyla because I loved her and wanted to spend the rest of my life in her company. And I wasn't afraid to marry her because I believed my conservative Christian friends and family who said or implied or somehow managed to convey to me the following dangerous misinformation: "If you're struggling with homosexuality, a good woman will take care of it." It was that lie that led to so many of the joys and sorrows that followed for both of us.

When the last bite of wedding cake was eaten and the last wedding portrait posed, after the presents had been gratefully received and the last good-byes tearfully spoken, after the mad dash through the hailstorm of rice and confetti and the long drive with Ed and Nancy Scrivner to the International Hotel in the landing path of the San Francisco Airport, we were alone at last. Lyla disappeared into the hotel bathroom to change into her beautiful new lime green peignoir set, and I whipped off my clothes and jumped into bed.

That night I learned that with a lot of love and huge doses of imagination, sex can be beautiful and exciting even between a hopelessly heterosexual woman and a confused and embarrassed gay man, even when they're exhausted. But I also learned that though I was able to perform sexually with Lyla, the process in my head was complex and exhausting. She was young and beautiful. She was playful and sexy in bed, but I was a gay man. No matter how hard I tried, I did not respond "normally" as a heterosexual male.

From earliest adolescence, my normal, automatic, subconscious sexual responses were to beautiful young men. To make love to Lyla, I had to focus my imagination on male bodies and on male faces. And though I needed those sexy male fantasies to keep our sex life going, they made me feel guilty and sinful. That made it twice as difficult to perform.

Gradually, the very fantasies that would help me fulfill the sexual side of our marriage drove me deeper into confusion and despair. Before long, even thinking about going to bed made me feel nervous and on trial with Lyla, with my goals to alter and abolish my homosexual longings, and with God, who I feared was condemning me for my failure.

But on that honeymoon flight to New York, I was hopeful that everything would work out all right. My whole heart, mind, and soul was focused on my beautiful new bride. When Lyla broke down for a moment and cried into my handkerchief on that long transcontinental flight, I knew that she was just tired from the fury of those last few hectic days. Nevertheless, I felt every tear.

I was determined to fulfill my wedding vow "to be faithful to her alone as long as we both should live." Lyla had been faithful to me during those five long, painful years of ambivalence. Even when she was dating other classmates, she was loyal to me. In our senior year, several men proposed to Lyla, but she never stopped believing in me. In light of all those years of love and loyalty, I was resolved that the old double-minded ways had to go. I would discipline my mind and my body so completely that no one would distract me. Our love was sacred. Nothing would get in its way.

But just a few days later, during our five-day Atlantic crossing on the *Queen Elizabeth,* I went alone to the pool for a swim before dinner. A young Frenchman in a thin bikini swam up beside me and engaged me in conversation. He was a tourist from Le Havre returning home after a summer in America. I suppose he just wanted to practice his English, and because the pool was built like a box half-filled with water with no deck or deck chairs, we dog-paddled or swam slowly in place side by side.

He was playful and often touched my hand or grabbed my arm and pulled me around to face him when he was making an important point. We were often thrown together when the ship moved through a large ocean swell. Once, he embraced me, laughing as the entire contents of the pool shifted us up against the wall. For a long, sensual moment we rode the waves back and forth up one wall and down the other, clinging together and laughing hysterically.

During dinner that night, I saw the handsome, young Frenchman sitting at a nearby table. His smiling, sensual presence left me feeling guilty and uncomfortable; yet I was drawn to him by a powerful, natural force. And though I fought it with all my heart, I longed to feel his wet body in my arms one more time. I was totally committed to Lyla and to my new marriage, and yet I felt grief and jealousy when that young man left the dining room arm in arm with another young Frenchman.

Now, I know that heterosexual men even on their honeymoons may also be attracted to a shapely body or a pretty face. Being momentarily stimulated by a beautiful (or a handsome) stranger is part of the human condition. Feeling momentarily infatuated by someone whose legs, face, smile, or laughter perfectly fits that mysterious sensual grid that each of us has imprinted on his or her brain is neither wrong nor uncommon.

"Beautiful people aren't that common," a wise friend once said to me. "Consider it one of God's little gifts when a real beauty passes by.

Enjoy it like any other aesthetic experience. Pretend you're viewing a magnificent Greek sculpture or a sensual nude sketch by Michelangelo. Then go on with your life."

I can do that now, but in those painful days when I was sexually stimulated by a beautiful man, it terrified me. I thought I was a sinful heterosexual with an "evil obsession," when, in fact, I was a natural, healthy homosexual being stimulated as God planned it. And though I managed to conceal my desperate feelings from most people, guilt and fear followed me like the dark, gray cloud that hovers over Pig Pen's head in the *Peanuts* comic strip. I told no one about my struggle to "overcome" homosexuality. Not even Lyla knew at first.

Every time I saw a handsome man who attracted me I felt all the more unnerved, guilt-ridden, and afraid. I was terrified that one day I would succumb, that one day I could resist no more. And I was convinced that once that happened, my reputation would be ruined, my marriage would end, my ministry would be destroyed, and my God would abandon me forever.

As a result of not being able to accept my sexual orientation with gratitude and grace, I was often moody, distracted, and plagued with guilt. It's a wonder Lyla could tolerate my uptightness in those days. On that same honeymoon cruise to Europe, for example, an older couple at another table close by sent over a bottle of expensive champagne "to toast the newlyweds."

"We can't drink it," I whispered to Lyla after reading the note and nodding gratefully in the direction of our benefactors.

Lyla just smiled patiently and waited for me to work out my old evangelical Christian guilt. She grew up in a home with beer in the refrigerator, a wine rack in the pantry, and a liquor cabinet in the living room. Having a drink was not a sin. Prohibition was not a virtue. But when she began her spiritual journey, Lyla decided to tolerate the strange and sometimes even silly rules that I still held so dear and spend her time on the real issues of love, justice, mercy, and truth.

In my sixteen years of childhood, there was never a can of beer or a bottle of wine in our house. My father even declined the posh Mayor's Suite at a San Francisco convention of state leaders one year because liquor would be served there. As children we often kidded each other with these words: "I don't drink. I don't smoke. I don't chew. And I don't go with girls who do." And though I, too, tried to focus on the important spiritual issues, even after marriage I was still caught up in the old strictures from my childhood.

Consequently, I sent the champagne back with a note of thanks to that generous, confused couple. I have always regretted that ungrateful, arrogant act. Toward the end of our European journey, Lyla and I stayed for two weeks in a small hotel on the Costa Brava on the magnificent Spanish Mediterranean. For $5 a day, we had a room overlooking the beach and three good meals. At dinner our first night, the management sent a carafe of white wine to our table. After three months in Europe and the Middle East, I decided to drink my first glass. The waiter hovered dutifully. Lyla grinned. And I picked up the carafe to pour. At the same moment, we all saw the dead fly lying drowned and rather swollen at the bottom of the carafe. I said jokingly, "It must be God's will that I never drink." Lyla groaned. The waiter disappeared in a flight of embarrassment.

I didn't take my first glass of wine for at least another year. And for more than a decade, I managed to sublimate, to deny, to put off, to control, to pray and fast into submission, to postpone, to hold in fearful bondage, to restrain, repress, regulate, bully, and intimidate my homosexual needs and longings. I may be a homosexual, I thought to myself during those painful days, but I will spend the rest of my lifetime fighting my homosexuality like an alcoholic in a twelve-step program fights his or her need to drink.

Determined to spend those three months in Europe thinking only of my wonderful, loving wife, I prayed long and hard every morning and every night. Almost every hour of every waking day, I tried to discipline my eyes, my thoughts, and my actions. But from day one, it was a difficult and demanding game that I could not win.

By the time our trip had ended and we finally set sail back across the North Atlantic on the *Maasdam,* a little Dutch liner, I was a nervous wreck. That December cruise—nicknamed by Lyla the Thirteen Days of Nausea Special—was a kind of preview of the stormy times that lay ahead. We spent most of those two weeks on our stateroom bunks, seasick, frightened, surviving on apples and crackers our steward provided, clinging together when the ship plunged down into a fifty-foot trough, unsure we would make it through the storm.

The little white 1962 Volkswagen traveled with us deep in the hold of the SS *Maasdam.* After being greeted on Christmas Eve by carolers singing from a barge off Halifax, Nova Scotia, and after sailing past the Statue of Liberty into New York Harbor, we packed our few belongings in the bonnet of our faithful little Bug and drove from New York to Santa Cruz in the dead of winter.

Crossing the Colorado Rocky Mountains, the wind blew so hard against us, we seldom made better than ten or fifteen miles an hour. After a seven-day, snowbound, wind-whipped, icy crossing of the continental United States, we made it home tired, eager to settle down, and flat broke. Surviving another round of good-byes and perked up by another Swedish-pancake breakfast and by the earnest prayers of Noni, we packed up our wedding gifts, drove to Portland, Oregon, and rented our first apartment on Mt. Tabor near the Warner Pacific College campus.

To support us, I continued my work at Portland Youth for Christ, emceeing the Saturday-night rallies and producing and hosting the "World of Youth," our weekly television program. While Lyla finished her baccalaureate degree and earned a teacher's credential in English at Portland State University, I completed my master of arts in communications at the University of Portland. We also produced two 16mm films that year.

It was a busy time, but staying busy was the way I survived. Instead of telling Lyla about my struggle to "overcome" homosexuality, instead of being honest with myself, my wife, my closest friends, confidants, and even my counselors, I tried to push the whole ugly nightmare out of my mind with a schedule that kept me working day and night.

My subconscious must also have been working overtime those days because the two 16mm films I produced during the 1963–64 year were both about young people having the courage to be honest. My master of arts thesis film, *Dream Island,* was the story of two teenagers, Mike and Kathy, who were struggling with their decision about premarital sex. I played the youth director to whom the kids confide. Lyla played my wife. Unfortunately for me, the stereotypical but well-intentioned dialogue was preserved in my master's thesis in the university library.

At a meeting of Mike and Kathy's Youth Fellowship group, the youth director says, "We never faced the fact that Christian kids fight the sex battle, too, until it was too late for one of our own members." Then he goes on to tell the story of "Diane," who got pregnant because she never told anyone about her secret love and never asked the questions or got the answers that she needed.

Noni visited Portland during *Dream Island*'s production. We ferried her across the Willamette River to our island with its little shipwreck and its white, sandy beaches. As we raced against the sun to film the romantic scene between the two young lovers who were working desperately not to give in to their sexual passions, Noni watched with growing horror. She believed every word of their dialogue and wanted to rush in to stop the kids before they went "too far." When we tried to explain it was only a movie, Noni, who had never yet seen a theatrical film, stood up in the sand and stated for cast and crew to hear, "This filmmaking isn't very conducive to spirituality, is it!"

Noni never did understand films or filmmaking, and she certainly didn't see it as a kind of ministry. We finally convinced Noni and Grandpa to attend a 70mm screening of *Ben-Hur*. At intermission, just after the famous chariot race, Grandpa sat blinking in the silence, looking stunned and disoriented. Noni headed for the exit like a soldier retreating from a war zone. "It isn't over," I said. "It is for me," Noni answered.

After years of avoiding movie theaters like the plague, Noni and Grandpa finally got a television set "to watch Billy Graham," she said, along with her other soon-to-be-favorite religious and news programs. One afternoon, she greeted me excitedly at the door. "God is going to answer my prayers," Noni said confidently. "I've finally found a way to support my missionaries." Grandma spent most of her day raising flowers or baking fruitcakes to sell in order to support young couples on the mission field. Noni had been watching "The Millionaire," a fictional TV series featuring a rich old man who gave away a million dollars every week. "I've asked God to lay my burden on the heart of that fine old millionaire," Noni said, fully believing it would happen, "and I'm just waiting for the day."

That same year, I collaborated with three good friends—Dr. Winfield C. Arn, the director of Portland YFC, Kirby Brumfield, an accomplished local actor and television personality, and Dan Dunkelberger, our YFC cameraman—on the first of our *Charlie Churchman* series. Kirby, in black mustache, baggy pants, and bowler hat, looked remarkably like Charlie Chaplin. We shot in grainy black and white and sped up the action to match those wonderful high-speed, slapstick performances by Chaplin, Buster Keaton, and the

Keystone Kops. We added titles and a honky-tonk piano to complete our first religious satire, *Charlie Churchman and the Teenage Masquerade*.

Again, I wrote and directed the motion picture without even realizing how accurately it reflected my secret struggle. At the beginning of the film, our cast of normal, robust, happy teenagers speed through a hilarious school week. But on Sunday, when they enter church, each puts on a translucent mask, wears the mask through the youth fellowship meeting, and when the meeting ends, takes off the mask, leaves it at the door, and rushes back into the real world.

Portland's Civic Auditorium overflowed with thousands of teenagers the night *Charlie* was premiered. After the film, Dr. Arn introduced our cast and crew to the enthusiastic audience. When he introduced me, the young people came to their feet, cheered, and applauded. Religious films had a reputation in those days for being notoriously dull. *Charlie* had them laughing and cheering with recognition. But even as I received their applause for making such an honest little film, it didn't occur to me to practice what I preached on the big screen, to take off my own mask and get about the business of living out my gay life with gratitude and integrity.

Toward the end of our last summer vacation in Santa Cruz, my fourteen-year-old kid brother, Dennis, asked permission to drive with us back to Portland. Our decision to take him for a short visit north led to a terrible family tragedy. Like his older brother, Denny loved theater, music, and film. He wanted to attend the Shakespeare Festival in Ashland, Oregon, and to see his big brother making movies and hosting his own television program. Dennis was exactly ten years younger than I and five years younger than our brother, Marshall. Marshall and I both loved Denny. He was smart, eager, enthusiastic about everything and everyone, and he loved us back with abandon. During my visits home during the past years of college and grad school, Dennis would race from the open front door, run toward me down the sidewalk, and throw himself into my arms.

"He can go with you," Mom said with a worried look in her eyes, "but you have to promise to take good care of him."

"Of course I will," I answered, never dreaming how those words would haunt me to this day.

After the magnificent drive north through San Francisco, across the Golden Gate Bridge into the wine country of Napa, Sonoma, and

Mendocino counties, and the deep green forests of the low Sierras, Lyla, Denny, and I spent two nights in Ashland at the Shakespeare Festival sitting on the grass, eating hot dogs, listening to the sounds of renaissance instruments, watching and discussing plays. I had a film to direct or we might have stayed forever in that idyllic place.

Back in Portland, Denny enjoyed touring our television studios and watching us film *Charlie* on the southeast side of Mt. Tabor in Portland. When he got bored, I borrowed a bicycle from our neighbor and waved as Denny bicycled down the well-marked, beautifully landscaped mountain trails. Less than an hour later, a police car drove up with an officer inquiring about a twelve- or thirteen-year-old boy on a bike. When his description sounded exactly like Denny, we raced to a nearby emergency hospital where I found my little brother lying on a gurney soaked in blood.

Orderlies restrained me as I tried to get through the crowd of nurses and doctors around his broken, unconscious body. Denny had been riding down an unmarked trail that ended unexpectedly where a new road had been carved out below. He had ridden his bicycle into space and had fallen at least thirty or forty feet before hitting the tarmac.

Lyla held me in the lobby and we wept together as we waited for the long, difficult surgery to end. The doctor finally approached us with the good news. Denny would live, but he would be in the hospital several weeks before we could transport him home. I stayed those two long weeks with Denny in his hospital room while his young body mended and his scrapes and gashes healed. For several days we worked together on my keynote speech for our International Youth Fellowship Convention that would be held in Louisville, Kentucky, a few weeks later. He was determined to hear me give that speech and I promised that we would fly him there if the doctors approved.

Finally, Denny was cleared to travel home. Mom and Dad supervised the delicate journey. We were all relieved to see him tucked safely and comfortably at last into his own bed. The family doctor would watch over Denny's final weeks of healing. Lyla and I prepared to go to Louisville. On the phone, Denny nagged me to take him along. I promised that if he was well enough, Denny would have a front-row, center seat in that huge convention center in Kentucky.

Feeling confidant that Denny was well enough to be left in Noni's care, Mom, Dad, and Marshall began the long drive to Louisville.

Instead of getting better, suddenly my little brother's condition wors-
ened seriously. Apparently, a physician had taken him off antibiotics
too soon. Without warning, Noni found Denny in his bed doubled
over by intense pain. The doctor diagnosed spinal meningitis. They
rushed Denny to a special intensive care unit in San Jose where he
died just hours later.

If you have ever received one of those late-night phone calls where
a stranger announces the worst news possible, you will know exactly
how Lyla and I felt that night when we were awakened from our sleep
with the terrible words, "Your little brother, Denny, is dead."

I screamed in pain, and together we rushed frantically to the Portland airport. Jesus had raised Lazarus from the dead. He would raise
my brother Denny, I was certain. We landed in San Jose at sunrise,
rented a car, and raced to the hospital.

"Take me to him," I told the doctor.

"But he's gone," the poor exhausted man replied.

"But I must see him anyway," I shouted impatiently, not realizing
that my emotions were perilously close to collapse. He was my kid
brother. I had promised to take care of him. He could not be dead.
And if he were dead, God would bring him back to life. Until that
awful day, I had never even thought of praying such a prayer. But
while we drove and flew that night, I was obsessed by it.

The doctor advised me strongly against looking at Denny's body.
When I refused to heed that advice, he led me through the morgue
into a silent, sterile room. An attendant opened a door in the wall and
pulled out a heavy, sliding tray. A young boy's body lay on the tray
covered by a heavy, white sheet. The doctor and the attendant left me
alone with that precious little body. I pulled back the sheet and stared
down at my baby brother. I had entered the room crazy for a miracle,
but one look at Denny's face and I knew he wasn't there to be revived.
He had gone to be with Jesus and I was alone.

"Oh, Denny," I cried. "I am so sorry."

After a few moments of terrible anguish, the doctor returned to lead
me from the room. Wisely, Lyla had waited in the hall. She drove me
back to the San Francisco airport where Dad, Mom, and Marshall
would be arriving from Denver, Colorado, where we had found them.
One day earlier, at a campsite along the highway, Marshall had fallen
from a tree and broken his leg. He hobbled off the plane on crutches
just behind Mom and Dad. I reached out to take all three of them in

my arms, and we stood in the airport concourse weeping as we had seen so many others weep before.

Just days later, I stood to deliver my keynote address to five thousand teenagers in a Convention Center arena in Louisville, Kentucky. Denny and I had written that speech together. I could not fail him. Halfway through my opening remarks, however, I looked down from the huge platform and noticed one empty front-row, center chair. Denny promised me he would be there, sitting in that reserved seat, smiling up at me. But the seat was empty.

For a moment, I couldn't speak. I just stood there staring down at that empty chair, choking back my tears, feeling guilty, sad, and alone. Then, suddenly, I knew in my heart that he was there, smiling up at me as he had promised. And Denny was not alone. He was being held in the arms of his loving Creator. I believed that then. I believe it now. In our darkest moments, God comes through to lead us back into the light.

From Genesis in the Old Testament to Revelation in the New, Jewish and Christian writers in all sixty-six books of the Bible make this one thing clear. We are not alone on planet Earth. In the midst of our pain, God is there to comfort us whether we feel God's presence or not. The Psalmist David said it best in the Twenty-third Psalm: "Though I walk through the valley of the shadow of death . . . thou art with me." How many times in my life, blinded by tears, feeling helpless and alone, have I thrown myself on that promise? And every time, the Creator's loving Spirit has been there to see me through.

But during the weeks and months that followed, it was easy to get distracted and to forget that ancient promise of God's loving presence in our lives. For more than a dozen years, at least half my life, I had lived with fear and guilt brought on by not understanding my God-given sexual orientation. After Denny's death, that fear and guilt was compounded by another misunderstanding.

It is difficult to admit this, but during those first years after the tragedy on Mt. Tabor, there were desperate, irrational times when I thought maybe God was punishing me for my homosexual thoughts by letting my brother die. I knew then as I know now that our God of love and grace and forgiveness doesn't work that way. But then I was distracted and confused.

In the evenings for those last months in Portland, I often walked alone on Mt. Tabor, reliving those tragic memories, trying to deal with my guilt, struggling to understand and overcome my need for male intimacy, praying to God to take away my homosexual feelings, to end the longing, and to ease the pain. I knew that the young gay men who often passed me in the shadows were just searching for companionship as I was searching. But their smiles of recognition left me in growing terror. After a nod or a smile passed between us, fear would sweep over me in waves and I would rush down the mountain, enter our little apartment, and fall on my bed weeping in despair.

Upon graduation, Lyla and I moved to Los Angeles where she taught English at Crescenta Valley High School while I made films and began work on my Ph.D. in communications at the University of Southern California. I was drinking liquid Maalox on the hour and a combination of milk and cream on the half-hour hoping to heal my stomach, inflamed by acid churned up by all the conflict. It had to end. I had carried this burden alone too long. Someone had to share it.

Through the religious grapevine, I learned that Dr. Don Tweedie, a well-known Christian psychologist who taught at Fuller Theological Seminary, was also taking private clients. My career as a Christian filmmaker, television producer, and writer was on the rise. I was afraid that telling Dr. Tweedie my deepest, darkest fears would destroy everything. Where does this dark, irrational fear of homosexuality come from that makes homosexuality a "sin" worse than all the others? Why are we so frightened to even discuss the issue with our counselors? It took me weeks to get up my courage even to talk about my personal struggle with a professional.

I can still remember sitting in his little reception room, waiting to be called into Don's office. What would I say? How would I say it? I was in an absolute panic when he called me in. Trembling, I entered his office and practically collapsed with fear on his old leather recliner. Dr. Tweedie just sat there silent and smiling. "It's your buck," he said with a grin. "What can I do for you?"

"I think I'm a homosexual," I blurted out, breaking down the wall of silence and fear I had carefully constructed to isolate my secret struggle these many years.

Don didn't blink. He just sat there smiling and waiting for me to continue. Lightning didn't strike me dead. No voice from the skies spoke out to condemn me. I didn't hear anything but my heart, and it was beating with the speed and power of a jackhammer.

"Have you told your wife?" he asked quietly.

"No," I said, hoping I would never have to tell her.

"Then tell her today." And with those four words, he stood up from his desk, walked to the door, and thanked me for coming.

"That's it?" I said dumbfounded by his instant and terrifying advice. "Tell my wife?"

"That's it, and tell her today. Don't put it off one more hour if you can help it. Then, when you've told her, come back, and I'll refer you to someone who is sure to help."

I staggered to a pay phone. Lyla was teaching at Crescenta Valley High School. "I'm on my way," I told her. "I have something to tell you."

On that drive up Foothill Boulevard, I went through the whole cycle of fear again. How would I tell her? Worse yet, how would she reply? Would she want a divorce? Would my life and my vocation end up in ruins? I wanted to postpone this terrible moment, to find a way of escape. "Tell her," he'd said, "and tell her today." He was a well-known counselor and a professor of psychology. Certainly he knew what he was doing.

Lyla looked concerned as she moved into the front seat beside me. We drove back down Foothill Boulevard in silence. Although it was only four P.M., I suggested that we stop for a bite at a strange little Chinese restaurant near Pasadena. Lyla looked surprised, but quickly agreed. Again we sat in silence sipping tea while I tried to get up my courage. I told her about seeing Dr. Tweedie and every step leading up to that moment.

"I think I'm a homosexual," I finally whispered, looking across the table into her eyes.

Lyla didn't even blink. She just took my trembling hands in her hands and smiled with such love and confidence that my worst fears vanished.

"Mel," she asked quietly, "what do you want to do about it?"

"I want to work it out," I answered honestly. "I want to have a home and family. I just don't know what to do about the sexual thing."

"We'll work it out together," she said, and with those words, I began to hope again.

The young German pastor Dietrich Bonhoeffer, who was hanged by the Nazis just before the end of World War II, said these words to his students in the underground resistance seminary: "When I go to my brother [or sister] to confess, I am going to God. . . . In confession, the breakthrough to community takes place."

"Evil," warned Bonhoeffer, "demands to have a man by himself. It withdraws him from the community. The more isolated a person is, the more destructive will be the power of evil over him, the more disastrous his isolation. . . . Evil shuns the light. In the darkness of the unexpressed it poisons the whole being of a person. This can happen even in the midst of a pious community. In confession the light of the Gospel breaks into the darkness and seclusion of the heart. . . . It is a hard struggle . . . but God breaks gates of brass and bars of iron" (Psalms 107:16).

Lyla was for me that day the voice and the arms of God. Although I had feared judgment and rejection, she reached out to me in love and acceptance as we walked from that little Chinese restaurant into the rest of our life together. At long last, the days of silence were over. There would be difficult times ahead, but I was no longer alone, and that has made all the difference.

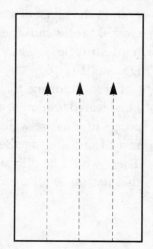

Chapter 6

1964–70,

Learning About Friendship

$\mathcal{E}$*arly in 1964, I sat with a group of graduate students in a film-*criticism class taught by Arthur Knight, a columnist-critic for *Saturday Review* magazine. Late every Tuesday afternoon, I drove from our apartment in Pasadena to attend his seminar at the University of Southern California campus where I was studying for a Ph.D. in communications.

Because of his national clout as a critic and film historian, Arthur managed to con the biggest names in Hollywood to make guest appearances in his graduate seminar to show and discuss their films. Already I had spent long stimulating evenings with the likes of Alfred Hitchcock *(Psycho)*, George Stevens *(Giant)*, and Otto Preminger *(Man with the Golden Arm)*. That night we were all rather disappointed to see an unfamiliar young Greek sitting in the guest-director's chair.

"This is Michael Cacoyannis," Arthur began. "Michael has produced a film that all of the major film distributors have turned down."

"They hate it," Cacoyannis cut in good-naturedly, "but they are wrong, all of them."

Cacoyannis spoke with a lilting Greek accent. And though he looked exhausted and a bit wary, his eyes sparkled and his enthusiasm was contagious. After investing millions of dollars in borrowed money and years of his life in the project, Cacoyannis wanted desperately for someone to appreciate his film. Knowing his student's arrogant, would-be-film-critics ways, Arthur smiled sympathetically, but promised nothing.

"Based on a Nikos Kazantzakis novel," Arthur Knight continued, "the film features Alan Bates as a young English writer on the island of Crete who is befriended by a rather overly gregarious Greek fisherman, played by our old friend Anthony Quinn. I think it's a film you might enjoy. All the director wants in return for this preview is your *enthusiastic* recommendations for him to present to the last studio in town that hasn't already turned him down."

The students laughed politely and pulled out their pens, notebooks, and small flashlights. The screening room dimmed, and for the first time, at least that we knew, *Zorba the Greek* was publicly shown in America. In the beginning, I halfheartedly watched the story unfold, but by the time Zorba and the uptight young English writer stood in the ruins of their shattered dreams, I was enthralled. "Teach me to dance," the young man says to Zorba, overcoming his fear and timidity at last. Slowly at first, free arms out, palms up, faces turned to the ashen sky, the two men twist and turn, faster and faster in a traditional Greek dance, signaling the acceptance of their unhappy fate and hopeful resignation to what might follow.

As the two men began dancing together down the beach, I began to weep. When the lights came on, the rest of the students were scribbling furiously on their notepads such words as *melodramatic* and *pretentious,* while I sat in the back of the screening room sobbing and blowing my nose into a wad of paper towels I had snared from the rest room.

I said nothing during the long, critical discussion that followed. Barely able to hold back more tears, I sat in embarrassed silence until mercifully Arthur Knight dismissed the class. As I tried to sneak out the door, Cacoyannis rushed up to me, grabbed my hand, shook it enthusiastically, and said for all to hear, "Thank you for your review!"

It was typical, especially in those days, for me to have overrelated to the young English writer, for those were melodramatic times for the world and for me. That year, when the Beatles invaded America, conservative Christians were quick to warn the nation's families about the sinfulness of rock and roll, but slow to recognize the real sin of racism and bigotry that threatened to undo the nation.

For the last decade, since 1954, when segregated public schools had been outlawed by the Supreme Court in *Brown v. Board of Education of Topeka,* the civil rights issue had been heating up in the South and across the country. In 1956, after Martin Luther King led his successful boycott of public transportation in Montgomery, the Supreme Court struck down Alabama's laws requiring segregated buses. In 1957, Arkansas governor Orval Faubus prevented integration of the public schools in Little Rock by calling out the state militia. In 1958, the governor closed down the schools of Arkansas to prevent integration in that state. In 1959, his act was declared unconstitutional, and hundreds gathered near Little Rock's Central High to protest its integration.

Tension and violence increased across the South and around the nation. Martin Luther King and other courageous Christians, clergy and laity alike, led their congregants in marches, pray-ins, sit-down strikes, boycotts, freedom rides, and demonstrations to speed the end of segregation in this country. The enemies of integration answered with riots, beatings, arson, lynchings, and assassinations.

In 1960, President Eisenhower's Civil Rights Commission announced that Americans in twenty-three states had filed complaints about being denied their right to vote. In 1961, President Kennedy created referees to promote and supervise voter registration. On August 28, 1963, hundreds of thousands of Americans filled the mall between the Lincoln and Washington memorials to protest segregation and to hear Dr. King's famous words, "I have a dream." On November 22, 1963, President Kennedy was assassinated.

Early in March 1964, still grieving and in shock from their young president's death and with his death the loss of so much promise, hundreds of Christian leaders, clergy and laity alike, marched on Selma, Alabama, to demand the end of bigotry and segregation in that state. Jerry Falwell, the thirty-one-year-old pastor of the Thomas Road Baptist Church in Lynchburg, Virginia, publicly responded to the civil rights crisis in a sermon entitled "Ministers and Marchers." Jerry's response was typical of most evangelical, fundamentalist churches and churchmen in those days.

The new thousand-seat sanctuary that Jerry Falwell and his congregation had dedicated that year was filled to capacity as Jerry reminded his people that a Christian's citizenship is in heaven. "Our only purpose on this earth," he insisted, "is to know Christ and to make Him known." Jerry went on to admit that "believing the Bible as I do, I would find it impossible to stop preaching the pure saving Gospel of Jesus Christ and begin doing anything else—including the fighting of communism or participating in civil rights reforms."

"Preachers are not called to be politicians," he added, taking direct aim at Martin and the other activist clergy, "but to be soul winners. If as much effort could be put into winning people to Jesus Christ across the land as is being exerted in the present civil rights movement, America would be turned upside down for God. . . . I feel we need to get off the streets and back into the pulpits and into the prayer rooms."

One week later, President Johnson encouraged Baptist leaders to join the battle for civil rights. He appealed directly to Christians in the South to get behind the passage of the new civil rights legislation. Jerry refused. In an interview with the *Lynchburg News,* he said the bill had been misnamed.

"It should be considered civil wrongs rather than civil rights," he claimed. "It is a terrible violation of human and private-property rights." To a local newspaper reporter he added, "I've spoken against this bill in the pulpit and I will continue to do so."

On a Sunday morning four months later, four young men, three white, one black, members of CORE, the Congress of Racial Equality, held a kneel-in on the steps of Jerry's Thomas Road Baptist Church. They carried a sign reading "Does God Discriminate?" After the demonstration, Jerry joked about the boys, saying nothing was wrong with the young demonstrators that a good haircut wouldn't cure.

Years later, when I was ghostwriting Jerry Falwell's autobiography, I uncovered these events in the local press and asked Jerry to explain his side of the story. When he answered, Jerry spoke quietly and thoughtfully. "Now I wish I had taken another approach entirely," he admitted. "We resented those teenage boys for their interference in the lives of our community; but looking back, they were courageous, and it is time that I for one admit it."

According to Jerry, it wasn't the marches or the demonstration on his steps that changed his mind about segregation. It was at least in part the Christian witness of Lewis, an elderly African-American man who held the last chair at Lee Bacas's shoeshine business on Main Street in Lynchburg. It was Jerry's Saturday-morning ritual to have Lewis shine his shoes exactly at ten A.M. "He could set his watch by my appearance," Jerry told me.

"The Lord is so good, isn't he," Lewis would say each Saturday morning and Jerry would nod and smile in agreement. But one Saturday morning, not long after the young men from CORE held their pray-in on the steps of Thomas Road Baptist Church, Lewis asked a question that helped change Jerry's life forever.

"Say, Reverend," he began softly, so that no one else could hear, "when am I going to be able to join that church of yours over on Thomas Road?" Already in 1964, Jerry's sermons were broadcast on radio and on television. Lewis listened faithfully. "I don't want to cause you no trouble, Reverend," the old man said quietly as he finished polishing Jerry's shoes that day, "but I sure do like the way you preach and would like one day to join there with you."

Jerry told me that the old man's question hit him "like a boxer feels a hard blow to the stomach." Thirty years have passed since the man who shined Jerry Falwell's shoes asked when he could join Jerry's church. Now, another friend is asking. When can I join your church, Jerry, and still not be forced to hide my God-given sexual orientation? When will your church accept me, your old friend and confidant, the man who wrote your autobiography, into leadership in your church as an openly gay man, let alone be willing to ordain me into ministry?

During all those years at Thomas Road Baptist, Jerry represented a "Bible-based" tradition of exclusion on the basis of race that he now acknowledges to be wrong. Today, he represents another kind of exclusion, this time based on sexual orientation. Both policies were backed by a misunderstanding of the Scriptures. Both policies require courage to confront, let alone to change. He had that kind of courage once. I wonder if he will have that kind of courage again.

Because homosexuality isn't a sexual preference, but a sexual orientation that cannot be changed, that we must live with all our lives, to live with integrity and grace we need the Christian community to love us, to understand us, to accept us as we are. Instead, my sisters and brothers in Lynchburg and across the country have to lie about themselves, their friends, and their relationships even to join their fellow Christians in worship. When will the lying end? Right now the hate they feel coming from the church and its leaders keeps them from the love of Christ. One day soon, I hope Jerry will show gay and lesbian people, as he finally showed Lewis, what real love looks like.

In 1968, the first black family applied for membership in Jerry's church. The board of deacons decided unanimously to accept them. But in June 1964 when 250,000 people marched on Washington to lobby Congress on behalf of a civil rights bill, and in July when President Johnson signed the civil rights act outlawing discrimination in all public facilities, Jerry was a fiery and unwavering spokesman for the opposition.

That same month, James E. Chaney, twenty-one, an African-American, and two white friends, Michael Schwerner, twenty-four, and Andrew Goodman, twenty-one, were murdered by racists in Mississippi. The young freedom riders had traveled across the state registering voters and fighting discrimination. On a dark Mississippi country road, they were arrested "for speeding," jailed, fined, and released. It was the last time the boys were ever seen. Their bodies were later found buried in an isolated earthen dam.

About that time, at USC, I sat in Arthur Knight's class weeping as Zorba the Greek and his young friend danced down the beach. That young, uptight English writer seemed so much like me. For most of my life, I had spent endless time and energy feeling guilty and afraid, struggling against my homosexuality, trying to please God and my friends and family. I longed to dance free of that struggle even if it meant standing in the ruins of my dreams. I remember thinking how much more noble it would have been to be buried in that earthen dam in Mississippi with James, Michael, and Andrew than it would be to go on using up my life in the endless struggle to overcome my sexual orientation. But with Lyla at my side, I determined again to go on struggling.

After reporting back to Dr. Don Tweedie that I had told Lyla everything, he referred me to a counselor on the staff of Clyde Narramore's new Rosemead Counseling Center near our home in Pasadena. Immediately, I made an appointment. Dr. Parker was a psychiatrist who had also written widely on the power of prayer. At his suggestion, I began my long series of "treatments" in his office with a time of prayer, asking God to deliver me from this "burden of homosexuality."

"If you have enough faith," the doctor promised, "God can do anything."

Remembering those painful sessions in Dr. Parker's office, at first I felt angry that this Christian professional, a man who had earned doctoral degrees in medicine and psychology, would be so uninformed about sexual orientation. However, in fairness to his memory, until recent years that kind of ignorance about all sexual matters was fairly widespread among the whole medical and psychological community. Until the evidence showed differently, homosexuality was considered a "disorder" by the American Psychological Association in the 1960s. Dr. Parker was undoubtedly sincere in reflecting the views of his medical colleagues and his Christian associates, but sincerity is no virtue when it comes to psychological or spiritual malpractice whether in the office of an accredited psychological clinic or in the crusade and healing tent of Oral Roberts or Katherine Kuhlman.

That same year, my parents took Lyla and me to see the charismatic preacher and healer Katherine Kuhlman in action. Neither Dad nor Mom had any idea then of how sincerely I wanted to be "healed" of my homosexuality. They didn't even know that I was gay or that I was in weekly "therapy" to overcome my gayness. They just came to see their kids in southern California. Mom and Lyla bustled about the kitchen while Dad unpacked his toolbox to help me patch, paint, and plumb.

My parents loved to attend the Kuhlman meetings at the Shrine Auditorium in downtown Los Angeles. We obliged them once each visit to go along. The four of us sat in the first-row, left-hand side of the balcony looking down on the endless wheelchairs and portable beds filled with sincere seekers waiting for the time of healing.

When the enthusiastic singing, clapping, and hand-waving had ended, when the sermon and the altar call were through, Ms. Kuhlman moved to the front of the stage and called on the congregation to "pray the prayer of faith" as the endless line of suffering souls marched past to be touched, prayed for, "slain in the spirit," and healed by God's Spirit through Katherine's "anointed hands."

Using the same words my Christian psychiatrist had used, Kuhlman promised that "if you have enough faith, God can do anything." I grasped Lyla's hand tightly and strained forward in my chair in the

Shrine Auditorium exactly as I had strained forward in my chair in the Rosemead Counseling Center. I begged God to heal me and believed with all my heart, soul, mind, and strength that God could do it. And in both cases, I rose up from that time of prayer determined to do exactly as I had been instructed. "Whatever you feel, act as though you have been healed," they told me, "and God will honor your faithfulness and heal you for certain."

It's the same primitive, misleading line used by many in the "ex-gay" movement today. "If you have enough faith," they promise, "God can do anything." In those days, I believed it. Now, I know how dangerous and misleading the whole process can be. I left that place determined to prove my faith in God. For the next years, I read and memorized biblical texts on faith. I fasted and prayed for healing. I believed that God had "healed me" or was "in the process of healing me." But over the long haul, my sexual orientation didn't change. My natural attraction to other men never lessened. My need for a long-term, loving relationship with another gay man just increased with every prayer.

After months of trying, my psychiatrist implied that I wasn't really cooperating with the Spirit of God. "He is trying to heal you," the doctor said, "but you are hanging on to the old man and not reaching out to the new." After that, my guilt and fear just escalated.

In fact, the doctor was wrong. He had promised that if I had enough faith, God would completely change my sexual orientation. I was clinging to that promise like a rock climber clings to the face of a cliff. You can imagine how confused and guilt-ridden I became when my homosexuality stayed firmly in place and the new heterosexual man I hoped to become continued to elude me. Now I know that my homosexual orientation was another of the Creator's loving gifts. Then, I thought it was my punishment for not having enough faith.

That night watching Katherine Kuhlman at the Shrine Auditorium I saw an example of the heartbreak caused to people who are certain that they have failed when God "doesn't heal them." Lyla and I were both drawn to a young boy whose parents were pushing their wheelchair-bound son toward the stage for healing. The parents were weeping. The child was wide-eyed with fear and wonder. They held each other's hands and whispered urgent, desperate prayers as they waited in the line. They watched as before them a crippled man tossed away his crutches and a deaf woman praised God that she could hear again. Finally, the parents had positioned their son's wheelchair directly in front of Katherine Kuhlman.

"Do you have faith?" Ms. Kuhlman asked the little boy's mother.

"Oh, yes!" the woman replied, sobbing and reaching out to touch the healer's hands.

"Do you have faith?" Ms. Kuhlman asked the boy's father.

"Yes," he said quietly, rubbing his hand through the boy's hair and trying not to cry.

"And little one," she said, leaning dramatically over the boy, "do you have faith?"

The boy nodded and looked confused. Katherine Kuhlman laid her hands on the child and began to pray in tongues. With their arms in the air and their own prayers drowning out the prayers of Ms. Kuhlman, the audience surged with excitement.

"Now, child," Ms. Kuhlman said firmly, "you just come here to me."

The child tried to get up out of his wheelchair, but he couldn't move. His mother and father knelt beside him, urging him to take that "first step of faith." The audience prayed and wept and applauded as the boy leaned forward in his chair. But no matter how hard he tried, the boy couldn't stand. Finally, Ms. Kuhlman moved on to the next person in the line. The parents rushed the boy offstage. Lyla and I still remember the look of failure and embarrassment in the child's eyes and the anger we felt that such a thing could happen. We do the same to our gay sons and daughters when we force them to have faith that God will heal them. When, in fact, that isn't the way God works.

I believe that God still heals troubled minds and broken bodies. The Old and New Testament writers all talk about the power of faith, and I am totally convinced that the Spirit of God is present among us working to rescue and to renew this planet and her people. After all, I have seen God heal me of the anger and of the guilt I felt after praying the wrong prayer for more than two decades. Now, however, when I see well-meaning parents praying for the "healing" of their homosexual children, I am certain that they are praying the wrong prayer altogether. They should be praying to understand and accept their children as God has made them.

But back then, I was certain that God wasn't healing me because I didn't have enough faith, because I was doing something wrong. In my muddled brain, I thought perhaps it was God's way of getting me out of media and into the ministry. Even while I worked on my doctorate in communications, our film-production team was busy making entertaining films with a spiritual focus. The five-episode *Charlie Churchman* film series had become a great success. Pastors and teachers across America were showing it to their youth groups and at their Sunday-evening services. Nevertheless, I worried, maybe God wanted me out of the movie business and into ministry.

About that time, in 1965, I spotted an announcement on the registrar's bulletin board at USC announcing a Rockefeller Foundation grant for seminary scholarships to men and women working in other graduate disciplines. Thinking it another gift from God, I filled out the forms. An interview team including the renowned scholar and educator Dr. Pitney Van Deusen flew to California to interview several of us candidates.

Because Lyla had just signed a contract to teach English at nearby Crescenta Valley High School, I told Dr. Van Deusen that I was thinking of attending Fuller Theological Seminary in Pasadena, the largest nondenominational evangelical seminary in the world. When he grimaced slightly and suggested that I consider other great seminaries in that tradition, including his own, I remembered Noni's warning against "liberals" who "undermine" young people's faith with their emphasis on "social action" instead of the Bible. Later, I learned that many of the freedom riders who risked their lives with Martin Luther King were from those same "liberal" seminaries. It took a long time for me to understand how important it is for a Christian to integrate faith and action.

That summer, I entered Fuller's language program, to begin, as the seminary catalog promises, "a lifelong mastery" of New Testament Greek. The Fuller curriculum was committed to a thorough study of the Scriptures in their original languages. And though I whined a lot before I reached proficiency levels in both Koine Greek and ancient Hebrew, the five years of biblical scholarship were among the most exciting and transforming years of my life.

Why I left USC and my media studies to begin a whole new graduate program in ministry is still only half clear to me, although I do know that I had felt called to ministry from my childhood. Noni had often quoted this verse to me: "Unto whom much is given, much shall be required." "God has a special place in ministry for you, Mel," my whole family maintained. "Don't fail Him!"

But it wasn't just their inordinate pressure that caused me to begin my biblical and theological studies in earnest. I wanted sincerely to follow Jesus and to equip myself better for serving His church, but I was also desperate to prove to God how far I would go to deny, to discipline, to master my "homosexual sin." Following this path would certainly be proof to God that I had faith and that I was determined to exercise that faith in "healing my homosexuality" whatever it cost me.

During my second year at Fuller, President David Allen Hubbard offered me a position teaching speech and preaching at the seminary while I completed my master's and doctoral degrees. The little office he assigned me in the library basement was the scene of my next phase of guilt and fear-driven overachievement. I continued producing motion pictures and television specials. I traveled about the country as a guest preacher and teacher in Christian colleges and seminaries. I wrote articles for Christian publications. And at the same time I studied and taught at the seminary.

"It's coffee time," I heard one morning about ten A.M. simultaneously with a series of loud knocks on my office door.

Jim Morgan, a young teacher of ethics who began his tenure at Fuller that same year, had decided to make me his friend. It wasn't easy.

"No thanks, Jim," I said, looking up at him standing in the open door. "I have papers to grade, a lecture to write, and I'm facing a film-script deadline that is already passed."

"Please, sir, " he said rather sarcastically, getting down on one knee and pretending to beg, "couldn't you spare just fifteen minutes on a cup of coffee with a friend?"

We spent exactly fifteen minutes in the seminary cafeteria chatting, but when the big hand reached fifteen, I jumped up, paid my bill, and headed for the exit. Thinking I had fulfilled my obligation as a colleague for that semester, I was surprised when at exactly the same time on the very next morning, Jim was back at my door whispering loudly and pulling me toward the cafeteria: "It's ten A.M. Coffee time again."

Every morning for one week, Jim dragged me out of the library basement into the seminary cafeteria for "coffee time" at ten A.M., and I didn't even like coffee. On Monday that next week, I was surprised and pleased to see that ten A.M. came and went without Jim appearing again at my door. I've outlasted him, I thought. Now I can get a full morning's work done without interruption.

At 10:05 A.M. I noticed that my mind was wandering. I was thinking about Jim. Foolish. Back to business. By 10:10 A.M. I was beginning to worry. What happened to him? Is he sick? Should I check on him? By 10:15 A.M., after looking in the cafeteria and not finding him there, I walked to Jim's office and peeked through the little window in his door.

"You came!" Jim said happily, jumping up from his desk where he had been waiting and rushing across the room to embrace me. "I knew you would come!"

Red faced, but grinning, I hurried after Jim to the cafeteria to begin the second week of a tradition that would last the next three years. He was a husband, a father, a scholar, a writer, and two decades before Robert Bly, one of my first adult male friends. He pursued me, and in the process I discovered close male friendship. Like Zorba the Greek, Jim taught me to dance. After Monday faculty meetings in the Geneva Room, my other new faculty friends, Drs. Fred Bush, Cal Schoonhoven, Jim Morgan, and later, Lew Smedes, and I adjourned to a little bar near the seminary where the students wouldn't see us playing pool, throwing darts, or drinking a cold draft beer.

Actually, I was the only one in that illustrious, scholarly crowd who hadn't studied in Switzerland with Karl Barth, in Holland with Hans Kung, or in Germany with Helmut Thielicke or Emil Brunner. Jim and the others were from evangelical homes like mine, but they had learned to drink at least an occasional beer in the homes of their distinguished European mentors or in the cafés that lined the boulevards of Geneva, Heidelberg, or Paris. I had been "tempted" once on our honeymoon in Spain, but thanks to that fly at the bottom of the carafe, I was not tempted again until Jim and the others came along.

"I don't like beer," I said to Jim every Monday afternoon when he would order another tall, frosty glass for me.

"Drink it for me," he would sarcastically answer, with the others smiling on.

Weeks went by. Jim would order the beer. The waitress would set it on the table before me. And I would leave it sitting there untouched. While deep in a fascinating conversation one particularly hot afternoon, without thinking, I picked up the glass and drank its cool contents in one long swallow. Nobody noticed, thank God, or so I thought until Jim jumped up from the table with his glass lifted high.

"To Mel," he said, grinning broadly, motioning for the others to lift their glasses and join the celebration. "He drank the beer and lightning didn't strike him dead. He drank the beer and devils didn't appear to take him off to hell. He drank the beer and he's still the wonderful Christian saint and potential martyr that he always wanted to be. To Mel," he said again, and then in a whisper that no one could hear but me, he added, "I think he's just discovered grace."

The embarrassing scene made me so angry that for a fleeting moment I thought about stomping away. I'm so glad I stayed. As I sat around that table with my friends, I realized that Jim was absolutely right. I had been afraid to drink my first beer. Through this, and other acts of abstinence, I was trying to prove my virtue to a demanding God with a pistol pointed at my head and a very nervous trigger finger.

Jim saw that my God was too small, that I desperately needed to be emancipated from the fundamentalist notion that goodness is determined by what we don't do: smoking, drinking, masturbating, swearing, skipping a Sunday at church, leaving my salary check untithed, premarital sex, and above all, homosex. These were the sins of my childhood, and I grew up thinking that if I could just avoid those sins, I would be acceptable to God.

Besides, when I was just ten, Noni signed me up for membership in the WCTU, the Women's Christian Temperance Union. My parents never served alcohol in our home or drank beer or wine in other people's homes or restaurants. Growing up, I heard endless stories in church and Sunday school about the evils of drinking. In youth camp one year, well-meaning counselors tried to stage a little experiment that would keep us sober forever. I'm still laughing.

With straight-faced sincerity, our counselor submerged one fresh whole carrot in a jar of water and a second equally fresh carrot in a jar of beer. The jars were covered. At the end of the week, with great fanfare, the counselor unveiled the telling results. The carrot in the fresh water was healthy and hard. The beer-soaked carrot was shriveled up, gray, and flaccid. Years later, I asked Jim Morgan what the experiment taught us. "It's okay to drink," he answered, "but never dip your carrot in the beer!"

On April 4, 1968, Lyla greeted me at our apartment door with the news that my friend Martin Luther King, Jr., had been killed by an assassin's bullet. I still remember pounding on the walls with my fists and yelling angrily. It was Jim Morgan who comforted me. " 'History,' " Jim said, quoting Dr. King, " 'is ultimately guided by spirit, not by matter.' Dr. King is spirit now." I hoped and prayed then, as I hope and pray now, that the same loving Spirit of God who guided Martin was also guiding me.

Sixty days later, on June 5, Jim picked me up at the Los Angeles International Airport. We were listening to music on our long drive home when the broadcast was interrupted with the news that Bobby Kennedy had been gunned down at the Ambassador Hotel. We turned off Harbor Freeway at Wilshire Boulevard and drove immediately to the sight. Police barricades were in place. News media from around the world were already broadcasting from the scene. Jim and I sat in the car looking at the Ambassador Hotel bathed in lights, trying to wrap our minds around this growing wave of hatred, violence, and death, wanting to do something to help turn back the tide, fearing that it was already too late.

The next morning, I learned that Sirhan Sirhan, the Jerusalem-born Jordanian arrested for killing Bobby Kennedy, lived with his mother just four blocks from our home in Pasadena. I walked those four blocks, found the streets crowded with camera crews, reporters, angry demonstrators, and police. Later in the afternoon, I returned to find Mrs. Sirhan sitting on her porch with a few members of her family. She appeared devastated by the tragedy. I introduced myself and we talked for several minutes about her position at the nearby Presbyterian church, about her family, and about her terrible grief. Several times she apologized that her lawn had not been mowed. "He must have had other things on his mind," she said, mostly to herself.

Toward evening, Jim Morgan and I returned with our own gardening equipment to cut and trim the grass. As I finished sweeping the sidewalk and turned to leave, Mrs. Sirhan came out on her porch again, tried to speak, but could only smile, wave gratefully, and return to her grieving family.

Jim and I talked about that moment for months. He and his wife, Jean, were our first married-couple friends at Fuller. Soon our circle expanded to include Walt Becker, a Baptist seminarian whose studies for the ministry ultimately led to his Ph.D. in counseling. Walt's loving and spirited wife, Francois, had been born in Hanoi of French parents. Fran became a Christian in a Billy Graham meeting while visiting New York City. She, too, earned her counseling degree, and together Walt and Fran now run a counseling center in Ruidoso, New Mexico, for couples, especially pastors and lay leaders in Christian ministry. The third couple in our small circle of friends was Walt and Beverly Wright. Walt finished his Ph.D. in theology and now serves as president of Regent College in Vancouver, Canada. Beverly, an early-childhood specialist, got us all through the poorest years with her spectacular low-budget meals, her handmade pottery, colorful planters and fabrics, and her deep and loving commitment to us all.

Meeting regularly for more than twenty years with the couples in our first little circle of hope made an incredibly positive difference in our lives. At least once a week we gathered at one apartment or the other to talk, argue, pray, and study. We spent nearly every Thanksgiving holiday and most Christmases together. We watched each of our children born and were together as an extended family all through their elementary, junior high, senior high, and college years. All the kids—Shauna, Michelle, Heather, and Jennifer Morgan, Walt junior and Marcel Becker, Damon and Aaron Wright, Erinn and Michael White—were then and remain to this day such an important part of our lives, of my life.

During our first eight years of marriage, Lyla was pregnant and miscarried four times, the last time with twins. We both wanted children. How many months we waited only to be shocked and painfully disappointed once again when those terrible premature pains began. I still remember trying to comfort Lyla as she lay in pain on the sofa or in the hospital dreading the nightmares and the sadness. But with each new tragic loss, our circle of friends gathered around us.

When we decided to adopt a child, the whole crowd enrolled as unofficial godparents and waited with us while Lyla took a year off from teaching just to be ready when the glad day came. After waiting a year without a call from the adoption agency, Lyla signed another teaching contract. Then, on Friday, one week before Lyla was scheduled to begin teaching again, the phone rang at last.

"We have a little girl for you," the caseworker said calmly. "Are you still interested?"

Interested? We went berserk. Don't ever let anyone tell you that adopting a child is less exciting or meaningful than giving birth yourselves. The nursery had been painted and waiting for fifty-two long weeks. Clothes and toys for a little girl or a little boy were piled up around the room. We wanted her and we wanted her immediately, but the fourteen-day-old infant could not be released from her foster home until Monday. So, we spent the weekend with our friends working up a near fatal case of overexcitement. When they finally went home exhausted from lack of sleep, Lyla and I spent the last night watching the film *Alice's Restaurant* and wandering around Westwood Village, waiting for the sunrise, eager to see our new baby girl.

On Monday morning, Lyla and I arrived at the agency, jammed our car into the curb, and rushed in to discover one of God's greatest gifts to us. Erinn Kathleen was six pounds eight ounces. She made her mommy laugh and her daddy cry with joy. The evangelical adoption agency asked us to spend an hour alone with our new daughter in a room where no one would interrupt us so that we could "think and pray through" on this important decision. We spent five minutes looking at that beautiful girl and then bundled her up against the cold, rushed past the exasperated caseworker, loaded tiny, delicate Erinn into our car, and rushed her safely home.

Our son, Michael Christopher, was born exactly nine months later. "That's what happens when you both get up for a two A.M. feeding," Lyla explains. Actually, we've heard endless similar stories from people who have adopted and then conceived. Whatever happened, both Michael and Erinn were gifts from God, I'm sure.

After all those miscarriages, I paced the maternity ward with our friends, fearing the very worst. When the nurse rushed in with the news, "You have a beautiful baby boy," I answered without thinking, "What's wrong with him?" She laughed and scolded me while the others hugged me and danced about the room. The nurse was right. Absolutely nothing was wrong with our healthy son. Of course, we're prejudiced and a bit nearsighted, but those two nearly perfect kids brought incredible joy to our lives, and we will both be forever grateful.

While Lyla taught school, I tended babies, two at a time, with their simultaneous diaper changes, their uncoordinated napping and feeding schedules, and their fine-tuned curiosities, anxious to see, hear, and do everything. Erinn rode in the blue, aluminum-framed pack on my back. Because he was smaller at first, Michael rode in the black velvet harness on my chest and stomach. When it rained, with the parka thrown over the children, I looked like the hunchback of Notre Dame lurching through the streets of Pasadena. And when the sun was out, we walked everywhere, all three of us talking gibberish and pointing in different directions.

Lyla and I had everything. My films were winning prizes and our film business was making enough profit to pay the bills. Fuller's small salary gave us discretionary funds to take our friends to dinner or the movies. Lyla and I hired Blanche Buegler to be part-time nanny to our children. Blanche's husband, Ernie, was Fuller's chef. When he died, Blanche became part of our family.

We bought our first small home on Elizabeth Street and, with my father's help, created a happy, colorful living space for our very traditional family in the foothills above Pasadena. Lyla quit her teaching position to be home with the children. I worked at home, so we shared parental duties. We ate together as a family. Before each meal we held hands and said grace. On Sundays, we sat together in a front-row pew at church.

When our family extended to include Lyla's recently widowed mom, we bought an old Spanish home on Holliston with an extra bedroom. We entertained Fuller students at Thanksgiving and on Christmas. My longtime friend the talented fellow-filmmaker Dan Dunkelberger came to live and work with us during a difficult time in his life. Walt and Fran Becker and their children stayed with us while relocating. We had vacations every year with our children, three or four of them on Poipu Beach on the island of Kauai. Everyone saw us as the perfect Christian family. And in most ways we were. God blessed us with far more than we could have asked or dreamed.

But just below the surface, my confidence was shaking like the earth often shook beneath the streets of Pasadena. I had a beautiful, thoughtful, caring wife, whom I sincerely loved, and yet at night I longed to be in the arms of a man. God had given us two incredible children and a practically perfect home and family, but even during our happiest moments, I was torn apart by my growing need for another kind of long-term, loving relationship with another gay man.

The conflict was tearing me apart. How could I possibly leave my loving wife, break up my happy family, destroy my career, and end my ministry? On the other hand, if homosexuality wasn't something that could be fixed, how could I go on denying, repressing, sublimating, holding back, refusing to deal with all the natural, God-given passion at the very heart of my existence?

Just before Michael was born, Jim Morgan visited my office in the basement of the seminary library. His eyes were troubled. His hands were trembling. Jim paced the room, trying to get up the courage to share his own dark secret. "I have cancer," he mumbled. "I thought that it was gone, that the doctors got it all five years ago, but apparently, it is no longer in remission."

At that moment, Jim began to cry. Besides his wife, Jean, he had four beautiful young daughters, ages eight, five, three, and one. "My family," he sobbed quietly. "What will happen to my family?"

I stood up, walked around my desk, and took Jim awkwardly in my arms. We both stood there crying for the longest time. Then, suddenly, Jim pulled away. "I will not die," he said angrily. "God will heal me. This is the beginning of my life. I will not let it be the end."

Jim was still completing his Ph.D. in a demanding joint academic program between Columbia University and Union Theological Seminary in New York City. He had studied with Karl Barth in Switzerland. He had written and researched his dissertation in libraries in Europe and North America. Jim's career as theologian and academic was just beginning.

"And I won't hear any words of doubt or pity out of you or anybody else," he said, walking from the room. I followed him as he hurried from my office through the library stacks.

"Will you trust God for my healing?" he said, turning to face me at the basement staircase.

"Of course," I answered immediately.

"No doubt?" he added, walking back in my direction.

"No doubt!" I replied as we hugged one last time before he hurried away.

But after hearing from Jim's surgeon the extent of his cancer, I had terrible doubts. Before they rediscovered the malignancy it had spread throughout Jim's lower bowel system. This time the cancer was inoperable. I wanted to speak frankly to Jim about my fears for his life, but he saw it as a test of faith and refused even to think about the options.

In 1970, I was thirty years old. I had spent the last fifteen or sixteen years living on blind faith myself, trusting God for my healing from homosexuality. There had been periods of time, some of them years long, when I had been convinced that God had healed me. The love that Lyla and I had shared seemed invincible at first. Certainly, our love and the love we felt for our two beautiful children was a sign that

God had healed me. But not once in all those times of love and healing did my sexual orientation ever change. After all the prayer and professional therapy, I felt exactly the same way that I had from the beginning, only the longings for sensual male intimacy grew stronger. Like Jim, I had spent years praying to be healed. But I was growing more and more afraid that those prayers would not be answered for either of us.

One night after Lyla and I had taken Jim and Jean to dinner and a movie, I undressed and sat on the side of our bed, feeling terrible. Jim wasn't allowing us to talk about his cancer, even during these long, intimate evenings together with our wives. And yet there were obvious signs that my friend was getting sicker each day. He had lost weight. His shoulders stooped slightly. He had almost no energy. His once mischievous eyes looked tired and rather sad.

"He's going to die," I said to Lyla, "and he won't even talk about it." For a moment I sat there knowing what had to be done. Finally, I dressed and drove back to the Morgan home.

"Jim," I said, knocking on his door long after midnight. "I've got to see you."

"Come in," he said sleepily. "I'll fix coffee." Jim fixed the coffee. We drank a cup. But I couldn't find the courage to tell him. When I finally left, he looked confused and slightly angry.

About three-thirty A.M., after lying awake for two or three hours more, I got out of bed, dressed and drove back to Jim's house again. This time, he wasn't a bit happy to see me. He stood at the doorway half-asleep staring down at me.

"Can I come in?" I whispered, hoping not to awaken Jean again. Jim opened the door, moved back a few steps, and stood there waiting.

"Jim," I began with fear churning in my stomach, "I'm afraid you're going to die."

Jim looked angry. He moved forward to interrupt, to stop this show of no faith on my part, but I continued.

"Jim, listen to me. You have plenty of people praying that God will heal you. I'm just afraid that if you aren't healed, that if you die, I will never have the chance to say how much I love you and how much I'll miss you when you're gone."

Suddenly, Jim's resistance just melted. He groaned and his whole body slumped in place.

"Jim, I pray that God will heal you," I said, reaching out to hold him, "but if God doesn't, I had to tell you that if you die, there will be a hole left in the center of my heart that no one else will ever fill."

At that moment, embracing in the middle of his living room floor, we both began to cry. I don't know how long we stood there weeping, but finally, Jim pulled away, sat down on his sofa, looked up at me, and smiled.

"Thanks, Mel," he whispered. "I was dying to hear somebody say it."

The next morning, Jim was taken to the hospital. A group of students who visited him there reported that in their short conversation, Jim told them about that crazy, terrible, wonderful night and how grateful he was that he had friends who were honest, who gave him permission to get on with what needed doing.

Four or five days later, Jim passed into a coma and died. After his funeral, while Lyla helped Jean feed the endless stream of people who dropped by to express their love and sympathy, I drove back to our home on Elizabeth Street. I turned on the record player and slumped on the sofa. A Simon and Garfunkel record began to play: "So long, Frank Lloyd Wright. When I grow dry, I'll stop awhile and think of you."

Jim had blazed into my life like a comet on the evening sky. He introduced me to a pantheon of fiery saints and martyrs whom I had never known. The Jesus whom he loved and followed was a radical young teacher who preferred the company of sinners and outcasts, who raged at church leaders for their hypocrisy and demanded honesty from everyone. The Gospel that Jim preached was the Gospel of personal liberation, and those who had been liberated by that Gospel were called to liberate all others who suffered. Jim's lectures on Dietrich Bonhoeffer and his stand against the churches in Germany who supported the Third Reich helped me understand how religious leaders often protect and preserve the status quo while God raises up in every generation a handful of courageous prophets to confront the church and keep the truth alive.

Now, Jim was dead, and I knew for certain that if God chose not to heal Jim Morgan, then no one could be certain of healing. With Simon and Garfunkel singing in the background, I sat on the sofa weeping for Jim, and for all his lost promise and potential, and weeping for me as well. There was so much left to be done and I had so hoped that he would be there to help me through it.

"May I come in?" I heard a voice say quietly as I sat alone and grieving. It was John Nordquist. John's wife, Elizabeth, was a teacher with Lyla. We weren't close friends, yet, but John had sat through the funeral thinking about my friendship with Jim and the loss I must be feeling.

"I thought you might need a new friend," he said quietly, sitting down beside me, wrapping his arm around my shoulders, and holding me while I cried.

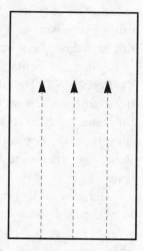

Chapter 7

1970–80,

Taking the First Steps

Toward Integrity

O*n a cold, rainy afternoon in Paris, January 27, 1973, in the massive* ballroom of the Hotel Majestic, Henry Kissinger and Le Duc Tho signed a truce agreement ending America's war in Vietnam. On Valentine's Day, February 14, 1973, the first planeload of our American prisoners of war landed at Travis Air Force Base in southern California. You may still remember those tearful, joyous scenes captured on network television as wives and families were reunited with their husbands and fathers after all those years of separation.

Five days later, I read this headline in the *Los Angeles Times*: "Faith in God Sustained Him, Ex-POW Tells Congregation." In ten short paragraphs a *Times* staff writer shared the moving story of Navy flier Howard Rutledge, who returned to his little Baptist church in San

Diego after seven years in a Vietnamese prison to "thank those who had prayed for his freedom." I was fascinated to learn that the ex-POW had spent much of those seven years in solitary confinement.

After reading the story to Lyla, I looked up Phyliss Rutledge in the San Diego telephone directory, called her home, and asked to speak to Howard. I told him that I was a Christian filmmaker and that his story had inspired me. Could we meet, I said, to make a documentary film together? There was a media blackout, Howard explained, until the other planeloads of POWs returning from Vietnam had landed. Call the Pentagon, he advised me. Maybe they can help.

I called the Pentagon and talked to the Navy admiral in charge of the POW airlift. He told me that no ex-POW could speak to the media until all their fellow prisoners were safely home. I explained that a film takes months to assemble, that all I wanted was a chance to begin the process. I could hear the admiral talking to someone else in his Pentagon office. Suddenly, the Navy chief of chaplains came on the line.

"Mel," he said, "I've wanted to meet you. Your films are being used in military bases, on submarines and aircraft carriers around the world. I've never had a chance to thank you on behalf of all the chaplains who use them. Is there something I can do to help?"

I waited while the two Navy officers discussed the matter. The next thing I knew, Howard Rutledge called me from San Diego.

"I don't know what kind of pull you have with Navy brass," he said, obviously amazed by the turn of events, "but I just talked to the head honcho at the Pentagon, and he said I was free to meet with you anytime or anyplace."

In the Presence of Mine Enemies, the film I made with Howard and Phyliss Rutledge and their four children, was shown in tens of thousands of schools and churches, telecast regularly on public broadcast channels, purchased by university and public libraries, and honored with gold ribbons, plaques, and citations by film festivals across America.

When Bill Barbour, the president of Fleming Revell Publishing, heard that I was the only journalist granted permission to meet with the POWs, he urged me to write a book as well. I had never written a book. Surrounded by graduate-school and seminary scholars, I knew that real books required years of study and research. "Then write a disposable book," Richard Baltzell, my new editor at Fleming Revell, suggested. "Think of it as a long news story and tell it from your heart."

I took the interview notes to the Laguna Riviera, a little hotel on the southern-California coast overlooking Laguna Beach, and wrote the 128-page book in seven days. Lyla and Richard cut, patched, and edited the final manuscript into shape. Four weeks later our book, illustrated by another POW, was delivered to bookstores across the country. Six weeks later, *In the Presence of Mine Enemies* appeared on the nation's best-seller lists.

In the beginning, I had no idea that the film would become a prizewinner or that I would ever write a book about Howard and Phyliss Rutledge. You can imagine the real reason I was so fascinated by Howard's story. I wanted to know how he remained sane in a tiny prison cell cut off from real human contact for seven lonely years. There was no comparison between his life and mine, but living in my closet for the past twenty years felt much like solitary confinement to me.

I was isolated, not by iron bars or guards in uniforms, but by fear. I was surrounded by my loving family and close friends, but there was no way to explain to them my desperate, lonely feelings even when we were together. I wasn't tortured by leather straps or cattle prods, but my guilt and fear kept me in constant torment. I wasn't deprived of the basic necessities, in fact I lived a life of plenty, but I was starving for the kind of human intimacy that would satisfy my longing, end my loneliness, and at least calm if not fulfill my unrequited passion.

By 1973, I was working triple time. I suppose it's too simplistic to say that I was taking on far more projects than I could handle in order to divert and distract myself from dealing with my "unhealthy" longings. In fact, I also loved my work, found it fulfilling, and felt called by God to do it. Whatever the mix of motives, we were on a roll.

That year, along with the book and film on Howard Rutledge and my normal seminary teaching load, Lyla and I accepted a contract from World Literature Crusade to produce a four-hour television special. Working with Dr. Jack McAllister, WLC's founder and director, his creative young son, Gordon, and their brilliant and indefatigable international director, Johnny Lee, we shaped one of the first successful religious fund-raising telethons.

To fill those 240 minutes with drama and pathos, we decided to film true stories of World Literature Crusade at work in nine countries on five continents around the globe. Before I could take film crews to all those exotic places, I had to find the stories and scout their locations. To accomplish this task, Lyla and I began a five-week, around-the-world odyssey with multiple stops on every continent.

In Europe, we interviewed fascinating leaders in London, Paris, Rome, and Athens. In the Middle East, we toured towns and villages in Israel and Jordan. In Africa, we visited Egypt, Uganda, Ethiopia, and Kenya before flying on to Djibouti, French Somaliland; Karachi, Pakistan; Bombay, India; and Colombo, Sri Lanka (Ceylon). In the Far East we visited the Philippines, Hong Kong, and Japan before the final flight across the Pacific to our children, happily in the hands of their nanny, Blanche Buegler.

On that mind-stretching, around-the-world journey, I experienced for the first time evidence of the international gay and lesbian community. Of course, I experienced it only at a distance and through my lens of prejudice and fear. But from the beginning, there was no doubt. We were everywhere. One by one, I found them or they found me. Once our eyes met, there was no need to question further. At first, I was afraid, thinking them prostitutes or gigolos. Then, I began to realize that most of them were as closeted and afraid as I was, maybe more. In every country, my gay brothers and lesbian sisters faced varying degrees of discrimination and bigotry, but everywhere I went, in hotels, restaurants, parks, city streets, and village plazas, I found them smiling up at me, reaching out, hoping for contact, wanting to know my story as eagerly as I wanted to know theirs.

Although we were cut off from each other by ancient and modern prejudice, and though I still could not accept them fully any more than I could accept myself, I knew instantly who they were. I was never alone in private let alone intimate with even one of them. I only spoke quick words in passing to a handful of gay men whom I met on that journey, but I smiled and nodded discretely to dozens of gay strangers, young and old, wherever we traveled. Whatever I thought about homosexuality, when I came back from that tour, I knew that I was not alone. There must be millions of us out there, I thought to myself, and if God made millions of us, maybe we weren't a mistake at all.

In 1973, shortly after returning to the U.S., I accepted an invitation to become the senior pastor of the Evangelical Covenant Church in Pasadena, California. Because of my on-going work as a writer and filmmaker, Lyla and I decided to share the pastoral load. The search committee agreed. Lyla would serve as the director of worship and special programs. I would preach and pastor. We walked up those stairs to our little offices in the tan, cement-block office building behind the church on Lake Avenue filled with hope that at last I had found my real niche in ministry.

Aided by Roland Tabell, the creative music director at Pasadena Covenant and by Lyla's team of enthusiastic volunteers, we created an exciting liturgical experience Sunday after Sunday that included original bulletin covers, banners, processions, trumpet fanfares, music, films, slide projections, drama, and even dance. One of our creative volunteers called it "devotion in motion," to keep our critics at bay. I prayed and preached my heart out.

One Sunday morning, our four-year-old son Michael decided in the middle of a service to join his dad on the platform. The whole congregation watched as he left his startled mother in a front pew, climbed up the carpeted steps, and sat down beside me, grinning. Not minutes later, Erinn joined him there. It became a kind of family tradition and made me proud.

For more than three years we worked to see that little church grow. Attendance doubled, then tripled. Soon, Sunday services were crowded further by hundreds of students, staff, and faculty from Fuller Theological Seminary along with other young people from Pasadena City College and from nearby Cal Tech.

The young crowd preferred our eight-thirty A.M. service. After every sermon, I left the pulpit and walked down into the congregation with an open mike to answer the people's honest questions about the text. And it wasn't always scholars and theologians who brought new insights to the biblical narrative. Many times uneducated, blue-collar folk and artisans, even elementary-school students, raised theological questions or told stories that informed and inspired us all. Those question-and-answer times were an enlightening (if occasionally threatening) experience for me and for the people of that great church.

During that first pastoral assignment, I was often shocked and surprised by the intolerance I discovered lurking in our very own pews. One of our young, unmarried women delivered a beautiful baby boy and asked that I dedicate her child on the Sunday after Thanksgiving. I agreed immediately. After finding herself pregnant, she had come to me for counsel. We discussed her options, and she had decided to keep her child. But when I announced that we would dedicate the child in a Sunday-morning service, key members of the church board were outraged.

"How could you dedicate an illegitimate baby?" one of them asked.

"No baby is illegitimate," I answered, but the discussion that followed was meaningless. Those two board members put up such a fuss that I finally dedicated the child on Thanksgiving Day in a nearby home, with the proud mother, her friends, and more loving members of our congregation in attendance.

I also learned about change, and how long it takes for people to wrap their minds around new ideas. Sometimes it was little things that we could quickly change. When I announced my first sermon title to the church secretary, for example, she said, "Oh, Dr. White, you can't call it that!"

Immediately, I got defensive. "Why not?"

"Because it has a capital *R* in the title, and we've run out of *R*'s for the outdoor bulletin board."

Other kinds of change were more difficult. Peter and Jenny were an attractive, committed young couple from our growing graduate-student population. Peter was working on a Ph.D. in psychology at Fuller Seminary. His wife, Jenny, was studying for the ministry. One Sunday morning before Communion, I asked them to join our other lay servers. I hadn't even noticed that until that day women prepared the Communion elements, but were never asked to help serve them. This time an official of the board took me out to lunch. During our meal, he grinned, patted me on the shoulder, and said, "You're young, pastor. You will learn that people just don't get a blessing from Communion when it's served by a woman." From that day on, I tried to have at least one woman help serve the elements every Sunday.

At the same time Lyla and I were pastoring, I was producing three other films for my Twenty-third Psalm series launched with *In the Presence of Mine Enemies*. It was part of my contract with the church. I didn't take a salary. They used that money to hire a church administrator to help with the organization load. I made films to pay the bills and because I believed that filmmaking was a part of my call to ministry.

Because I was still struggling with guilt and sadness over my little brother's death, I wanted to do a film on death and dying that would better prepare people like me for that shock that comes with sudden, unexpected grief. Lew Smedes, a colleague at Fuller and today one of

America's eminent Christian writers, suggested that I ask his good friends Tony and Win Brouwer to be my subjects. Tony was a professor at Calvin College in Grand Rapids, Michigan. He had only recently been diagnosed with terminal, inoperable cancer.

When I visited their home to discuss the possibilities of filming their story, I discovered that Tony's wife, Win, and their two loving daughters were also articulate and thoughtful. I have to admit that I felt embarrassed and pushy when I suggested bringing cameras into the private lives of these good people. "What if I don't die?" Tony asked with a grin. "Won't you lose your investment?"

"Then I'll be filming a miracle," I replied, "and that would make me a lot happier."

Though I Walk Through the Valley became one of the first films in history to document the last year in the life of a dying man and his family. Thanks to the honesty, the openness, and the thoughtfulness of Win, Tony, and their two daughters, *Though I Walk Through the Valley* was used widely across the nation in churches, schools, hospitals, and universities and honored by film festivals in this country and abroad.

I still remember sharing a hotel room in Grand Rapids with Lew Smedes the night before we buried Tony. For half the night, I watched this distinguished theologian and ethicist pace the room anxiously. Win had asked Lew to preach the funeral sermon for his old friend, but Lew was also doubled up with grief over Tony's untimely death. "What can I say about evil," Lew asked himself over and over again that night, "when there is nothing helpful to be said?"

The next morning, Lew's sermon was brilliant. It calmed and consoled us all, but the real lesson I learned was the lesson learned watching Lew struggle to make sense of evil when there is no sense to be made, and that in spite of that reality, with the morning's light, Lew could lead us into the presence of God, who comforts and consoles us even when we don't understand.

In 1976, I wrote and directed *He Restoreth My Soul,* the third film in my Twenty-third Psalm film series, the true story of Merrill and Virginia Womach. In a Thanksgiving Day snowstorm, Merrill crashed his private plane into an evergreen forest. Struggling to escape the blazing wreckage, Merrill was seriously burned over most of his body. I was fascinated by his positive attitude during all the years of pain and plastic surgery that followed.

"People stared at me on the street," Merrill told me, "like I was some kind of monster. But I was alive and that was all that mattered."

Even though terribly scarred, Merrill sang in public concerts and built a huge and successful music business. I walked with Merrill down busy city streets. The people who passed him often stopped to stare, whisper, point, and grimace. Strangers often walked up to Merrill to tell him that he shouldn't be allowed in public. During those first years of recovery, people even fainted when Merrill stood to sing.

Like so many of the people whose lives I filmed, Merrill's courage never seemed to waiver. I didn't have that kind of courage and I was curious about its source. At the close of his concert we filmed at the Veterans Hospital in Spokane, Washington, Merrill spoke these words to patients in the burn ward: "Doctors and nurses have needles and pills to help get you through the physical suffering, but what about the pain inside you that comes from loneliness or fear? They can't give you enough shots or pills to take that pain away. Only God can help you bear real pain. Remember, whatever you feel, you are not alone. God is with you. When you feel lonely, call out to God, and God will hear and help you. When you are afraid, reach out, and God will take your hand."

He Restoreth My Soul became another prizewinning film used in hospitals, schools, churches, and on television across the nation. *Tested by Fire,* the book I wrote about Merrill and Virginia, was translated into dozens of languages and became our second best-seller around the world.

He Leadeth Me, the last film in my Twenty-third Psalm series, was the story of Ken and Jane Medema. Ken was left without sight during childhood. A brilliant poet and pianist, his unforgettable performances left me weeping and inspired. After spending a whole day with Ken, Jane, and their young son, Aaron, talking about our very different lives, asking to film their story as a part of my Twenty-third Psalm series, Ken sat down at the piano and began to sing about me. "Psalm chaser," the song began, and his spontaneous, insightful poetry soon revealed that Ken, though unsighted, had penetrated my defenses and looked deep into my anxious soul.

The growing list of accomplishments had done nothing to satisfy my secret longings. I would have traded every prizewinning film and both best-selling books for one night in a man's arms. It is so difficult to explain what it feels like to be a homosexual, struggling to survive as something else. I was discovering that sexual orientation was at the core of my being. Some people are successful celibates and I admire them. Whether by choice or by necessity, other people stay single and even enjoy it. I envy their maturity. But for me the desire to love and be loved by my own kind, the craving for affection from someone who met my own mysterious sensual grid, who fulfilled my own need for warm, human intimacy, cried out to be satisfied from my earliest adolescence. And in spite of everything else I accomplished or possessed, until I was at least free to try to meet that basic human need, I could not be content.

Even in those times of longing, I was grateful for the overabundance of gifts God had given me. I enjoyed filmmaking, writing, teaching, and preaching. The occasional prizes and honors that came my way were gratifying. I was thankful for our good life and the luxuries we shared. Having Lyla and my wonderful family had given me great joy, but even their loving presence could only temporarily ease the painful longing and temporarily postpone the inevitable crises. Gradually, I came to realize that there were limits to my restraint, and as the years passed, I grew closer and closer to that time when I would reach those limits.

I felt longing compounded by guilt and terror whenever I stood to teach or preach before rows and rows of handsome seminarians. When young gay Christian men from Fuller or from my congregation came to me for counsel, I referred them immediately, but lived with fear that they might see the longing in my own eyes. After twenty-five years of denial, I was taking Valium just to get back on an airplane or through the night in another distant hotel. And when other gay travelers smiled silent invitations at me across a busy lobby or as we passed in the street, I felt my resistance weakening.

Still, I was determined to keep my commitments to God, to Lyla, and to my children at any price. I loved them. I wanted to stay with them. It wasn't their fault that I had needs they couldn't meet. I didn't want them to suffer because of my "immaturity" or "lack of will." So, not knowing what else to try, after ten years of prayerful, Christian insight therapy, I decided to take a whole new course.

Counseling based on the premise of "if you have enough faith, God can do anything" was only a temporary solution. In fact, as the years passed, it only made matters worse to hope for so much, to try so hard, to struggle so long, to believe so desperately, only to realize again that my sexual orientation was unchanged. So I decided to try another strategy to save my marriage and my family. At Fuller, I met a Christian psychologist who was a self-avowed, practicing behaviorist. He made another kind of promise. "If you have enough faith in yourself," he said, "you can do anything."

During the next week we discussed the options. I was desperate. I wanted to try any "cure" to overcome my homosexuality. When I suggested electric shock he frowned but didn't try to dissuade me. The counselor asked me to bring to our next session a selection of pictures from magazines or advertisements of men whose face or form aroused me. He also asked me to bring photos of myself that I found attractive.

Though it embarrassed me to do it, I spent several hours that next week cutting out pictures of handsome men from *Time* and *Life* magazines and from full-page ads in the *Los Angeles Times*. I even robbed our family album of a picture that Lyla had taken of me at Laguna Beach. I was standing in front of a little cottage we had rented for a week's vacation that last summer. I had blond hair in those days, lots of it (at least more than I have now), and I was tanned, trim, and healthy.

At my next appointment, into my pile of male photos my counselor mixed pictures he had brought of models, actresses, and famous women of great beauty. Maybe he asked me to bring those photos, too. I can't remember. Then he attached several electric cables to my body and placed a box with a dial in my hands. I was to shock myself whenever I felt stimulated in any way by a picture of a man, and I was to stop shocking myself immediately when the picture of a beautiful woman appeared.

I could control the strength and the duration of the electric shock. Needless to say, I was desperate enough in those days to turn the dial up until I thought my hair would stand on end. Maybe that's how I lost it. Electric shock was painful, and looking back, I might feel truly angry at the long, pointless process if it all weren't so pathetic. Believe me, electric shock didn't work to change, or as they say now, to "repair" my sexual orientation. In fact I remember being attracted to the therapist's graduate assistant even as I sat in the behaviorist's office turning up the juice.

After three and one-half years as senior pastor of the Covenant Church in Pasadena, I resigned. My excuse was simple. I wanted to make films and write full-time. It wasn't true. In fact, by 1977, I was teetering on the edge of a complete nervous breakdown. I had held my homosexuality in check for twenty-five years. Besides being a husband and a father, I was writing, filmmaking, pastoring, preaching, and traveling nonstop across the country trying desperately to please God and chalk up credits in God's little book on my behalf. I still believed that if I could do enough good for the world, God would forgive my homosexual thoughts. But the plan wasn't working. Instead of managing to pull myself together, I was falling apart.

In the past, Lyla and I drove happily from London to Jerusalem. In the present, I was squirming impatiently on a drive across town. In the past, I had directed documentary films and television specials in more than twenty countries. In the present, I could hardly get on an airplane or move into another hotel room without trembling with fear. When two 747 jumbo jets crashed head-on in the Canary Islands with 574 deaths, I wept uncontrollably while watching a live broadcast from the scene. Everything seemed to effect me emotionally. I wept too much, worked in a daze, and thought often of dying. Something had to give.

Early one evening, shortly after Jimmy Carter's inauguration, I landed at LAX, picked up my car, and drove up Harbor Freeway into Pasadena. Instead of bypassing the heart of the city, I drove directly to our high-domed City Hall, the only place I knew where gay men often walked at night. I was relieved to find the streets deserted and was driving slowly toward home when I saw a tall, slender man walking in the semidarkness. I had resisted these moments for a quarter of a century. Whatever it might cost me, I couldn't resist anymore.

The young, well-dressed African-American stopped and bent down slightly to peer in my front window as I drove slowly past. When he smiled, I put on the brakes and leaned over quickly to open the passenger door. Without saying a word, he got in and sat beside me looking straight ahead. He said his name was Mark. I told him my first name and confessed that I had never done this kind of thing before. He invited me to his little apartment on the second floor of an older apartment building on Colorado Boulevard.

By the time we parked, walked down the dirty, cluttered side street, climbed up the darkened staircase, and entered his apartment overlooking the site of Pasadena's New Year's Rose Parade, I was terrified beyond imagination. That year, my son and I had ridden a float in the Rose Parade. I had been a pastor and a professor in the city. On various occasions my face had appeared in articles and tributes in the *Pasadena Star News* and in the *Los Angeles Times*. I loved my wife and family and wanted never to dishonor or embarrass them; but I had postponed the inevitable far too long, and that night my passion boiled over, insisting that the wait must end.

In the darkness, Mark and I undressed and climbed into bed. I didn't know the first thing about making love to another man. Even the thought of anal or oral sex with a stranger repulsed me. The whole process seemed awkward and alien if not evil. I had internalized all the homophobia of my past, and I lay there condemning myself while desiring everything I condemned. But I was determined to go through with it. I had wanted to love and to be loved by another man for so long, nothing else mattered.

For several minutes I lay next to this handsome young stranger without moving. When he broke the silence, his voice was quiet, his words gentle and without reproach.

"You really haven't done this before, have you?"

"No."

"Are you afraid?"

"Yes."

"That's okay. I understand. Let me take care of it. You just relax and try to enjoy."

He got out of bed and returned a short time later with a jar of heated massage oil. As he rubbed the warm oil into my body, for some strange reason I remembered the woman anointing Jesus' body in the open tomb. I don't know why this erotic moment would remind me of Jesus' tragic death and burial. But even while I lay there worrying that this sinful act would be the end of me, something in my brain kept reminding me that after death came the resurrection.

For more than an hour Mark massaged me like a professional masseur. After I climaxed, he lay beside me and held me in his arms until I went to sleep. When I awakened a short time later, he was leaning on one elbow smiling down at me. I don't remember even touching Mark that night. He gave me an hour of exquisite sensual pleasure and asked nothing in return. Upon leaving, when I took money out of my wallet to give him, he looked surprised and saddened by my gesture.

For the next few weeks, I was hounded by guilt and fear. What if Mark sees me on the street? What if he calls to blackmail me or my family? What if he tells the world I'm queer? What if he's given me some terrible disease? What if I never see Mark again?

Several months later, I got up my courage to call Mark at the number he had given me at his work at the Jet Propulsion Lab in the foothills of Pasadena. He was a first-year engineer there, still struggling to pay off his grad-school bills, and he seemed genuinely glad to get my call. "Anytime you need me," Mark said, "just phone. Don't worry about anything. I understand."

I survived the next year in large part because of Mark's generous, loving spirit. What my friendship with Mark provided was far more than "recreational sex," a practice that doesn't fit into the ethical pattern of Old Testament Judaism or New Testament Christianity. I had postponed appropriate male intimacy so long that I was desperate. If Mark hadn't been there for me, I don't know what I might have done. I believe without any doubt that he was another of God's gifts. When I think of how my story might have ended and how many other stories like mine have ended tragically, it makes me weak with gratitude to Mark and to Mark's Creator, who heard my desperate prayers even as I walked up that dark staircase into my unknown and terrifying new life.

My friends on the religious right will read this story and accuse me of giving way to lust. "He only needs to confess his sins," they'll say, "and be reborn." Or, "He just needs a good dose of God's Holy Spirit to take away this sinful bent." In fact, I gave my life to Jesus at their altars in my childhood and I spent my lifetime in their churches, listening to their sermons and praying with my whole heart for God's loving Spirit to heal me. On several different occasions I even went to Christian healers secretly asking to be exorcised of my homosexuality. Catholic and Protestant exorcists alike knelt around me with their hands on my head and shoulders asking God to cast out the "demon" who had "haunted me from my childhood." In fact, it was their homophobic ghost who was haunting me. Like all the rest, their simplistic solution to my God-given sexual orientation only made matters worse.

The misinformation passed on to me by friends and family on the religious right kept me from coming to terms with my sexuality as an adolescent and as a young adult. And my fear and guilt kept me from learning the truth on my own. How many innocent lives have been lost because our religious leaders refuse to acknowledge homosexuality as God's gift, let alone to help young lesbians and gays to understand how to live responsibly with that gift?

If I had been allowed to mature as a homosexual when all my young heterosexual friends were dealing realistically with their sexuality, that night with Mark would not have been necessary. But because I had postponed the process until my late thirties, walking up those stairs was the beginning of real reconciliation with my sexuality and with the loving God who created me. But in those days, I, too, believed that it was just one more failure in my long struggle against "lust."

During his campaign for the presidency, on July 21, 1976, Jimmy Carter stood on the front steps of his home in Plains, Georgia, and confessed his own sexual struggle to reporters, who listened with surprise and amusement.

"I've looked on a lot of women with lust," Mr. Carter said. "I've committed adultery in my heart many times. This is something that God recognizes I will do—and have done—and God forgives me for it."

Jimmy Carter's confession was published in *Playboy* magazine (September 20, 1976) and made banner headlines around the world. Liberal readers laughed. Conservatives were scandalized. Whatever others may have thought about the candidate's confession, I found it helpful. That a candidate for public office would dare to be so honest may have cost him votes, but he had the courage to break the embarrassed silence about all things sexual, and I was inspired and informed by his courageous act.

Since meeting Mark, I had practically memorized the story of David and Bathsheba. Realizing the terrible price that the young king had paid for yielding to his sexual lust, I still took great comfort in the fact that God loved him anyway. Whatever God may or may not think about homosexuality, if God loved David and God loved Jimmy Carter, then God loved me, too.

Shortly after meeting Mark, Bill Barbour, the president of Fleming Revell approached me to write another book. "What are you thinking about these days?" he said to me.

"Sex!" I answered, half in jest.

"Then write about it. I'll give you a twenty-five-thousand-dollar advance right here and now if you promise me a book."

As we walked away from the Velvet Turtle Restaurant on Arroyo

Boulevard, I told my first publisher about Jimmy Carter's honest confession and how I would like to retell the largely untold stories of our
Old Testament heroes—Samson, the judge, Solomon and David, the
kings, Hosea, the prophet—and how they and their ancient sons and
daughters survived their struggles with sexual lust.

I also wanted to tell my own story then. I wanted to come out of my
closet, to be totally honest at last, to call for an open dialogue about
homosexuality, but I didn't have the courage. Now, I wish I had been
more forthright. The agony that Lyla and I faced those next fifteen
years might have been tempered or even avoided by dealing with the
issues honestly and openly earlier in our life together. But at the time,
I didn't have the courage to come out of my closet, let alone to write
about Darrel or Peter, Gordon or Mark.

On the *Donahue* show during my author tour for the *Lust* book, Mr.
Donahue suddenly turned to me and asked, "Have you ever struggled
with lust yourself?"

"Of course. Haven't you?"

"Yes," he replied honestly, "but you're the first minister I ever heard
admit it."

The audience laughed and applauded while I sat there feeling sad.
Why is it so hard to admit that we are human?

On November 18, 1978, shortly after the publication of *Lust: The
Other Side of Love,* I read another headline in the *Los Angeles Times*
that would change the direction of my life: "Christian Cult Kills Congressman. Mass Suicide Suspected." During those first confusing days
as rumors trickled out of Jonestown in Guyana, Lyla and I watched
the rising body count with growing shock and sadness. After three
days, I flew to San Francisco and drove across the Bay Bridge into
Berkeley to a yellow, wood-frame house at 3028 Regent Street. Called
the Human Freedom Center, this historic old house had become the
gathering place of family and friends of the 909 people who had died
in Jonestown. And to this place the world's press was coming to ask
survivors how such a terrible tragedy could have happened.

The concerned relatives inside were high on Jones's rumored re-
taliatory "hit list." They had urged Congressman Ryan to make the
trip to Guyana. After Ryan's murder at Jonestown, police and federal
marshals surrounded the house with barricades while SWAT teams
patrolled the neighborhood with high-powered rifles and binoculars,
protecting the people inside.

For the first few days, television crews, reporters, FBI agents, and police were in and out of the old building, adding to the noisy confusion of the scene. But when I arrived, the shades were drawn and the doors were locked. The media had portrayed Jim Jones and his followers as crazies, fanatics, and former drug addicts from the slums of San Francisco who had turned to communism. The complex and tragic truth about Jim Jones and the hardworking, well-meaning people who had followed him had been lost in a barrage of sensational and simplistic news reports. Out of grief and anger, the hundreds of survivors waiting inside for more bad news from Guyana had decided to grant no more interviews.

I walked through the crowd of police, media, and curious spectators, knocked on the door, and waited. Finally, a voice whispered, "What do you want?" I explained that I was a Christian writer and filmmaker interested in finding answers to the questions Jonestown raises for the church. Suddenly, the door opened wide and I was pulled inside.

In every room, weeping families poured over enlarged pictures of bloated bodies rotting in the jungle, trying to identify their missing parents, children, or friends. Jean and Al Mills, who had helped found the Center, took me directly to the room where Tim Stoen, once the second most powerful man in the People's Temple, waited to answer my questions.

I was surprised to learn how many well-established, sincerely Christian people had joined the People's Temple. Jones was an ordained minister in good standing in a major Christian denomination. Jean Mills had been a lay leader and Sunday-school superintendent in her Nazarene church before joining with Jim Jones. Her husband, Al, was an engineer for Shell Oil Company and a Christian lay leader. Tim Stoen had a law degree from Stanford University and had served as an assistant district attorney for San Francisco. His wife, Grace, had been raised in Catholic schools and had served faithfully as a young adult on Catholic boards and committees. Their only son died with Jones in Guyana.

For six long weeks, I stayed with the surviving victims of that terrible tragedy. I learned how easy it was for good people to be deceived and how our own churches helped prepare Jones's victims for deception. "From childhood, we sat in long rows every Sunday," Al Mills explained. "We listened to our pastors and Bible teachers tell us what is right and what is wrong. We never got a chance to ask questions or to think for ourselves. We gave our money and never really knew or cared how it was spent. We worked day and night to please God and to help the cause even if it led to our exhaustion. We stayed so busy attending services and meeting on committees that our children didn't see us and our family life suffered. Our pastors may have meant well and been trustworthy, but they never taught us to think and act on our own. So, when a Jim Jones came along, we were conditioned to be deceived."

My film *Deceived: The Jonestown Tragedy* combined insightful and poignant memories of Jonestown survivors, rare Jim Jones footage that we found in the abandoned Temple from the early days when Jim was still preaching and teaching evangelical Christianity, and heart-breaking exclusive footage from Jonestown. Both the film and the book, *Deceived,* were used in seminaries, schools, and universities, featured on the media, and recommended widely by the leading clergy of this nation, Catholic and Protestant alike. I was hired to work as a consultant on the prizewinning CBS miniseries on Jim Jones and the Jonestown tragedy.

Al and Jean Mills and their teenage daughter, Daphene, were so grateful that I had been able to tell the survivors' side of the story that they invited me to a special dinner after the film's premiere. When the meal ended, in the quiet of a private dining room in a restaurant overlooking San Francisco Bay, the Millses shared their fears that they would probably be killed for telling their story to me. I didn't take their warning seriously. A few weeks later they were each shotgunned to death in different rooms of their home in Berkeley. To this day, so far as I know, the crime is still unsolved.

A homicide investigator with the Berkeley Police Department told me that a fellow churchman, very likely a young friend or even a member of the Mills family, pulled the trigger. It is so ironic that through the ages Christians, who follow Jesus, who spent his lifetime talking about love, end up killing other Christians who dare to disagree with their "fundamental beliefs." Old and New Testament texts have been misused to justify excommunication, imprisonment, torture, and death. Millions of innocent lives have been lost through "Christian" crusades, inquisitions, trials, witch-hunts, reformations, and cleansings.

Those attitudes continue today. In that same spirit of inquisition, honest gay and lesbian Christians are being excluded from membership in the churches of their childhood, ridiculed, rejected, and rebuked by pastors, priests, and laity alike. Sincere Christian leaders have even called for the death of gay and lesbian people. All the hatred trickles down from pulpit and lectern into acts of violence and death.

No wonder gays and lesbians stay in the closet so long. No wonder we go on trying desperately to be what we are not intended to be. We stay in our closets to protect ourselves and the people we love, to maintain our lives, our vocations, and our ministries, to support and sustain our families and our causes. Then, when we finally get desperate enough, when we just have to love and be loved as God intended, we end up alone and feeling desperate in gay bars, bathhouses, or on darkened city streets.

In spite of what television preachers say when they condemn us, we are not driven to these dark, secret places by lust, but by the natural, human need for intimacy that their current homophobic policies deny us. We enter into those furtive, usually unfulfilling, and almost always dangerous sexual encounters because we don't know any other way to meet our basic human needs and at the same time to preserve and protect all that we hold dear.

The Club Baths in Los Angeles was just off the Santa Monica Freeway. For years when I saw its sign blinking through the night, I wondered what I might find there to relieve my growing need for male intimacy and affection. Actually, what I pictured was right out of Dante's *Inferno,* a place given over to "perverts" and to "perversion." In 1979, shortly after the Millses were murdered, I parked my car in the Club's parking lot, walked up to the window, traded my driver's license for a room key and a towel, walked quickly down halls filled with cubicles locked from the inside, and entered a tiny room with a clean sheet on a freshly made bed.

I lay on the bed trembling with fear, certain that Satan himself would knock on that door and welcome me to the pit of hell. After an hour or more of terror and fantasy, I put on my bathing suit and hurried to the pool past signs warning against alcohol or drug use on the premises, and little jars loaded with free condoms. At the pool, a handful of Club Baths regulars were gathered in the Jacuzzi laughing and talking. I dove into the pool and was swimming endless laps when I heard someone call my name.

I didn't know whether to dive to the bottom and drown myself from embarrassment or jump out of the pool, put my towel over my head, and run dripping for the parking lot. So, I continued doing laps until the person calling my name dove into the pool, swam alongside me, and shouted, "Hey, Flipper. You look a lot like Mel White to me."

The man in the pool—I'll call him Dr. Smith—was a nationally known Christian pastor and evangelist whom I had known and respected since my years at Fuller Seminary. He had distinguished himself as a leader in a major denomination and as a powerful and courageous elected official in a Northern state. Dr. Smith had a wife, a fairly young family, and a spotless reputation. He was as surprised to see me at the Club Baths as I was surprised to see him.

The Jacuzzi had emptied and we sat talking on the edge of the hot, bubbling pool with our legs dangling in the water. He laughed when I told him what I had expected to find in this den of iniquity and explained that Club Baths across the country had allowed him a place to have at least some male intimacy during all those decades in the closet. He hadn't told his wife or his family about his homosexuality, but through people he had met at the Club Baths he had created an informal, nationwide network of gay friends and acquaintances.

"I don't come here for sex anymore," he told me. "In fact that's never been my primary reason for visiting this place. I come here to be with gay people like yourself, and to talk about things no one else would understand."

During our long conversation, I told Dr. Smith that Lyla knew almost everything, that we were trying to be totally honest with each other, that I had not told her about Mark and I certainly wasn't about to tell her about the Club Baths.

He took my arm and spoke quietly. "Don't do what I have done. Don't spend your life pretending. It isn't worth it."

Once again, it was as though God had heard my desperate, guilty prayers even as I traded my license for a towel at the door. After several hours of frank, helpful discussion, Dr. Smith left for the airport and I drove home. Four years later, I heard by the grapevine that Dr. Smith had died unexpectedly from a sudden case of AIDs-related pneumonia. Only then did his family and friends discover that years before this respected man had been infected with HIV.

Apparently, people across the nation were scandalized that such a wonderful man had a secret, "sinful" life. I knew better. Dr. Smith had done his best to keep his commitments, to protect his wife and family, to maintain his powerful and effective ministry. In spite of everything he had tried in his effort to "overcome his homosexuality," he couldn't resist an occasional night of male intimacy and conversation with those who understood.

Dr. Smith grew up in the generation just before mine. There were no gay or lesbian community centers then, no Universal Fellowship of Metropolitan Community Churches, no gay choirs, political organizations, special interest or support groups, no place to find real counsel or comfort from the homophobes and gay bashers in and out of the church. So, he did what he had to do to get by. In the process he became another victim of that terrible virus that has killed so many good men who were doing their best to get by.

At Dr. Smith's memorial service, I wanted to stand up and tell that great, confused congregation about my evening at the Club Baths with their senior pastor. I wanted to explain how he had ministered to me as we sat talking in that "wicked" place. I wanted to thank him for his advice and tell him that one day I hoped to have the courage to act on it. I wanted to take his wife and children in my arms and tell them that he had died trying to support and protect them, and that this sudden flurry of embarrassment and grief was the last thing he would have wanted. I wanted to help them all understand what it means to be gay and in the closet and trying desperately to meet everyone else's expectations while you are starving for intimacy and affection and affiliation with your own kind.

Instead, I just sat alone on a folding chair that had been set up for the overflow crowd in the fellowship hall and tried not to cry.

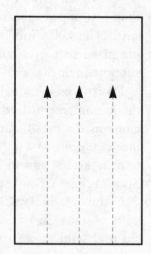

Chapter 8

1980–81,

Facing Reality

*J*ust *eight weeks before the new decade began, on November 4, 1979,* Moslem fundamentalists seized the U.S. embassy in Tehran. The Aya- tollah Khomeini made angry speeches condemning the Carter admin- istration, while militant Islamic students holding forty-nine American hostages screamed, *"Margh bar* [death to] *Carter!"* Across the world Moslem fundamentalists were rising up to join the right-wing Islamic revolution in "purging" their people's religious and moral practices and "cleansing" ethnic and racial impurities from their nations.

About that time, a fundamentalist Christian revolution was stirring to life in America. My clients on the religious right, whom I would serve as ghostwriter in the 1980s, were at the heart of that revolution. One of the reasons I didn't see the dangerous side of their neoconservative movement was that much of what they valued, I valued, too.

When Billy Graham used his television broadcast "The Hour of Decision" to call on all Americans to "turn from their sinful ways and get right with God," I felt moved and convinced. When Jerry Falwell used his "Old Fashion Gospel Hour" to help launch the Liberty God-parent Homes for pregnant teenagers and offered to pay all the expenses for an unwanted pregnancy, I applauded his desire to do more than just oppose abortion. On Pat Robertson's daily television broadcast, "The 700 Club," when he preached against homosexuality and promised that gays and lesbians could be healed, I sent in funds to support their 800 prayer-line ministry.

I wasn't wise enough to anticipate where all this talk of "cleansing the nation" might lead. I didn't foresee that one day those same religious media personalities and the political groups they would organize could become a dangerous threat to me, to my gay brothers and lesbian sisters, and to all persons who might disagree with their political, religious, and social agenda for our country.

In those early days, I never made the connection between the mentality of some Christian fundamentalists and their desire to "purge and cleanse" with the mentality of Islamic or other fundamentalist revolutionary movements. Nor did I dream that in the next few years I would be writing books, sermons, and speeches for those same fundamentalist Christian revolutionaries.

I was still pastoring and teaching in 1978 when the *Wall Street Journal* featured a front-page article on Jerry Falwell's national radio and television ministry. The author labeled this new phenomenon "the Electric Church." In fact, it wasn't a new phenomenon at all.

In December 1956, twenty-two years earlier, Jerry had launched his first live television broadcast from WLVA, Channel 13 in Lynchburg, with a $90 weekly budget, a guest soloist from the Methodist church, and his wife, Macel, at the upright studio piano. By 1978, Jerry was just one of the handful of powerful preachers on the religious right who were quietly and effectively building multimillion-dollar media empires "to preach the Gospel to every creature."

During 1978 and 1979, Jerry and a group of talented student musicians from his own Liberty University traveled across the country holding patriotic rallies on the steps of forty-four state capitols and in more than one hundred other American cities. The "America, You're Too Young to Die!" rallies featured spine-tingling trumpet fanfares, lively choral anthems, and Jerry's call for the nation to repent. "When God's people cry out for mercy, God sends them a deliverer," Jerry warned. "When they forget God again, their nation falls again. I think our country is now at the point where we could fall."

Over a portable loudspeaker to crowds that grew larger in every city, Jerry called for massive voter registration campaigns and urged the religious right to stand up and be counted. He preached against communism, abortion, pornography, divorce, moral permissiveness, our nation's military unpreparedness, the general breakdown of traditional family values, and as one specific example of that breakdown, Jerry preached against homosexuals and homosexuality.

There was no way for me to understand in those days that Jerry might be dangerous. He was just beginning to exercise his political activist muscles. He still dedicated most of his television sermons to the life, death, and resurrection of Jesus with only an occasional foray into politics. And though I felt restless and sometimes angry when he launched into his new political rhetoric, I still believed that in his heart, Jerry loved Jesus and wanted to make Him known to the nation. And though I was confused by his occasional tirades against homosexuality and homosexuals, they didn't really offend me. In those days, homosexuality was still on my own list of primary "sins" as well. It never crossed my mind to oppose him, let alone to see his words as dangerous and misleading.

In 1979, Jerry Falwell called a group of conservative leaders to meet in his office in Lynchburg, Virginia, to "draw up a plan to save America." At a lunch break, Paul Weyrich, a public-relations and mass-mailing genius, looked across the table and said, "Jerry, there is in America a moral majority that agrees about the basic issues. But they aren't organized. They don't have a platform. The media ignores them. Somebody's got to get that moral majority together."

Immediately, Jerry recognized the powerful possibilities in bringing together the "moral majority" of all Americans who shared his conservative political and social values. But with his lifelong, Bible-based fear of believers being "yoked together with unbelievers," Jerry wondered how he could conscientiously recruit into his fundamentalist army people from evangelical, charismatic, mainline Protestant, Roman Catholic, and Orthodox churches, as well as practicing and nonpracticing Jews, let alone Mormons, agnostics, and atheists.

He found the answer in the teachings of Dr. Francis Schaeffer, the man *Time* magazine called the "Guru of the Evangelicals." About that time, Schaeffer was traveling about this country showing his incredibly successful film series *How Should We Then Live*. Conservatives, Christians and non-Christians alike, packed arenas and large church auditoriums to see the films and hear Dr. Schaeffer's dramatic plea for the nation to turn away from "godless humanism" and return to "moral absolutes."

After the predictable standing ovation, enthusiastic audiences would spend the rest of the evening asking questions of this engaging, goateed guru in a white Nehru jacket and tan knickers, sitting on a table center stage, legs dangling comfortably, the Bible in one hand and *Time* magazine in the other, giving infallible answers with the authoritarian certainty once reserved for prophets and kings.

Francis Schaeffer was my first client on the religious right. In fact, I ghost-wrote and directed the final version of that same *How Should We Then Live* film series. On Monday mornings I commuted by United Airlines to Chicago and by Swissair DC-10 to Switzerland where Francis was an expatriate teacher and, on weekends, made the return, ten-thousand-mile journey to Pasadena, California, where I was pastoring the Evangelical Covenant Church.

To complete the series on time, Lyla and I and our two young children lived in Switzerland one summer in a beautiful little chalet overlooking the village of Thun. With Heinz Fussle, an expert filmmaker and my longtime friend, I commuted back and forth to the Schaeffers' study center above Geneva, to interview and film Dr. Schaeffer, and to a studio in Bern to complete our editing of the project.

During my six months with the Schaeffers, I learned to love Francis, Edith, and their artistic, young son, Franky. Their home in Switzerland had become a sanctuary to fundamentalist and evangelical Christians from around the world, who made pilgrimages to seek counsel from this compassionate and winsome man and to eat Edith's freshly baked orange rolls and apple strudel.

But Dr. Schaeffer had a dark, arrogant side as well. At a private "thank-you" luncheon he gave us at the Hotel Hyatt in Los Angeles, Lyla asked Francis what other trustworthy biblical theologians he liked to quote besides himself. After a long pause, Francis answered, "There are none."

During the next ten years of service to the "electronic preachers," I would remember that moment, for it came to symbolize the way all the self-appointed gurus on the religious right saw themselves. They were "special," uniquely called by God to "save the nation." They trusted no one to know or understand the truth as clearly as they themselves understood it. They didn't even trust each other.

In spite of his separatist spirit, it was Francis Schaeffer who taught Jerry Falwell how to mobilize an army of "nonbelievers" to accomplish "God's will for the nation." Jerry admired Schaeffer, and his political strategy was shaped by Francis's notion of "cobelligerents." In his books and speeches, Dr. Schaeffer declared that there was no biblical mandate against evangelical Christians joining hands "with nonbelievers" for political and social causes "as long as there was no compromise of theological integrity." In fact, Schaeffer pointed out, there are many Bible stories about God using pagans "to accomplish His purposes." Imagine the grin on Jerry's face the day he realized the potential for using "pagans" who happened to be political conservatives for raising money and mobilizing volunteers.

Once Jerry had been won over to Schaeffer's position of "cobelligerents," he began to discover the few key issues and/or fears that most if not all conservatives held in common: communism came to mind immediately, of course, but abortion and homosexuality were also at the top of Jerry's list of "national sins." On July 18, 1993, fifteen years after Jerry launched his new Moral Majority organization, Ralph Reed, the president of the Christian Coalition, Pat Robertson's version of Jerry's old Moral Majority, admitted (to a national convention of the Christian Coalition) that the conservatives shared opposition to gay rights and abortion had "built our movement and remain a vital part of the message." Isn't it ironic that the first political-action committee that Adolf Hitler organized in his successful attempt to conquer Germany was also the Committee Against Abortion and Homosexuality?

Three of the five men selected by Jerry in 1979 to serve on the first board of directors of his Moral Majority were D. James Kennedy, pastor of the Coral Ridge Presbyterian Church in Fort Lauderdale, Florida; Charles Stanley, pastor of the First Baptist Church in Atlanta, Georgia; and Tim LaHaye, pastor of the Scott Memorial Baptist Church in El Cajon, California. These men adapted quickly to the ways of "cobelligerency" and went on to use the issue of homosexuality to mobilize conservative armies of their own.

D. Kennedy, another of my former clients on the religious right, and Charles Stanley learned quickly to build powerful television ministries by uniting generous conservatives, "pagan" and Christian alike, around their mutual disapproval of abortion and homosexuality. Currently, Jim Kennedy is sending out antihomosexual "surveys," antigay petitions to the president, and inflammatory antigay videotapes to help pay his media bills. Charles Stanley regularly condemns gays and lesbians from his electronic pulpit. Tim LaHaye uses antigay rhetoric to support his conservative lobbying organization in the nation's capital, and his wife, Beverly LaHaye, uses her own genteel brand of homophobia and homohatred to mobilize and support her Concerned Women for America, the country's largest and most powerful right-wing women's organization.

In the mid-1980s, after a tense, combative lunch in Washington, D.C., with Tim and Beverly LaHaye, I declined the opportunity to ghost-write Beverly's autobiography. She and her husband seemed obsessed with "the homosexual menace." I wanted so badly to tell them that I was gay, that so many of their friends and coworkers were gay, that they were doing great damage to gay and lesbian people. Instead, I just turned down their offer and walked away.

That same afternoon, on a revealing ride across the capital in the two-phone, one-fax limousine of a high-level executive of the *Washington Times,* I also turned down the opportunity to ghost-write a book defending Sun Myung Moon's "positive contribution" to the neoconservative movement in America. It was during that ride with the *Washington Times* executive, a Christian fundamentalist whom I had met when he was a leader of Falwell's Moral Majority, that I learned that the *Times* was owned by Moon's Unification Church.

Looking back now, I wonder if Jerry is still convinced that he made the right decision to incorporate Francis Schaeffer's notion of "cobelligerents" into the credo of his Moral Majority. However he may feel now about the ethics of using "pagans" and "heretics" to help accomplish his political and religious goals, the results are now a matter of history.

Through his powerful Moral Majority organization, Jerry Falwell established himself as a major player on the nation's political scene. In fact, when I was ghost-writing for Jerry in 1985 and 1986, it was his standing policy to call one senator and two congressmen or women every day. Even when we were flying across the country in Jerry's private jet, nothing kept him from making those two influential phone calls, and never once while I was with him did the people in power refuse or even postpone his calls.

At the last Republican National Convention in 1992, after being warmly embraced by Ronald Reagan and George Bush, and after congratulating the Platform Committee for conforming the party platform to his deeply felt, Christian values, Jerry Falwell sat in his place of honor looking down on the convention floor, grinning his full approval. But in 1979, when Jerry launched the Moral Majority, no one, not even Jerry, ever dreamed how fast or how far his new strategy would take him. Nor did any of us even imagine how important his antihomosexual rhetoric would be for raising funds or for mobilizing his volunteers, "pagans" and Christians alike.

Now, fifteen years later, Jerry is still using homosexuality to raise money and mobilize support. I hate that his ignorance and superstition leads to the suffering and death of my brothers and sisters, but I understand how he was so terribly misled. Like myself, Jerry is a victim of other victims. We both grew up surrounded by well-meaning, Bible-believing Christians who had never really tried to understand in our modern context the ancient passages used now to condemn homosexuality. In those days, we were all victims of blind, unreasoned fear and hatred of homosexuality that had been passed down generation after generation without much thought and almost no careful historical, cultural, or linguistic study of the ancient biblical record, let alone of the new data being gathered by the medical, scientific, and psychological communities.

We didn't know the difference between sexual "preference" and sexual "orientation." We thought homosexuals were perverted heterosexuals who *chose* for some "sick reason" to have sex with men. We didn't realize that homosexuals were mysteriously imprinted with the need for same-sex intimacy and affiliation in their mothers' wombs or in the first few years of childhood, and that, try as they might, their sexuality, like heterosexuality, was a permanent condition.

Because we didn't understand the real nature of homosexuality, we feared the rumors that heterosexuals could be "recruited" into homosexuality, that homosexuals abused children, that homosexuals shouldn't serve in the military, that homosexuals were more promiscuous than heterosexuals, that homosexuals could be "healed" or "cured," that homosexuals who committed their lives to Christ and to heterosexual marriage and family could escape this "terrible sin."

Now, thanks to a host of well-known studies, we know the truth: That heterosexuals (young or old) can't be recruited into homosexuality. That child abuse is primarily a heterosexual phenomenon usually committed by members of the child's own family and close friends. That gay and lesbian soldiers, sailors, marines, and air force personnel have fought with honor and courage in every war and that Pentagon studies reveal that homosexuals are as capable of controlling their sexual needs on leave or under fire as their heterosexual colleagues, maybe more.

We know now that the average homosexual is no more promiscuous or no less responsible sexually than the average heterosexual. That homosexuals are not "healed" by God or by "reparative" therapy, in spite of all the misleading and short-lived testimonials of the current "ex-gay" movement. And that homosexuals who enter into heterosexual marriage to "cure" their homosexuality are more likely to cause terrible suffering and inevitable grief for their partners and for themselves as well.

I believe further that sexuality, homo or hetero, is a permanent part of the mystery of creation; that each of us, gay and nongay alike, is called by our Creator to accept our sexual orientation as a gift; and that we are called to exercise that gift with integrity, creativity, and responsibility. I know all this now, but I didn't know it then.

About the time Jerry Falwell was beginning to discover the benefits of stirring up the ancient homophobic ghost, I was running as fast as I could to escape that same evil spirit. Haunted by the ancient lies, I still believed that homosexuality was evil and that practicing homosexuals were condemned by their "lust" to misery, disease, and death. I was convinced that if I ever "gave in" to the "evil spirit," my life would be ruined, my family would be destroyed, my vocation would be lost, my spiritual journey would be derailed forever, and my soul would be condemned to an eternity in hell. So when I heard Jerry condemn homosexuality and homosexuals, I just piled up more guilt, prayed again that God would heal me, and tried to live a productive life in spite of the growing load of fear and frustration that I carried.

However, in spite of that growing fear, after trying for twenty-five years to change or overcome my sexual orientation, the truth was slowly dawning in my befuddled brain. Homosexuality is not something you change or heal or overcome. After trying desperately to be the world's best son, husband, father, student, professor, pastor, writer, and filmmaker, it was becoming more and more obvious that there was nothing I could accomplish that would replace or end my constant longing to be in a long-term, loving relationship with another man. Lyla and I were both beginning to realize that we could not postpone forever the painful decisions that lay ahead.

In the summer of 1979, just as Jerry Falwell called leaders of the religious right to Lynchburg to launch his Moral Majority political-reform movement, Lyla and I took Erinn, nine, and Michael, eight, to a much deserved vacation on Poipu Beach on the island of Kauai in Hawaii. For one idyllic week, I walked the beaches with my beloved family. Almost every day at dawn, Michael and I hiked out on a spit of sand curving into the Pacific to watch the sunrise and see the dolphins leaping in the morning light. From a wrinkled, old Hawaiian native, Erinn and I learned to weave hats from fallen palm fronds and string shells and colorful Hawaiian beads into leis. Both children learned to snorkel that summer, lying on my back, holding to my neck, and peering through their goggles at the bright yellow tang, the black-and-white-striped sergeant majors, and the rainbow-colored parrot fish.

In the evenings, Lyla and Erinn dressed in matching muumuus while Michael and I put on our white pants and colorful aloha shirts. As the sun set over the Pacific, we walked through the Waiohai Hotel's tropical gardens to the nearby Plantation House Restaurant where we sat on the veranda listening to sudden rain squalls beat on the old tin roof while we ate fresh grilled snapper, fried bananas, and pieces of homemade macadamia-nut pie.

At night, after the children were asleep, or during the day while they splashed in the gentle surf, Lyla and I walked the beaches or sat in the sand and talked and argued, laughed and cried. Even in paradise where everything seemed so picture perfect, we knew in our hearts that something had to be done to resolve the painful, ever-present conflict. I was a homosexual man drawn inexorably to my own kind for intimacy and affiliation. Lyla was a heterosexual woman. Try as she might, Lyla could not meet my sexual needs or satisfy my longings for intimacy.

We loved each other deeply. We were committed totally to our marriage and to our family. Every day for almost twenty years of marriage we had prayed for God's guidance and for God's strength to see us through; and year after year we thought we saw evidence that the crisis had finally passed, that the victory had been won. Then, little by little, my old needs would reappear, accompanied by fear, guilt, and increasing hopelessness.

During that week in Hawaii in 1979, I felt a growing sense of despair. After a quarter of a century of trying, it was obvious that my sexual orientation could not be changed. After twenty-five years, I knew that celibacy was not possible for me, and occasional secret encounters with a man only left me feeling more dissatisfied, more in need of a long-term, loving relationship. In spite of the ongoing conflict, I promised Lyla that I would never leave her or the children, and I made that promise fully believing that I could keep it. My marriage and my family were sacred commitments, and I was determined to keep those commitments until the day I died.

Late at night, during our Hawaiian vacation, after Lyla and the children were asleep, I walked the moonlit beaches struggling to find my way out of this impossible predicament. If I couldn't leave Lyla and my family, and if I couldn't overcome my desperate needs for physical and psychological intimacy with another man, there seemed to be only one solution. If I could die an accidental death, Lyla and the children would get my insurance benefits and we would all be spared the embarrassment and the disgrace that I feared would follow the revelation of my sexual orientation.

Earlier that year, when I mentioned suicide to one of my counselors, he warned me that taking my life would cause my wife and children terrible psychological suffering. But, if I died at the bottom of the sea, or so I told myself in Hawaii, no one would know why or how it happened, and after a time of grieving, my wife and children could move on to new lives in financial security.

At seven-thirty A.M. on our fourth morning in Hawaii, I took my first scuba-diving lesson from a sixty-year-old woman who smoked long, thin cigars and cursed like a sailor. For three days, Mary quizzed me on the scuba-diver's manual and dive charts. She lectured me about Boyle's law and the dangers of diving alone. And she even shamed me into buying my own regulator, air and depth gauges, buoyancy vest, wet suit, and weight belt.

I didn't realize it then, but this short, stocky woman would save my life and lead me into a world of quiet, exquisite beauty where God would speak to me again.

By Saturday, the day our family was scheduled to return to California, I was just a few lessons away from official certification as an open-water diver. Lyla had to get our children back to school, but she urged me to remain a few days alone on Kauai to finish my scuba lessons. After driving my family to the Lihue Airport, I hugged my tanned and happy children, kissed Lyla good-bye, and drove back to Poipu to finish my lessons and end my life.

It wasn't exactly that black-and-white, of course. I didn't really want to die. In fact, I loved life and felt grateful for all the blessings God had given me and my family. I knew that it wasn't God's will that I should die, and in the back of my brain, I even knew that I could trust God to see me through this nightmare, but momentarily I was blinded to my loving Creator's presence by my fear and depression. I was exhausted from trying too hard. I had run out of hope and I just didn't know how to resolve the endless conflict in any other way.

That evening, as I drove back to Poipu, I thought about Lyla and the children flying somewhere over the Pacific, and for a moment I was almost overwhelmed with the love I felt for them. I wondered if I would ever see my family again. I felt lonely and afraid and lost.

As I walked from the parking lot to my little thatched cottage on the beach, I saw a young man standing in the shadows. He followed me as I walked up on my porch and stood beside me as I fumbled for my key in the semidarkness. I had seen this same young man several times at the Sheraton pool when Lyla and I and the kids had gone there for breakfast or lunch on the open patio. That same afternoon in the parking lot, our eyes had met as I walked the family to our rental car. I had smiled and he had returned my smile. Apparently, he had spent the afternoon watching and waiting for my return.

The stranger was tall, tanned, and built like Mark Spitz, the young Olympian swimmer. He wore white shorts and a white tank top, and his sun-streaked, sandy brown hair was brushed back casually over his ears. He looked slightly embarrassed by this direct encounter. He smiled nervously, held out his hand, and spoke quietly.

"I'm Tony."

He was about twenty-five, a Mormon from Utah who was finishing his second missionary tour to the islands.

"Your family is gone back to the mainland?"

"Yes. I'm staying a few days to finish scuba certification."

"I'm a diver, too. I love the sea."

For a moment we stood beside each other in the silence looking at the waves rolling gently onto the beach just a few steps away. The dancing waters sparkled and glowed with reflected light. I had stepped onto that porch wanting to die from loneliness, but the moment Tony, a stranger, but one of my own kind, stood beside me, I wanted desperately to live again.

"Can I come in?" he asked.

"I'm feeling like a swim," I answered, thinking that I couldn't let him into that cottage without dangerously threatening my resolve.

"Good idea." He stripped off his white shorts and tank top and stood naked beside me on the porch. I started for the door, mumbling something about my bathing suit.

"Have you ever gone for a swim at night, butt-naked in the darkness?" he asked.

"No, I haven't."

"Try it," he said, running down to the sea and diving into the warm, dark waters. Without a moment's hesitation, I stripped off my own shorts and dashed into the sea before any late-night stroller might happen by. Tony swam just a few strokes ahead of me. There was enough reflected light to see his body moving gently through the water. I was swimming hard to catch up when suddenly Tony stopped, rolled over on his back, and floated on the water.

The coastline of Poipu Beach stretched out before us painted in sparkling lights. Music from a live jazz band in the Sheraton bar echoed across the water. The sky was streaked with stars. I backstroked in place beside Tony trying not to think how much I wanted to touch him, feeling the old waves of guilt and fear pulling me down like that dark, black sea.

When the first chill came, I began a long, slow swim back to the beach. Tony swam beside me through the surf and ran behind me up the beach to the cottage. I opened the door, and before I could even think to object, Tony was inside, headed for the shower. While I was puttering awkwardly around the still-darkened bedroom looking for dry underwear and long pants, I could hear Tony adjusting the shower controls. Suddenly, he was standing naked in the doorway, framed by the light from the bathroom.

"Save water. Shower with a friend," he said, turning and at the same time gesturing for me to follow.

Desperate with desire, somehow I managed to decline this fantasy come to life. While Tony showered and dried, I succeeded in getting dressed and was searching through the refrigerator for something to drink when he emerged half-dry and gleaming in his damp, white shorts.

"I want to make love to you," he said, and I almost collapsed with surprise and fear.

"I can't do it, Tony." I felt waves of ambivalence.

"Why not?" He moved me gently toward the king-size bed.

"Because, I have a wife and family. I have commitments . . ."

Tony took both my arms and lowered me gently onto the edge of the bed. He was playful but determined. He knew that I wanted to make love, and he was doing his best to help me get past my guilt and fear.

"I want to make love to you, too," I confessed, "even if I don't know you, but I just can't do it. Please, try to understand."

Gently, playfully, Tony lifted my legs and put them up on the bed. I fell back onto a pillow feeling mixed emotions somewhere on the scale between absolute terror and absolute ecstasy. He crawled across me and lay beside me on the bed.

"I've watched you with your family," he said. "I know you love them and it's pretty obvious that they love you. I'm glad for you and even jealous, but what could be so wrong in making love tonight?"

For two hours I lay there trying to explain why I couldn't make love to Tony and at the same time wanting it desperately. Finally, he just gave up. I remember the exact moment it happened. He had been holding my hand and pleading with me to loosen up and to enjoy life a little. He had leaned up on one elbow and stroked my face trying to explain why he was suddenly worried about me. He had even paced the room, trying to help me understand why making love to strangers is the only option so many gay men have. But after two hours of useless struggle, he suddenly bolted from the bed and walked angrily from the room.

"Will I see you tomorrow?" I asked, feeling suddenly desperate, hoping for another chance.

"I'm leaving for the big island tomorrow," Tony answered, not looking back, and before I could speak, he was gone. I stood at the door praying he would return, but he didn't come back. I never saw Tony again.

About that time, Lyla called to report their safe arrival on the mainland. We chatted for a brief time, and after saying good-night to my wonderful wife and children, I lay back on the bed more certain than ever that death was the only way to end this terrible, secret conflict.

The next morning, I rode in Mary's rusty, war-surplus jeep to Poipu Landing, a tiny harbor on Kauai. After checking and double-checking our gear, after being certain we both understood Mary's dive plan, I climbed into her old Boston whaler and held on for dear life as she gunned the fifty-horse outboard engine down the coast toward the Sheraton Hotel.

Mary checked my equipment one last time and signaled me to follow as she flipped backward out of the boat and moved slowly down the anchor chain. Once I had righted myself, cleared my ears, and moved beyond the curtain of my own escaping bubbles, I could see forever through the light blue water. As I descended, I could count the barnacles growing on the metal bottom of Mary's little dive boat bobbing just above us. Below, it was perfectly clear why this popular dive spot was called the Sheraton Cathedrals. Great craggy clusters of rock loomed up at us like the spires of Notre Dame. As we descended into these towers, the morning sun streaked down through holes in the rocks and reflected off the backs of colorful fish darting about, giving one the sense of stained-glass windows come to life.

Mary hovered just above the anchor watching me descend. Her arms were folded and her fins moved slowly without touching the precious coral or even stirring up sand or silt from the bottom. She signaled, okay? I returned her okay signal. But I was not okay. I had come to the bottom of the sea to die alone in a safe, dark place, but Mary wouldn't leave me and the place she had chosen for my first open-water dive was not a dark cave or sunken freighter suitable for dying, but an underwater cathedral, a place to celebrate life shaped by the Creator's hands with hot volcanic lava cooled by the open sea, with earthquakes, hurricanes, and tidal waves, with tiny growing coral heads and curious, nibbling creatures, and with centuries of silent, moving waters.

Even as I swam slowly through this amazing natural cathedral sixty feet beneath the ocean, I thought of these words from the 139th Psalm: "This is too glorious, too wonderful to believe! I can never be lost to your Spirit. I can never get away from my God. If I go up to heaven, you are there; if I go down to the place of the dead, you go with me. If I ride the morning winds to the farthest oceans, even there your hand will guide me, your strength will support me."

In the absolute silence of that moment, the still, small voice of God was clear. Our Creator didn't abandon us at birth. We are not alone in this amazing universe. God's Spirit goes with us even to the bottom of the sea. And though we be confused and depressed and tired of life, God is still present to comfort and to guide us.

Mary waited to clear the anchor as I ascended slowly to the top of the anchor chain. Just a few feet below the surface, a school of dolphins raced by churning the water playfully. I clung to the ladder and watched them pass, grinning to myself and thanking God for life.

Safely back in Pasadena, several weeks later I walked up a narrow, wooden staircase to the second-floor office of Dr. Phyliss Hart, a psychologist at Fuller Theological Seminary. At the time, I didn't know exactly why I had decided to see Phyliss. I do know now. After listening patiently to the story of my lifelong battle to overcome my sexual orientation, Phyliss leaned across her desk and said quietly, "Mel, you aren't sick. You're a gay man. You just need to fall in love with another gay man, and get it over with!"

At first, I thought she was just being flip. But she had reviewed my twenty years of counseling, the shock therapy, and the Valium overuse. She had studied my psychological profiles. She had questioned me carefully as I told my story. I was stunned at first, even angry when she called me "gay" and suggested that I accept that fact and try to live my "gay" life with integrity. I walked back down those steps and across the parking lot feeling terribly confused. What about Lyla? What about my family? What about my vocation? Slowly, the truth filtered through all those years of resistance and denial.

"Mel, you aren't sick," Phyliss had said, and those simple words began to breathe new life into my crippled spirit. Suddenly I realized that this was not about Lyla or my family or my vocation. This was about me. For twenty-five years I had been in a kind of bondage, judging myself, hating myself, trying to change something at the heart of me that could not, should not, be changed. All those years feeling dirty, ugly, sinful, sick, rejected by God, by myself, by my community; then in Phyliss's little office, good news broke into my fearful soul with all the light and music of that amazing night in Bethlehem. It has all been a bad dream. I am not sick. I am well. Her words brought liberation.

"You're a gay man," she had said, and she was smiling. Never before had I heard those words spoken without a sneer. She spoke those words as though I could be proud, as though my sexual orientation, too, was a part of God's plan. I didn't see shame or judgment in her eyes. I saw celebration. She was congratulating me. My Creator hadn't made a terrible mistake. I wasn't some kind of tragic deviation from the norm. I was a gay man. There have been millions of gay men and lesbian women before me. Millions more will follow. We are a part of God's mysterious, loving plan for the universe. We, too, have gifts to offer. Her words brought pride!

"You just need to fall in love with another gay man," she had said, and the idea literally exploded in my brain, blowing away all the terrible years of tight-lipped, desperate resistance to what my heart had been telling me from the beginning. I could dance with Darrel. I could hold Peter in my arms. I could kiss Gordon without feeling embarrassed or ashamed. I could fall in love with Mark or Jeffrey or Tony. It didn't matter if people sneered or turned away in disgust or yelled "faggot" when I passed. I could trust my heart, whatever anyone else did or said in response. Phyliss's courageous words brought hope!

"And get it over with!" she had concluded. At first, the urgency of her advice made me angry. Phyliss knew Lyla and my children. How could she set my feet on a course that might take me away from them? Then I remembered that morning in Hawaii just days before, when death seemed the only practical solution. Phyliss was not setting my feet on a course away from them. She was holding life out to me. Choosing life would cost me and my family dearly, but choosing death would cost us more. Ignorance and misinformation had brought us to this painful place. Truth would set us free. She seemed confident that we would all survive. Was it possible? Could this lifelong struggle end? Her words brought joy!

Chapter *9*

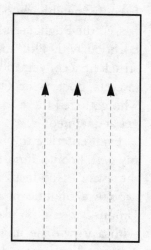

1981,

Surviving Infatuation

and Isolation

After ringing Philip and Janet Yancey's doorbell seven or eight times without response, I wrote a note, dropped it in their mailbox, and walked quickly down Clark Street to the Bughause. I had been commuting back and forth to Chicago from Pasadena on a major film project. The Yanceys had invited me to use their second-floor, brownstone condominium near Lake Michigan as a downtown base on these sudden, unplanned visits.

Philip Yancey was a best-selling author, respected columnist, and the editor of *Campus Life* magazine. His wife, Janet, was the director of a senior-citizen center ministering to the physical and spiritual needs of the poor and elderly in the heart of Chicago's skid row. For the past several years they had been close friends and confidants, listening to my desperate, late-night phone calls, alternately confronting me with hard, helpful questions and then comforting me with words of wisdom and of hope. We closed a lot of fancy restaurants after midnight with our intense, often tearful conversations about homosexuality and its potential effects on my life and on the lives of Lyla and our family.

Near the Yanceys' condo, just four blocks south on Clark, was a friendly, neighborhood bar frequented primarily by gay men. I had passed the Bughause several times on my long walks about the neighborhood with Phil and Janet, but I had never entered the bar nor struck up a conversation with another gay man in that crowd of young lawyers, doctors, accountants, blue-collar workers, and grad students who gathered there in the early evenings to talk shop, play pool, and get acquainted.

Even entering the bar required an act of courage and defiance on my part. I could almost see Noni's ghost standing at the door, warning me away. "Goodness sakes, grandson," she would have whispered, "you're a lifetime member of the Woman's Christian Temperance Union. Bars are no places for Christians. You know that." And then, with a frown she might have mumbled to herself, "Where is Carry Nation when we need her?"

When I was still a child, after buying my "lifetime" membership in the WCTU, Noni told me how that formidable woman, nearly six feet tall, weighing 175 pounds, dressed all in black, would march into a saloon alone or accompanied by hymn-singing women and proceed to pray, hurl biblical-sounding warnings, and smash the bar fixtures and liquor bottles with a hatchet. According to Noni, Carry Nation was imprisoned many times but managed to pay her fines from lecture-tour fees and souvenir-hatchet sales.

"She was threatened, beaten, and jailed," Noni once told me, "but her courage led to the Prohibition Amendment attached to the U.S. Constitution in 1919 and to the creation of the Woman's Christian Temperance Union of which you are a part!"

If entering a bar was such a risky, sinful act to Noni, imagine what she might have thought about her beloved grandson entering a gay bar. She wasn't present that late afternoon in 1981 when I walked into the Bughause, but she had passed on to me all her fears and prohibitions. Alarm bells were ringing in my head even as I walked up to

Mel White, age five.

A family photo, 1957. (Grandpa) Melvin, (Mom) Faythe, (Grandma) Noni, (Dad) Carl, Mel (seventeen), Dennis (eight), Marshall (twelve).

The graduating senior in a 1958 Santa Cruz High School yearbook photo.

September 7, 1964.
Mel and Lyla begin
their married life in
Santa Cruz, California.

In 1964, Mel leads
3,000 high school
students in a
"singspiration" at
the weekly Saturday
YFC rally in
Portland, Oregon.

A cast photo for Mel's first television series, *The World of Youth,* originating for NBC at KGW-TV in Portland, Oregon, 1958–1965.

On a film location with Dan Dunkelberger, Mel's long-time friend and cameraman/editor.

The obligatory photo on a camel while directing a television special near Jerusalem.

Mel and Lyla with their children, Erinn and Michael, 1975.

A Christmas family photo, 1982.

Mel and Lyla in
their home in
Sierra Madre,
about 1979.

Mel and Lyla with
their daughter, Erinn,
on her wedding day,
June 15, 1991.

In 1989, Mel in the Philippines with President Corazon Aquino while writing the story of his heroes, Ninoy and Cory.

Mel with his friend and speechwriting client, Ollie North.

In 1993, Mel was arrested in front of the White House while protesting President Clinton's decision not to end the ban on gays and lesbians in the military. (Photo by Annalisa Kraft)

With the Reverend Michael Piazza, Senior Pastor of the Cathedral of Hope, just before Mel's installation as Dean of the Cathedral on Gay Pride Sunday, June 27, 1993.

A family together at granddaughter Katie's first birthday, 1993. Standing: Michael, Gary Nixon (Mel's partner), Erinn, Lyla and Mel; seated: Katie, Bob (son-in-law), Faythe White, Carl White.

Gary Nixon and Mel in New York, two Californians caught in an East Coast blizzard.

Unless otherwise noted, all photos are from the author's collection

the bar, ordered a diet Coke, and stood blinking into the smoky semidarkness.

There was no going back now. For too many decades I had been nearly paralyzed by my need for male intimacy and by my fears of where that need might lead. I had resisted my own deep, personal longings for far too long. It was time I took my first steps toward understanding and accepting myself. But I was still torn by questions and fears. What would happen to Lyla? Would she and the children survive? Would our lives be ruined? I had spent those last years thinking more and more about death. It was time to choose life, to admit my desperate needs, to begin the search for a way to meet them, and to trust God's grace for all the rest.

Unfortunately, I didn't even know where or how to begin the process. On that fall evening in 1981, I didn't know about the Universal Fellowship of Metropolitan Community Churches where lesbians and gays gather to worship and to fellowship. I had never heard about gay/lesbian Christian groups such as Dignity, Integrity, or Affirmation, unofficially affiliated with Catholic or Protestant churches. There were gay and lesbian community centers then, too, but I didn't know about them. There were gay/lesbian bookstores, gyms, special interest groups, dating services, phone lines, bulletin boards, camps, conventions, hotels, retreat centers and resorts, books, magazines, even emergency twenty-four-hour hot lines, but I had missed them all. Bars and bathhouses were the only places I knew where gay men gathered, and so I fought back all the terrors that I had inherited from my youth and entered that little, neighborhood bar in Chicago, praying that God would lead me to someone who would understand.

The room was filled with young, middle-aged, and older gay men gathered into small groups talking, laughing, sipping their drinks, and eyeing each other playfully. In the back of the bar, other men gathered in twos and threes around the pool table and a row of noisy, brightly lit pinball and poker machines. Standing directly to my right, a rather obnoxious carpet salesman had cornered a young lawyer, who was listening politely to his endless spiel. When the carpet salesman looked away for one split second, I smiled at the lawyer sympathetically and his eyes cried out, "Rescue me from this guy and I'll follow you anywhere."

"My name is Mel," I said suddenly, shaking the carpet salesman's hand first and then reaching out to greet the startled young lawyer. "And I hate to interrupt your conversation, but it's important." With that mysterious greeting, I simply guided the young man toward the door and out into the late-afternoon sunlight. "Let's go somewhere else," I said quietly. "There's no way to get acquainted in such a place. I'm Mel White and I want to know everything about you."

"I'm Tom Montgomery," he said, shaking my hand and looking both amused and astonished. He looked into my eyes, grinning. "And if I know my luck, you're married, have children, and have never done this kind of thing before."

Thomas was twenty-eight, a recent law-school graduate with a specialization in tax law. He was tall and thin with hazel eyes, curly brown hair, and a grin that implied he knew far more than he was saying. During the next few hours, I told Tom everything. He listened with an occasional comment or question. When I confessed how much I loved Lyla and the children and how afraid I was of hurting them, Tom put his arm through my arm and walked close beside me along the shore of Lake Michigan. While we walked and talked together that first evening, the sun set and the lights began to glow in the high-rise condominiums that loomed above us. Tom was bright, articulate, honest, and fascinated by my story. I was twelve years older, fearful, confused, and rapidly falling head over heels in love, or in lust, with this handsome, intelligent man.

Thomas had tickets for an open-air concert by the Chicago symphony that night. I had a recording session scheduled. When I couldn't accept his invitation to join him in the park, Tom asked where I was staying, and just before putting me into a cab, asked if he could call. I went to the recording session fully believing that I would never see Tom again. At three-thirty the next afternoon he phoned, and during our brief conversation, agreed to meet me at the Lincolnshire Marriott twenty-five or so miles out of Chicago where I was staying that night. We had dinner, watched *South Pacific* performed live in the hotel's theater, and en route to Tom's car, stopped for coffee, more conversation, and a late-night dessert in the hotel coffee shop.

"It's a long way home," Thomas said finally as we stood to leave well after midnight.

"You could stay here with me," I replied. "I have a large room with two beds."

What happened next was dreamlike and unreal. The minute

Thomas entered my room, he put up the *Do Not Disturb* sign, closed and locked the door, tossed off his clothes, and jumped into bed. I hung up my suit and shirt slowly, moved to the other bed, and was pulling back the covers when Tom said, "Get over here." Frightened and yet exhilarated, I dropped the covers and climbed into bed beside this handsome, young stranger.

I had dreamed of this night for decades, but when it actually happened, I felt awkward, embarrassed, and guilty. We lay on our sides, face-to-face, embracing. Sensing my ambivalence, Tom just held me gently. As I felt him slowly pressing closer, my body responded eagerly, naturally, automatically, but my brain went into fearful overload. Suddenly, I felt chilled. I began to tremble. Even while I was thanking God for this good fortune, I was begging God to forgive me.

This was by anyone's standards an act of adultery. I was married. I loved my wife. I had promised to be faithful to her as long as we both should live. And in spite of my sexual orientation, until that night I had managed to keep my commitment with desperate, little compromises along the way. Then, suddenly, unexpectedly in my suite at the Marriott, as I was about to make love to a man, really make love, I realized that I was breaking my promises to Lyla and betraying her trust.

But even as I lay there debating, I knew as well that no matter how hard I tried, my natural, God-given sensual needs could not be ignored, postponed, and denied forever. As Thomas held me, I begged God to forgive me and to grant me this one moment of ecstasy. Gradually, the trembling stopped. As I lay there feeling Tom's arms around me, I began to imagine his arms as the arms of God.

I wasn't crazy. Even in my chaotic mental state, I knew that it was Thomas holding me, but lying in Tom's arms, praying my desperate, foxhole prayers, I felt again my Creator's loving, guiding, protecting presence. Thomas was God's gift that night, and as I relaxed and thanked God for the gift, I began to experience a quality of relief that I had never known before. I was a lost child who had suddenly been rescued by a loving adult, a fugitive who could stop running at last, a weary traveler who had finally found his way home.

As I lay in Tom's embrace, waves of gratitude and relief swept over me. The nightmare was ending. I had been diving in a dark, cold sea when suddenly this surge of joy like a sudden, warm deep-water current took hold of me. I could be myself at last. I felt at home in my body for the first time. My brain calmed. My body grew electric. Every place we touched, little brush fires of excitement and energy began to burn. Before long, it was a raging fire and I let it consume me gladly.

No longer did I feel awkward or embarrassed. I felt alive and free. When, finally, we made love, what I didn't have in experience, I made up in passion. The sun was rising before it ended. Tom finally went to sleep, and I lay on one elbow staring down at him, senses tingling with delight, amazed at the perfect, pure pleasure that had been released in my cramped little soul, awed by this stranger's power to enchant and inflame me even as he slept.

"Are you feeling guilty?" Thomas asked me as we lay beside each other later that morning.

"Yes," I replied, happy to be in his loving arms and at the same time frightened that this moment of ecstasy would cost me everything.

There is no way to reconstruct the difficult conversations that Thomas and I had that next night or during the tempestuous year that followed. Nor can I do justice to the painful, loving, endless dialogue between Lyla and me during the next years of struggle. Everybody suffered, especially my wife. It's no wonder that people in similar circumstances get quick, angry divorces or just run away from the ones they love.

Many times I thought it would be easier if I had died or just disappeared. Instead, we talked and cried, made terrible accusations and returned to beg forgiveness, threatened and retreated from our threats, felt massive doses of anger and of love until our brains and bodies ached from stress and our hearts neared breaking.

As with a bad case of poison ivy, everybody had a home remedy. "You are unhealthily intermeshed," a psychologist cautioned us. "Quit hanging on," another advised. "Get on with your separate lives," friends and counselors cajoled regularly. "You're talking this thing to death," a close friend admonished. Of course, the most common label people pinned on us was "codependent." The term was just coming into popular fashion, and Lyla and I were crowned by friends and strangers alike "the king and queen of codependence." Whatever co-dependence means, we were certain of one thing: we loved each other and we loved our family. And we were determined to find a way through this nightmare if it could be found.

On a recent television program when Lyla was asked how she managed "to stick it out," she answered simply, "We never stopped trusting each other." Lyla knew me (and probably goes on knowing me) better than anybody else in the world. In the very worst of times, she never quit believing that I was doing the best I could, and she never asked more from me than that. And I was doing the very best I could.

But I had learned that my best didn't mean that I could make everyone happy. You can genuinely love and respect a person. You can enjoy that person's company and celebrate that person's friendship. You can share that person's values and determine to be loyal and committed to him or her for a lifetime. But when there is no sexual attraction, no erotic fascination, no potential for authentic physical passion, no sensual pull, no amorous play, no romantic component at the heart of it, there can be no intimacy, at least not the kind of intimacy required to begin and to maintain a long-term, loving relationship, let alone a marriage.

"If you couldn't change your sexual orientation," people still ask me, "why didn't you decide on celibacy?" I studied celibacy and the history of practicing Roman Catholic celibates for more than a dozen years hoping that I could chose that option. I even tried to enroll in a monastery for a long-term program with a spiritual director to help me overcome my homosexuality. The wise priest just shook his head sadly and said quietly, "You won't find it here."

Admittedly, there are devout celibates who have "the gift of celibacy." Others have succeeded in mastering the loneliness and "taming their sensual passions," at least for a while; but as the studies show, most who try celibacy will eventually fail at it. In fact, a lifetime of celibacy is not possible for most people. Why don't we admit it and allow Roman Catholic priests to marry? Why can't we see that encouraging gays and lesbians to enter into long-term, loving relationships is the answer to loneliness and promiscuity exactly as it is for our heterosexual friends and neighbors?

Shortly after meeting and falling in love with Thomas Montgomery, I told my parents that I was gay. The honest confrontation was long overdue. And though they were in their late sixties, they were both still healthy and alert. They had spent the last year in South Africa as volunteer missionaries. I picked them up at the Los Angeles International Airport and brought them to our home in the foothills above Pasadena.

After Sunday dinner, I asked Mom and Dad to join me at the pool.

Until that day they had no idea that I had struggled all my life to change my sexual orientation. They listened in silence as I tried unsuccessfully to explain. They were shocked and horrified by the news. My dad asked if I was "a top or a bottom." At the time, I didn't even know what he meant. My mother's eyes filled with tears and her hands trembled when she finally managed to whisper, "I never thought I'd lose another son." Mom still remembers those terrible moments after hearing the news, wishing she could drown herself at the bottom of the pool. My dad reached out to comfort her. But to this date, there has been no way to bring genuine comfort to either of them. My father is afraid that I've been misled by a demon. My mother still feels as though she's lost her firstborn son. I am sorry they don't understand. One day, I hope they will!

In the meantime, my parents, too, are victims of the ancient misinformation about homosexuality currently so popular with the religious right. When televangelists and religious talk-show hosts talk about the origins of homosexuality, they still fall back on that tired, old, long-since-discredited idea that a weak or absent father or a strong, dominating mother is the cause. Behind that misleading stereotype is the notion that gay and lesbian people chose their sexual identity. One false notion leads to another. In fact, as Jesus exclaimed, the truth would set them free. Once my parents understand that sexuality is a gift from God, then they can be free to accept me and to accept themselves again.

Recently, my mother told a television journalist that she couldn't comprehend why sex would still be so important to me at fifty years of age. But as I watched her interview on television, I saw her lean against my father for strength and for comfort. He patted her gently when her eyes filled with tears. She lay back against his arm. Their relationship was never perfect, but they found something in each other's presence that was far more important and life-giving than having sex.

It was clear that she had no comprehension of the reality that homosexual love, exactly like the love she felt for my father, isn't just about sexual organs, that it is also about the spiritual strength and the support one person draws mysteriously from another. I can't explain why the comfort I find in a gay man's arms is greater than I could find in those of a heterosexual woman. It's not an act of sex. It's an act of love. It's not about sexual gratification. It's about spiritual survival.

Yet I know I could find either of these only in a relationship with someone who shared my sexual orientation.

In acknowledging my homosexuality and in finally taking those painful steps toward fulfillment, I was not risking everything just for the right to have sex with a man. My mother was right. After fifty, although the sex act is still important and life-giving to heterosexuals and homosexuals alike, it is not nearly so frequent or so urgent or so impassioned as it used to be. What is important is the comfort you get from just sitting or lying there beside the person you find most compatible.

After years of shared disappointment and grief, Anne Morrow Lindbergh described her lifelong marriage partnership with these words: "Both of us are groping and a little lost, but we are together." I was just asking for the same right my parents or the Lindberghs had enjoyed during their more than half a century of complex and difficult relationships, the right to hold hands, the right to caress or embrace or lie beside the person whose very presence mysteriously gives me comfort and makes me feel at home.

I had feelings for Thomas that I had never known before. He lived in Chicago in a little bachelor condo at 2626 Lakeview overlooking Lake Michigan. I lived with my family in Pasadena. We were more than two thousand miles apart. I couldn't stop thinking about him. And each thought left me more consumed with loneliness and melancholy.

On Saturday evenings, when I pictured Thomas out with his friends, I couldn't eat or sleep. I figured the two-hour time difference and tried to picture the exact moment he would arrive safely home. Usually he answered with patient, good humor. "Hi, Mel. Yes, I'm home. You can quit worrying now." There were nights when I dialed his number every fifteen minutes for hours at a time, certain that I had lost him, sure that he was lying in someone else's arms. My stress levels rose simultaneously with our phone bills.

"You are a crazy man," he would say. "I love you. I don't need anyone else. I spent Saturday night with my parents in Springfield." Or, "I spent the weekend with my brother and sister-in-law and their kids in Minneapolis." Or, "I took the phone off the hook to get some rest." I knew that he was trustworthy, but I lived in constant, unnecessary terror of losing him.

At every possible opportunity, I flew to Chicago just to be near

Thomas. Even now, ten years later, when I see the skyline of Chicago from the window of a jet or when I approach an Avis car-rental counter at O'Hare or when I drive up the Kennedy Expressway toward Tom's old condo in the high-rise balanced precariously on the shore of Lake Michigan, I can still remember the excitement, the terror, and the raging, unreasonable passion.

Thomas, on the other hand, had been open about his homosexuality since childhood. He had passed through his infatuations as a young man and was amused by, but sympathetic to, my runaway feelings. He tried to help me see beyond my temporary sexual obsession to the wider reality of life as a gay man. "You aren't in love with me," he told me often. "You're in love with love." I didn't understand then. I do understand now. Thomas was absolutely right.

I was experiencing a classic case of infatuation. It is dangerous to postpone as I had postponed the dating and courtship that leads to healthy, loving, mature relationships. Infatuation is natural and right for children and adolescents. Teenagers can fall in and out of love on their way to maturity without being crippled by the process. When they are young, broken hearts mend quickly. But infatuation at forty is a dangerous, even deadly journey.

When I finally allowed myself "to fall in love" with Thomas, all that pent-up passion like a flood broke down the dam that I had carefully constructed to contain it and roared through my life threatening everything in its path. I still loved my wife and children, and I struggled to hold on to them, but at the same time I was swimming against a raging current that threatened to drown us all.

All my life, I had tried my best to please everyone else. Suddenly, I was allowing my heart to lead me, and though it was a wild, painful ride at first for everybody, it was a ride I had to take to discover who I really was. Thank God for Lyla, who didn't shoot or poison me in the midst of all that runaway passion. And thank God for Thomas, who patiently opened for me the window on a whole new world. I was terrified that "giving in" to my passions would lead us all to darkness and despair. In fact, the gay and lesbian community turned out to be so much more than smoke-filled bars and dark, lonely bathhouses. Through Thomas and his friends I learned that life as a gay man had promise and potential that I had never dreamed of.

Tom's network of gay and lesbian acquaintances stretched across Chicago and around the nation. His friends—both in and out of the closet—inspired and amazed me. They were responsible, creative, productive citizens: doctors, lawyers, and tax accountants, ministers and teachers, blue-collar workers, models, even a famous athlete. Many had long-term, loving relationships. Through Tom, I met gay and lesbian couples who had been together ten, twenty, thirty, even forty years and more. They had adopted children and raised families. They had served responsibly as room parents and Scout leaders. And they could decorate an apartment or cater a brunch or (as his lesbian friends liked to mock themselves) change a tire as fast, as well, and as cheaply as any heterosexual.

Thomas himself had helped organize the first gay chapter of Toastmaster's International in Chicago. He was a faithful member of a gay hiking club that spent weekends backpacking in the wilderness or picking up trash along idyllic country streams. Thomas had been certified as a scuba diver in a dark, water-filled rock quarry near Chicago and dreamed of diving in Hawaii. He loved to ski, to listen to jazz piano, to call his friends together for a spontaneous brunch, to write long, impassioned letters to his elected officials, to run in benefit 10-K races, and to shop.

Although he was angry at the religious right for their growing invective against gay and lesbian people, Tom was also deeply spiritual, a Presbyterian layman who sang in the choir, taught a Sunday school class, and read hungrily from the writings of ancient Christian mystics and contemplatives. It was Thomas who invited me to attend my first gay and lesbian Christian church, the UFMCC (Universal Fellowship of Metropolitan Community Churches) congregation meeting at the Methodist Church on Wellington Avenue in Chicago.

On a cold Sunday morning in December, I remember walking into that predominantly gay and lesbian congregation in shock and disbelief. I had never been in the company of so many gay and lesbian Christians before, and to have them hug me at the door and welcome me to their service, to hear them sing, to see them pray, was a wonderful surprise. After living through all those years of guilt and self-condemnation, to think that you could be gay and Christian left me trembling with hope. Thomas and I sat alongside approximately two hundred other gay and lesbian Christians singing and praying together. The gay pastor and lesbian associate minister led us in a beautiful and thoughtful service of worship and of praise.

The service and the sermon moved me deeply, but when the Communion elements were uncovered and the prayer of dedication prayed, I was surprised to see individuals, couples, and small groups of friends, gay and nongay, going forward together to receive the bread and wine. The pastors and lay leaders who served Communion paused over each person or couple to pray. As Thomas and I stood to take our turn at the altar, the congregation began to sing: "Just as I am without one plea, O Lamb of God, I come to thee."

Thomas guided me, already blinded by my tears, to the altar and put his arm around me as we knelt. "Jesus died for you," the pastor said. "Take and eat in memory of Him." Even as he offered us the bread and wine, I thought of Lyla and the children at worship in Pasadena and of how much I loved and missed them. I thought of Thomas, too, kneeling beside me, already trapped between my love for them and my crazy infatuation for him.

My hands were shaking and my heart was beating furiously as the congregation sang, "Just as I am though tossed about with many a conflict, many a doubt, O Lamb of God, I come." When we had received Christ's strength for our journey, the pastor put his arms around both of us and began to pray. "Jesus," he said quietly, "let your perfect love conquer fear in these two hearts now and always. Amen."

Those frenetic, half-crazed months with Thomas were the best of times and the worst of times for me and a period of terrible suffering and conflict for Lyla. I had told her immediately about my crush on Thomas. She thought it a case of "retarded adolescence" but tried gamely to understand. In one of her long, loving letters of support and confrontation, Lyla described those days as the Log Ride at Knott's Berry Farm: "My heart and stomach seem always too close to my throat." In spite of everything, somehow we both managed to stay productive and together.

About that time, Word Books hired me to write the biography of Mike Douglas, the television celebrity, producer, and talk-show host. Lyla and I flew to London to interview Mike and Genevieve Douglas in their immense Trafalgar Suite as we sailed back across the Atlantic on the *Queen Elizabeth II*. Mike was taping five different TV shows on board that spectacular 55,000-ton ocean liner, one each day, with his regular cast and orchestra and special guests Ben Vereen, the singer/dancer/actor who had just received acclaim for his starring role in Bob

Fosse's film *All That Jazz,* and the 1981 Golden Globe Award–winning singer/actress Pia Zadora.

The Cunard Lines gave Lyla and me a first-class stateroom with a large window on the sea and an attentive, twenty-four-hour steward. We ate our meals in the posh Queen's Grill with a tuxedo-clad maître d' and a picture window overlooking the North Atlantic. Somehow Lyla had learned that diners in the Queen's Grill never needed to touch a menu. They simply ordered, and voilà, as if by magic, even the most esoteric entrée or dessert would appear.

That first night as we sailed down the English Channel past the white cliffs of Dover toward the open sea, I picked up the menu just to amaze myself with the endless array of fine food and wines (without any prices listed, of course). A elegant older woman nearby saw us pick up the menu. She leaned toward our table and spoke softly to Lyla: "Don't use the menu, dear. Order what you will." Lyla, always game for an adventure, whispered back, "Why don't you order for us."

The stranger smiled, nodded to us both, motioned for the steward to approach, pointed at our table, and said without pausing, "The newlyweds will have the following: beluga caviar and Nova Scotia salmon, Caesar salad, chateaubriand for two, steamed asparagus, and *pommes frites.*" She paused, placed her index finger to her lips thoughtfully, and then continued, "And for dessert, bring them fresh blueberries in double cream, with white cake soaked in cognac."

Lyla never looked at the menu again. Before that first evening ended, we rubbed shoulders with the powerful and the privileged, danced to a full orchestra in the Double Down Room, chatted with Ben Vereen over a roulette table in the Queen's Casino, and snacked for the umpteenth time that night from another spectacular buffet, complete with ice carvings and graceful French pastries, that we discovered on the open deck. We concluded that eventful night in our posh suite giggling through another bottle of free champagne from the Cunard Lines, thinking that at any second James Bond would come crashing into our stateroom and wishing the night would last forever.

Six days later, after going out of our way to avoid a winter storm that buffeted the ship with wind and waves, we limped into New York Harbor on Friday night already a full day overdue, too late to clear customs until morning. I had promised to see Lyla safely to her plane for Los Angeles before I flew directly to Chicago to finish work on a client's film and (without telling Lyla) to see Thomas again.

When I couldn't get off the ship, I panicked. Even the phones weren't connected. I had no way to explain to Thomas why I would not arrive that night for a party he had planned for us. When I discovered that Pia Zadora's wealthy husband had arranged for a helicopter to fly them to their private jet at Kennedy Airport where they could pass through customs, I wrote Thomas a note, rushed to the helipad, and asked Pia to call him for me.

Then I rushed back to Lyla, who had guessed the cause of my sudden panic and was struggling with grief and anger. When we finally escaped the ship, I took Lyla to Manhattan and checked her into a hotel room where she could wait more comfortably until her early-evening flight to California. She begged me not to leave her there alone, but I was determined to go. I was absolutely obsessed with meeting Thomas. She cried. I cried. Finally, I just bolted from the room, flagged down a cab to the airport, flew to Chicago, rushed to 2626 Lakeview Drive, and tried to explain to Thomas what had happened. He was still confused by a woman who had called him pretending to be Pia Zadora. "That was Pia Zadora," I explained. I'm not sure he ever believed me. "Just another day with Mel," he said, taking me into his arms and holding me at last.

When Thomas finally fell asleep, I sneaked to a pay phone and called Lyla's New York hotel, hoping she would be safely on her way to the airport. "She has checked out," the desk informed me. Immediately, I paged her at LaGuardia. I was so relieved when she came to the phone. I could hear the terrible distress in her voice. I promised that I would fly immediately to Los Angeles and meet her at the airport if she would just get on the next plane. I wrote a quick good-bye with a bar of soap on Tom's bathroom mirror, rushed back to O'Hare, and flew to LAX just in time to meet Lyla's plane.

With both of us exhausted and half crazy from stress, we found our car parked in Lot C and drove home arguing all the way. On that drive, I tried to explain why I needed to be with Tom, but how could she understand the craziness of my infatuation? Even I could not begin to understand it. She begged me to stay. Weeping, I left her again, drove back to the airport, flew to Chicago, and tried to justify another disappearance to a dazed and baffled Thomas.

Some unknown ancient Latin poet combined the word *fatuous* or foolish with the little prefix *in* to describe *infatuation*, that state of unreasoning passion we mistakenly call love that all too frequently consumes us and leaves us looking foolish and so absorbed with the object of our passion that we become blind to almost everyone and everything else. For me, infatuation was a kind of mental illness, a state of chaos and passion that I had to pass through to find myself. The love I felt for Thomas was a crazy kind of love, but I couldn't see or understand it then, and like David's love for Bathsheba, I was willing to sacrifice everything to possess it.

Finally, after a year of endless painful struggle, I decided to move to Chicago to be with Thomas permanently. I sent books and clothing on ahead and flew to Seattle where I was scheduled to lead the faculty and student body of Seattle Pacific University in a week of spiritual emphasis and renewal. By then I was an emotional basket case, but somehow, I was still producing films, writing books, and traveling across the country lecturing at Christian colleges and seminaries.

I prayed every day and every night that in spite of everything, my loving Creator would be present in my life and honored through it. And God answered those prayers. In the darkest night of my soul, God never failed me. When I was consumed by guilt and driven by infatuation, God was there, understanding me, loving me, forgiving me.

After five standing-room-only lectures to the student body of Seattle Pacific University, the teaching staff asked me to spend an hour that last afternoon talking to them about the art of communicating with young students. They didn't know that in just a few hours I would be leaving my wife and family and flying to Chicago to begin a new life as a gay man. Suddenly, the university president's secretary interrupted my lecture to announce that Dr. Billy Graham wanted to speak to me on the telephone. "It is urgent," she said, and the whole faculty looked surprised and impressed.

"Who is this really?" I asked when I heard that famous voice or a very good imitation of it on the telephone. My friends knew that Billy was my childhood hero. I expected one of them to be imitating that slightly accented, Southern drawl to get me to the phone. It was Dr. Graham. I had met him only once before when he was on the board at Fuller Seminary and had without warning dropped by my office to ask me to critique his preaching. I laughed aloud at the ridiculous prospect. Graham had preached effectively to more people than all the prophets, priests, and saints in history combined. He had outlived all the heroes of our century and remained the one man in the world who was recognized on every corner of the globe.

"My publisher says you can help me, Mel," Dr. Graham began. "Can you join me in Acapulco, Mexico, tonight and work with me on completing an important book?"

The serendipity of that call took my breath away. I was certain that God was using Dr. Graham to change my plans about flying to Chicago, moving in with Thomas, and leaving my family. I staggered from the telephone, finished the lecture, left a long, sad message on Tom's answering service, called Lyla, told her that after a time in Mexico I would be coming home, and got on a plane for Mexico.

By the time the eight- or nine-hour flight had ended, I was popping Valium pills like candy and sobbing bitterly. I couldn't leave my family and I couldn't live without Tom. Billy Graham met me in a little jeep. On the way into Acapulco, he explained that he had called an emergency meeting of his executive committee for the weekend, but that I would have an ocean-front room on the beach and piles of unfinished manuscript to tackle in the meantime. He dropped me off at the Holiday Inn. After calling the airlines, I discovered I could make it to Chicago and back before Billy knew that I was gone. After a quick cab ride back to the airport, I flew twelve hours to Chicago and hurried through the darkened streets to 2626 Lakeview Drive.

Thomas had invited all our friends to his home for a party to announce my move and to celebrate our relationship. The message that I had left on his phone service canceling everything had been the last blow. I had disappointed him one time too many. What was left of the party was in progress when I arrived. Thomas wouldn't even let me in. We were both weeping and shouting through the locked door. It could have been a bad scene in a B-grade soap opera. Finally, I returned to O'Hare by taxi and flew back to Acapulco without seeing Thomas or having the opportunity to explain. I arrived in the middle of the night, just in time to shower, shave, and meet Billy Graham for breakfast.

During a walk on the beach with Billy and his wife, Ruth, she suggested that I go parasailing. A young Mexican strapped me into a harness while Ruth rushed into the little borrowed beach-front condo to get her camera. While Ruth Graham was shooting pictures of my rapid ascent into the air, I was suspended three or four hundred yards above Acapulco wondering how I could unfasten the harness and escape it all.

During my next weeks in Pasadena, my frenzied depression reached new lows. I thought about death constantly. Determined to find real help, Lyla called five of our friends together, each a psychologist in Fuller's School of Psychology. We tape-recorded that long evening in a noisy booth at Bob's Big Boy restaurant. During the evening Phyliss Hart suggested that I fly to Tacoma and spend three weeks at Gig Harbor in Washington's Puget Sound with Dr. John Finch, a Christian psychologist and a board member of Fuller Theological Seminary.

Dr. Finch conducted stress-management seminars for some of the nation's top executives. I would live alone in a cottage on Fox Island, a small island in the Sound. There would be no radio, television, or cassette player to distract me, no books, magazines, or newspapers to read, not even a Bible. Without a telephone or a post office, I would be cut off from the outside world. It was Dr. Finch's notion that dealing with stress "head-on" was the best way to conquer it. I would keep a diary recording every thought or feeling during these three weeks of horror. He would meet me one hour every day to listen to my thoughts and respond with advice.

One of my most loyal and loving friends throughout that entire decade's long ordeal had been the Reverend Dr. Marguerite Shuster, now a professor at Fuller Seminary. When I was most desperate, I had called her, often in the middle of the night, from pay phones around the world, seeking her wise counsel. She refused to let me see her as a counselor. "I am your friend," Marguerite said simply. "Call me anytime you need me." And though her skills as a pastor and coun-selor saw me through so much of my ordeal, it is her friendship that I will cherish forever. When Marguerite heard that I was going to Gig Harbor to spend three weeks with Dr. Finch, she said simply, "Don't do it!" I wish I had listened.

It was the worst twenty-one days of my life. Dr. Finch began by suggesting that homosexuality was not "a feature of my original on-tology" but an illness that we would "cure together." At the first session, with only a few pages from my application to consider, he decided that something was wrong with my relationship with my father. "Go back to the island," he ordered. "Pretend your father is with you. Talk to him. Tell him everything you feel."

I did everything the doctor ordered including ranting and raving at my father. Needless to say, the therapy was only making matters worse. After ten days of isolation and terror, I was falling apart. Some-how, Lyla felt it, broke the rules, and telephoned through to me. We talked several times on the cottage phone. When suddenly Finch called Lyla and told her angrily not to intervene, we knew he had the telephone bugged. At the end of the second week of rain and cold and almost total isolation, except for an hour a day with a man determined to rid me of my homosexuality, I was close to an emotional breakdown.

After walking for miles, I found a pay phone on the island and called Lyla again. She urged me to hitchhike to the airport, but I was so desperate to get help, to overcome my homosexuality, that I stayed. I still can't read the thousand-page diary that I wrote during that hellish nightmare on "Devil's Island" without feeling again the painful, almost fatal waves of loneliness and despair. My friend Phil Yancey says the diary reads like Augustine. To me, it reads like Stephen King.

Late one desperate night, I decided that I would jump off the bridge that connected Fox Island to Gig Harbor. I wrote suicide notes to my wife, to my children, and to Thomas. It was raining and cold. I had walked and cried and written most of the day. As I climbed over the railing of the bridge, I heard a voice say, "It's a mean night for fishing, but come on down and we'll talk." When my eyes finally focused against the darkness and the rain, I saw an old fisherman sitting under a bridge abutment waiting patiently for his first bite. "Don't know why I chose tonight to fish," he said, shaking his head and trying to light his pipe.

In my heart, I knew why. I don't understand why some people die and others live. I can't make sense of evil in the universe and why some suffer endlessly while others live in luxury and ease. But don't ever try to convince me that our Creator doesn't care, for that night I knew that God was there sitting on the bridge beside me holding a fishing rod in one hand and an unlit pipe in the other.

Chapter *10*

1982–83,

"It's Going to Be

All Right, Dad!"

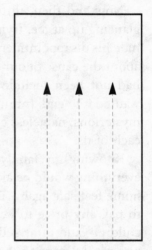

*A*fter three excruciating weeks isolated on Fox Island with a Christian psychologist determined to "cure" me, after those twenty-one endless days and nights of desperate introspection and fearful, frantic prayer, after writing a thousand-page diary during that short time recording each mountaintop certainty and each low valley of despair, after sending from the Gig Harbor post office one final letter to Thomas ending all possibilities of renewing our relationship, I returned home determined one more time that if Augustine could sacrifice his sensual passions for the sake of God, so could I.

Upon my arrival in southern California, my whole family greeted me at the airport. I embraced them eagerly, certain that never again would I risk the wonderful life we had together. As we walked to the parking lot, Lyla looked exhausted and afraid, but I could see at least a spark of hope in her tired eyes. At thirteen, Erinn was already becoming a beautiful, gregarious young woman. On the drive to Pasadena, to help us push back the uncomfortable silence, she chatted easily about her friends at school, about ballet lessons, and her girls soccer team; while Michael, our twelve-year-old writer and contemplative, sat in the backseat reading.

Now and then, through the rearview mirror, I could see my son glancing up at me, trying to show his love and support, but unable to hide his disappointment that we were not being more honest with him about the cause of our obvious discomfort. Michael was angry that he had not been included in the problem-solving process. Erinn just wanted it to end. Intuitively, both children had growing fears that this mysterious, nameless conflict might have long-term consequences for each of us.

Knowing my family's pain, I longed to assure each of them that everything would be all right. I wanted to end their fear and make our home feel safe again. This time, I would not look back. I was willing to pay any price to keep my commitments to God, to my wife and children, and to myself. In spite of all the evidence to the contrary, I was set on proving that sexual orientation can be changed or sublimated or held in check. With God's help, I would keep my Fox Island resolve to be an "ex-gay" permanently. With the exuberance of a drug addict who had conquered his addiction cold turkey and was determined never to get high again, I announced to my wife and closest friends that I was home forever.

Early each morning, I climbed to the green water tank high on the steep hills above our home in Pasadena to watch the sunrise over the Los Angeles basin and to pray for God's strength and guidance. I read and reread my Fox Island diary for renewal and support. I bought more books on "overcoming homosexuality" by Christian pastors and psychologists. Using a false name, I attended "ex-gay" meetings in Orange County and contributed money that helped lead to the founding of Exodus, a national organization dedicated to helping homosexuals "escape their sinful lifestyle."

Determined to maintain normalcy in our family life, I often fixed breakfast and ate with the children, drove them to and from their schools, served with Lyla as class parents, chaperoned field trips, and attended every possible school-parent function. We went to films and plays, concerts, and community celebrations together. Our friends the Beckers, the Wrights, the Hattems, my sister-in-law Sharon, her husband, Grant, and their children often joined us for weekend swims and barbecues in our backyard. Every Saturday, I took Erinn to her horseback-riding lessons and cheered as she entered and won ribbons in various equestrian events. I played the piano for my son's first neighborhood musical review, featuring Stephen Sondheim tunes, and bought him an 8mm camera for his first homemade film production. I even encouraged him to join a soccer team and went to every practice until one day in exasperation, Michael asked, "When are you going to have enough of this father-son soccer stuff, Dad?" We never kicked that ball around again.

On Sunday mornings, Lyla, Erinn, and Michael sat beside me in our usual third-row, left-side pew in the magnificent rock, wood, and stained-glass gothic sanctuary of the All Saints Episcopal Church in Pasadena. When the pipe organ prelude played or the trumpet fanfares sounded and the voices of our magnificent Coventry choir echoed an anthem of praise, I tried to hold back or hide my tears. The courageous and timely sermons of George Regas, our rector, never failed to move me and give me hope. Somehow, every Sunday, he managed to bring biblical truth down from the clouds into the real world where God loves us without condition but at the same time calls us "to do justice" for those who suffer. After the sermon, when our family knelt together at the Communion rail, Dr. Regas offered the bread and wine with these words, "Christ's body and blood, strength for your journey."

During that long year after Fox Island, though heterosexuality was getting my best effort, in rare moments of clarity I knew that I was still a homosexual to the core. Nothing had changed, not really. I was no more "ex-gay" than I could be "ex-human." Lyla and I loved each other, but I loved her with the love of a sister or a best friend. She was beautiful, sensual, and willing to do almost anything to make our marriage work, even in bed, but I couldn't even get an erection without thinking about making love to a man. And though we made love regularly, once again I was discovering that being gay is about so much more than having sex.

When Lyla and I attended parties or receptions, when we mixed and chatted with heterosexual couples, I began to feel like an alien who had been abandoned on a strange planet. I knew all the right words, but I had lost all interest in saying or hearing them. Living rooms and dining rooms, restaurants and lobbies, became foreign, unfriendly places. All my life I had performed on cue, making people feel comfortable, being the perfect host and sensitive conversationalist. Weary of pretending to be someone I was not, tired of hiding my feelings, angry that most of these same people would turn against me "once they knew," sick of queer jokes and homophobic insults, I longed to be with my own kind, with gays and lesbians who could understand my real world and speak to the real issues that involved or interested me.

In all that pretense, my once lively spirit was shriveling like a raisin in the sun. Every day, I was tormented more and more by what might have been. With Thomas, I had known a world that was real. I had been with people like me where I didn't have to wear a mask, where I didn't have to fake it, where my native tongue was spoken. After Fox Island, I had gone back into a dark, lonely closet and I knew that if I stayed there, I would die.

In the evenings when I was exhausted from another day of trying too hard to be what I could never be, I thought of Thomas and longed for the real comfort that came from being with a man. I began to feel distracted by every gay person I passed who happened to meet my own mysterious sensual grid. It was more than sexual attraction. The intensity of that sudden, unavoidable longing left me feeling terrified and guilty. How long could I withstand it? What terrible consequences would follow if I gave in to it again?

It was becoming all too clear. In spite of my love for Lyla and the children, I had real needs they couldn't meet. And though I tried continually to minimize those needs, to discipline and deny those desires, to ignore those longings at the center of my soul, with every new day I was growing more miserable.

When the desperation and the loneliness surged, I escaped on long walks in the foothills, accompanied only by Sheltie, my Shetland sheepdog. On those walks, when I imagined how the rest of my life would be, cut off from my own kind, not free even to pursue happiness let alone to meet my real needs, I felt trapped and terrified. When I sat down on the trail to cry, Sheltie would immediately run back to me, put his head in my lap, and let me stroke him until I recovered.

When I realized that, even with all my resolve, the old conflict had returned with new intensity, I felt embarrassed and ashamed. I found it impossible to explain to Lyla why being true to my homosexual self was the only possible way I could survive. I knew that within days, weeks, or months my resistance would crumble, but I couldn't bear to see again that look of disappointment and grief in her eyes. Knowing that my infatuation with Thomas had cost her far too much, I decided on a more pragmatic course.

I had tried being honest, but honesty had caused everyone too much suffering. This time, I would not be honest. I would protect my marriage. I would save my family. I would guarantee my vocation as a Christian writer, filmmaker, and public speaker. For everybody's sake, I would go on living in the closet forever, but to make it possible, I would find a secret lover who would help meet my needs as well.

The Boulevard was a friendly, neighborhood gay bar on Foothill Boulevard just two miles down Madre Street from our family home. Late one night, when the children were doing homework and Lyla was at a meeting of volunteers at All Saints Church, I drove to the Boulevard, parked on a side street, and sneaked inside, hoping no one had seen me enter. My resistance had crumbled, but even as I struggled with my sense of failure and guilt, I was praying that God would forgive and guide me once again. I knew there were more appropriate places for meeting gay men whom I might find compatible, but a bar seemed the only "safe" place to meet someone in secret and not be discovered.

There was one empty seat at the bar, and without looking right or left I sat down, ordered a diet Coke, and waited for my eyes to focus in the darkness. When I looked up, the young man on my right was smiling and holding out his hand in greeting. He had an ethnic look: curly black hair, dark eyes, perfect white teeth, and a smile that lit up the darkness and set my heart racing. He grinned and invited me to play the Joker Poker machine. As we took our drinks and moved to the end of the bar, I couldn't decide if his roots were Hispanic or Mediterranean. He was tall and built like an athlete. He carried himself with the casual sophistication of a Spanish don, but his easy, confident smile and open, friendly manner made me think of my friends in Mexico.

We stuck two quarters into the machine and one by one took our turns at Joker Poker. His name was David. His family owned a large film-processing plant in Hollywood, which he helped manage. He was a Mexican-American, born in this country with ancient family roots in

Spain. David loved to go to movies and the theater. He never missed Sunday mass at his local Roman Catholic parish, and he loved to dance.

Our shoulders touched as we stood side by side at the machine. When I played a full house and then doubled it, the screen lit up with my winning score. Spontaneously, David put his arm around me and laughed happily. You are a winner, he announced, and before the allotted time could elapse, he managed to put our names together— Mel & David—on the winner's list.

Just being with another gay man in that crowded gay bar, just seeing his smile and feeling his touch, lifted my spirits and gave me hope. But when I began to realize that I was becoming infatuated with another handsome stranger, panic swept the good feelings away. I was afraid to let it all happen again. With just a mumbled, halfhearted explanation, I said good-bye to David and left him standing alone at the machine. When I turned at the door, he was still standing there, looking in my direction. He smiled and waved. I rushed into the darkness.

Halfway home, I began to wonder if David might be a solution to our problem. I had run from our encounter at the bar because I wanted more than casual sex with a handsome stranger. That first stage of my coming out was over. During my half-crazed infatuation with Thomas I had seen gay men in long-term, loving, committed relationships. I wanted to be in such a relationship, but I wasn't willing or able to sacrifice my family in the process.

As I drove up my hill that night, a new kind of plan began to take shape in my brain. David was a responsible, caring, attractive adult male. He was living happily in the closet. What if he would consent to a closet relationship that would keep my family safely intact? Maybe it was possible to maintain my marriage vows in every way but one. I could be a responsible husband and father with a committed gay lover "on the side."

My family had arrived home. Before greeting them, I rushed into my office, phoned the Boulevard, and asked the bartender if David was still at the bar. He came to the phone, surprised but pleased by my sudden, unexpected phone call. We exchanged numbers. I promised to call him the next day. When Erinn came into my office, I hung up the phone, grabbed my daughter up in my arms, and danced her all the way to her bedroom.

David and I did enter into a secret relationship. He was amazingly sensitive and caring. As I grew more and more despairing, he was always there to listen. Every time my ambivalence threatened to overwhelm what little sense I had left, David took me to his church, knelt beside me at the altar, lit a candle, and prayed. Often, we sat in his van and just held hands in the darkness as I tried to think through what should happen next. We met once in a sleazy little motel that charged by the hour. The experience left us both feeling embarrassed and chagrined. We were grown men. We felt genuine love for each other. To be sneaking around, hiding out, terrified of discovery, was just too demeaning.

From the day I decided on this new closet strategy, I knew that I could not be dishonest with Lyla for very long. Trust was at the heart of our relationship, and risking that trust, even to protect her from pain or "to save our family," would threaten everything. Finally, I told Lyla about David. I assured her again that I was determined to keep all the marriage vows that I could keep. I asked her to consider entering into a kind of "time-share" relationship. That way, I could try to meet at least some of my needs for intimacy and at the same time keep our family intact.

She agreed to meet David and liked him immediately. He was closeted and innocent, a Roman Catholic from a macho ethnic culture with ancient hostility for homosexual people. He needed to stay in the closet to survive. Lyla could see that David was no threat to her relationship with me. They became coconspirators of sorts. Lyla brought champagne to our first meeting. David divided his time between his home in Pasadena and a little apartment we found in Sierra Madre. During our year together, David learned to love my family and encouraged me to keep it intact.

Unfortunately, during that year together, it became more and more apparent that I couldn't be true to the needs of my wife and family, let alone to my own real needs, through some kind of secret, closeted relationship. Why did it take me so long to learn that closet relationships are inadequate at best? Worse, they are often demeaning, dehumanizing, and destructive to everyone involved. Consider the comparison. Would a heterosexual man be able to spend his life living as the husband of a gay man, having occasional sex with a woman on the side? Marriage for heterosexuals is about so much more than sex. It is the same for us. Homosexuality, like heterosexuality, affects every dimension of our lives. For me, to think one can be satisfied with occasional sexual encounters, even with someone as loving and loyal as David, was a dangerous, misleading myth.

From the beginning, it was impossible to live in a closeted secret space between two worlds. It shouldn't be too difficult to understand why. As the months went by, our plan spiraled downward. I felt trapped between two people I loved deeply. Each tried his or her best to understand and respect the other's needs, but there was not enough time or money or energy to do it all. There were frantic telephone calls in the night, times of anger and disappointment, growing tension and stress. It had to stop. I had to be true to my God-given sexuality. To go on pretending was far too costly to us all. And though I loved and appreciated him deeply, this closet relationship with David had to end. But how could I tell Lyla? She had gone through this cycle of hope and despair too many times before. I just couldn't disappoint her again. And how could I tell David, whom I also loved and who loved me deeply in return?

Putting off the inevitable one last time, I plunged into work and worry in a kind of growing frenzy. Besides trying to be a loving husband, an attentive father, a responsible churchman, and a good lover on the side, I was also writing speeches for Billy Graham, producing television specials, scouting locations or directing film crews in Europe, Asia, and Africa, writing articles for various national periodicals, and consulting on film production and distribution.

Jay Jarman, one of my students at Fuller Seminary and a close, personal friend had established a network of house churches in Hawaii. He introduced me to Margaret Kaupuni, one of the last victims of Hansen's disease to leave the leprosarium at Kalaupapa. Fascinated by this beautiful old woman who had become an outcast at thirteen, I decided that in addition to everything else going on in my life, I would begin commuting to the Islands to write her amazing story, *Margaret of Molokai*. The more I researched and wrote about leprosy, the more I thought about AIDS and the similar ways that the Christian church and the new Reagan administration were treating gay people who had contracted that horrible virus.

When the book was released, I asked Margaret how she would like to celebrate. "Take friends Kahala Hilton," she said, half in jest. "Eat fancy food, dance hula, sing, praise God in big way!" Margaret laughed, knowing the irony of her suggestion, picturing twenty-five lepers at a buffet luncheon at one of Oahu's most exclusive resort hotels. I called Fleming Revell, our publisher, and they pledged $8,000 for the occasion. The Kahala Hilton also volunteered to help. Shocked and excited beyond belief, Margaret phoned her best friends, many still scarred by leprosy, from her tiny walk-up apartment in the Oahu Towers. I called the governor of Hawaii, the mayor of Honolulu, Margaret's special friend, Jay Jarman, and about fifty of Hawaii's leading citizens.

Just days later, in a spectacular dining room overlooking the sea around a long buffet table loaded down with tropical flowers and culinary wonders from the Pacific rim, I stood up before Margaret, her friends, and special guests and told the story of the thirteen-year-old girl showing early signs of leprosy who was taken by a bounty hunter from her first hula recital in city hall to a lifetime exile on the island of Molokai. During her half century there, she lost three husbands to leprosy. Her four children were taken from Margaret at birth and delivered to adoptive families on the mainland. On Molokai, leprosy mangled her feet, face, and hands. I spoke briefly of her suffering and her courage. "Margaret never thought she would dance again," I concluded, "but today she honors us and her loving Creator in a hula dance of praise."

The crowd applauded wildly as tiny Margaret hobbled to the center of the stage, barely able to see over the dozens of flowered leis that had been draped around her neck. "First, I sing song," she said quietly. "I no sing on key, but no matta." Even the waiters stopped to watch and listen in amazement as that scarred but still beautiful woman began to sing.

> My Lord, I made this song for You.
> To thank You for all what You done for me.
> I know I cannot repay You.
> So, God, thank You so much.

Still singing, Margaret lifted her arms and began to dance. Her movements were jerky and hesitant. She couldn't dance the graceful dance of childhood. She danced instead an old woman's dance of gratitude and grace.

> In times of pain and suffering,
> I turn to You for Your help.

You're always there to help me, Lord.
So, Lord, thank You so much.

As Margaret danced and sang, I looked around the room. Everyone, waiters and busboys included, even members of the press, was smiling and blinking back tears. After fifty years of suffering, Margaret was home. For most of her life, she had been a victim of misinformation, discrimination, and fear; but as she danced, we could feel her forgiving the ignorant, the insensitive, and the cruel who had driven her from home and family and left her to die on that isolated peninsula on a distant island. At the same time, Margaret's bent and gnarled hands were waving in praise to her loving God, who had somehow managed to see her through those awful years of loneliness and pain.

It was clear that Margaret knew so much about life that I had yet discovered. As a child, she, too, had carried a painful secret. Because ignorant people claimed that leprosy was God's punishment for something she had done, she, too, found herself an outcast, living in fearful isolation. But at Kalaupapa, Margaret had learned to accept herself, to celebrate her uniqueness, and to trust her Creator day by day for strength and guidance.

Still afraid that my homosexuality was some kind of punishment from God, I couldn't possibly accept myself. Instead of falling back into the loving arms of my Creator, instead of loving and trusting myself, I went on fighting and denying the very longings that would lead me home. In my frenzy to please God, to honor my commitments, to support my family, and to keep distracted from my needs and desires, Valium became my only real source of comfort. I sedated myself with growing quantities of those little, yellow pills. I used them to get on and off airplanes, to enter a film studio or recording session, to meet with a client or even to attend church.

The Valium left me in a kind of manageable daze. Worse depression followed. Lyla knew me like a book. I didn't have to tell her that I was spiraling downward. She knew every symptom. Once again, the difficult running dialogue began. We whispered frantically in our bedroom and shouted and cried our way through Pasadena's favorite coffee shops and restaurants. Waiters who knew us brought Kleenex to our table with the menus. One day, while Lyla drove us slowly beneath the Foothill freeway at our turn on Madre, I got so angry that I jumped from the car, slammed the door, and ran alongside it yelling.

Lyla yelled back, and our argument careened across Foothill Boulevard and up Madre with pedestrians staring and cars squealing to a stop.

One late afternoon, Lyla and I were in the middle of another heated debate. Suddenly, my emotions snapped. I opened the closet, pulled out a wire hanger, and unwound the twisted head. With the sharp, curled end of the wire, I began to slash my wrists. Lyla screamed and rushed to intervene. I couldn't stop slashing. Raw, bloody flesh collected on the end of the hanger. I was crying and slashing and wanting to die. Lyla got very calm. Slowly, she convinced me to put down the hanger. She got a towel and wrapped it around my wrists to stop the bleeding.

We loved each other or we would never have tried so hard. It wasn't just pathology that kept us in a relationship during those last two years of marriage. It was also love. And though we wanted desperately for our family to stay together, we didn't do it for the children either. We fought and cried and held on because we loved each other. Finally, something happened that made us realize that even love was not enough to change some things.

On a drive back from Laguna Beach across Orange and Los Angeles counties to our home in Pasadena, I began to imagine how good it would feel to jerk the steering wheel and crash head-on into a semi truck or into a cement pillar holding up a freeway overpass. In one quick, painless ball of fire, the nightmare would be over. No one would know that I had killed myself. The insurance would guarantee my family's security. Neither Lyla nor the children would have to bear the terrible reality that I had died by my own hand. No one would be embarrassed or ashamed.

I turned up the music on my car stereo and pushed the accelerator to the floorboard. Death would be such a relief. The talking could end at last. The guilt and fear would be over. I didn't care any more about displeasing God or facing hell and judgment. I just wanted out! Going north on Highway 57, my speedometer hit 100. I began to cry. The car was veering to the left. The steering wheel began to chatter. But there were no cement pillars and I didn't want to kill or injure anybody else. I drove faster, but my resolve began to fade. I didn't really want to die. I just didn't want to go on struggling.

At a 7-Eleven, I found a pay phone and called Lyla. We were expecting dinner guests and she was glad to get my call. I was paralyzed with fear. My voice trembled. "I don't know how to get home from here," I whispered. Tears rolled down my cheeks. I was trying not to scream. "Tell me where you are," Lyla said, trying to be calm. "I'll come get you." I couldn't talk about it with Lyla, not this time. Those conversations had become just too painful. "Tell me the name of the psychiatrist Don Thomas recommended," I answered. "I'm going to call him."

"Dr. Warren Jones here," the voice said calmly. "Whose calling?"

Sensing my terror, Dr. Jones' secretary had put me through. Jones listened. "I can see you tomorrow," he said quietly.

"Tomorrow?" I knew I couldn't make it through another night.

"Tomorrow at eight A.M."

Something in my heart said I could make it, after all.

That next morning, after a short, sedated night, I rode up the elevator to Dr. Jones's counseling suite on the fifth floor of the Mutual Savings Building in Pasadena. Jones was a psychiatrist with a specialization in dream work. Our friend Dr. Don Thomas, the director of Huntington Hospital's Emergency Services, had heard Dr. Jones at a special seminar on creativity and madness. Don had warned Lyla that Dr. Jones's counseling schedule was full years in advance, but said that he had many psychologists and psychiatrists on his staff to recommend. After our first interview Jones made a generous offer. If I would arrive at his office every morning at eight A.M. for the next year, he would come to work an hour early to see me.

Immediately, Dr. Jones took me off Valium and taught me how to breathe. He introduced me to endorphins, the body's natural tranquilizers. I had been breathing off the top of my lungs in tiny little gasps. He taught me how to inhale for four slow counts, to hold the breath deep in my lungs for another four counts, and then to release the air slowly while I counted to eight. I was to practice breathing slowly, deeply, several times a day and always when I felt a surge of stress or depression.

During the next year and a half, Dr. Jones seldom gave me advice. He just listened and asked questions as I recalled the last night's dreams, the previous day's events, my last waking thoughts, and my feelings about the dreams. Although we dream about other people, Jones explained, every character in our dreams also represents a similar dimension of our personality. If I dream about Hitler or Teresa of Calcutta, I am also dreaming about the tyrant or the saint in me. If I dream about a child, it is also the little gay child in me who needs a parent. What comes to mind when you think about that person? Jones would ask. How are you alike? What could the dream be suggesting about that part of you?

Dr. Jones believed that dreams are the mind struggling to heal itself. Like a broken bone put in traction, when we sleep, we give the mind a chance to file the day's memories under their appropriate categories in our brain's magnificent memory bank. When the file drawers are opened, old, unfinished memories pop out, demanding our attention. Unfinished memories cry out for resolution. Unhappy memories ask us to understand. Unhealed memories beg for healing. The dreams that result mix events, places, and people from our past and from our present. The result is a kaleidoscopic montage of related memories that may seem confused and unrelated in our dreams, when, in fact, the fragments are wonderfully related for the purpose of resting and renewing our minds. By playing Dr. Jones's dream game, we were extending the mind's nocturnal healing process. With our help, little by little every memory would be put to rest in its appropriate place.

At first I was suspicious of psychiatrists in general and of Dr. Jones in particular. When he talked about "learning to breathe" and "healing our memories," I was afraid that I had been turned over to another quack. But I was determined to find a way out of homosexuality. Nothing else had worked. The Christian counselors and their short-term solutions had ended in long-term despair. Dr. Jones was a specialist in creativity and mental illness. His résumé was long and impressive. His spirit was gentle. He listened carefully and remembered everything I said. Little by little I relaxed into his care. It wasn't long until I discovered that playing the dream game every morning with Dr. Jones was another of God's great gifts to me.

When we were approximately halfway through our sessions, a nightmare awakened me from a deep, troubled sleep. In that morning's dream game every second of the nightmare came back to me in vivid detail. I was eating dinner with Lyla, Erinn, and Michael when a truck pulled up outside our home and menacing soldiers in black leather boots and Nazi uniforms pounded on our door.

Even as I stared at the approaching menace through the half-open curtain, I knew intuitively exactly what I should do. I should rush my family out the back door and into hiding. Instead, I knelt on the floor and asked God to deliver us. As I prayed, the soldiers burst in and herded my family and me into a truck already jammed with other families just like mine. We drove through the night, pausing occasionally for the soldiers to smoke or relieve themselves.

At one stop in a familiar, heavily wooded section of highway, when the soldiers were laughing and talking at a distance, again I knew what I should do. I should help my family down from the truck and rush them into the nearby woods where underground partisans would find us and bring us to safety. Instead, I knelt in the truck and asked God to deliver us.

At dawn we were unloaded at a busy railroad crossing. The soldiers told us that we were being transported to safety in Switzerland, but as the train pulled into view, once more I knew what I should do. I should rush my family through the crowd and hide them in the nearby village until we were rescued and taken to freedom. Instead, I knelt down on the gravel and prayed for God to deliver us.

On the train ride, as we held our sleeping children, I could see the haunting fear in Lyla's eyes. When the train paused at a busy crossing and I discovered that the door of our boxcar had been left ajar, I knew in my heart exactly what I should do. Instead, I prayed another long, earnest prayer for God to deliver us.

We were unloaded from the train and marched toward a large camp with familiar words in German mounted on a sign across the entrance: WORK MAKES RIGHT. When an escape attempt distracted our guards and left us alone in the shadows of the forest, I knew again exactly what I should do. One last chance to save my family; instead, I prayed that God would deliver us.

Almost immediately, we were rounded up and marched through the camp to a large, ominous cement building where we were stripped and ordered inside for showers and delousing. Lyla and the children obliged quickly, believing our captors' lies. Even as we walked into the "shower room" together, I understood the terrible, deadly mistake I had made.

The iron door slammed shut. Poison gas hissed into the airtight room. Screaming with pain and terror, our friends and neighbors began to die. One by one, my wife and children died weeping and clutching each other for comfort as I knelt on the floor praying one last prayer for God to deliver us. Even as I prayed, I felt the poison invade my lungs, and after one last gasp for life, I died in agony and despair.

After sharing this nightmare with Dr. Jones, he passed me the Kleenex box and waited. For a long time I sat across from him in silence, thinking about that terrible nightmare, so disturbed by the suffering of my family that I couldn't play the dream game. "What were your last thoughts before going to bed?" Dr. Jones finally asked.

Lyla and I had spent that past evening talking about our marriage. She had been brave enough to suggest that maybe we should begin separating. We both hated the idea of divorce. It wasn't a word that described the reality of our situation. Whatever happened to our marriage, I was determined to keep the vows that I had made to Lyla about loving, honoring, and caring for her as long as we both should live. After all, we still loved each other. And though I was gay, we had married believing that with God's help, our love would be enough. That night, Lyla was afraid for my life. You have done your best for twenty years, she told me. You didn't want to be gay, but you never really had a choice.

After that sad but realistic conversation, I went to bed determined that if I would just pray harder, that if I would just have more faith, God would deliver us. I knew in my heart exactly what I should do, but I fell asleep praying that God would perform some kind of miracle. Suddenly, the dream made sense. It wasn't a nightmare at all. A part of me had to die that night. It was that part of me that went on praying for a miracle instead of listening to my heart and acting with courage. God was ready and willing to deliver us; I just needed to get off my knees and lead my family on that long, painful journey to freedom and to safety.

Just days later, Lyla met with Dr. Jones. She asked him how serious I was about suicide. He told her that on a scale of one to six, I was a five and a half. We met for lunch after their conversation. She sat across from me toying with her food, trying to get up the courage to say what needed to be said. Her eyes were filled with love and fear when she finally admitted that we had both tried long and hard enough to save our marriage. From that day, an even more painful discussion had to begin. Now we would need the same kind of love that had kept us together to help us let each other go. In spite of her love for me, she suggested that we should seriously consider ending our marriage.

We left the restaurant torn in two by our ambivalence. Whenever I had contemplated really leaving Lyla and the family in our home on

Sierra Madre Villa, my heart almost broke with grief and anxiety. But moving everything into my little office-apartment in Sierra Madre Villa was a natural next step. We had already moved my library, my computer, and my working files into a corner of the living room with a picture window looking out across a field of eucalyptus, pine, and gnarled native oak. In a kind of daze, we tried to explain to the children that I needed a private space for a while, to write, to think, to work on personal issues. I promised that I would be there for them in the future as I had been in the past.

Erinn was fourteen. She wanted desperately to believe that everything would be all right, that we would always be a family. Many of her classmates had already gone through divorce. "We've been the Brady Bunch all too long," she said, putting the most positive spin possible on the news, hugging me, smiling through her tears, glad she finally had something dramatic in her life to share with her friends. Thirteen-year-old Michael simply stared across the distance at me, loving me desperately but unable to hide his sense of anger and betrayal.

As I drove away from them that first night, I began to scream and pound the steering wheel. I couldn't stop imagining Lyla, Erinn, and Michael in their rooms grieving just as fiercely. Wondering if my freedom could possibly be worth their suffering, I felt waves of guilt and panic that made me want to die. Crying out to God in absolute despair, I prayed that with the sunrise we would all waken from this terrible dream.

My capacity for melodrama in those days still amazes me. After entering that lonely, little apartment and wallowing around for a while in my grief, I called Lyla. She was working on the 100th Anniversary project for All Saints. Erinn had been on the telephone chatting with her teenage friends, and Michael was listening to Sondheim on his Walkman and working on a class project.

The children still joke about how I overcompensated in those days. Motivated by love (and, admittedly, by guilt), the very next morning I appeared early on the home scene. Lyla had gone to All Saints for a morning meeting. I rushed into the kitchen, prepared to be the perfect dad and make the perfect breakfast. But if my children's memories of that day are correct, and who would doubt them, I made huge quantities of the worst French toast they had ever eaten, oversoaked in egg batter and drenched in cold syrup. Apparently, the bacon came out underdone and clogged in grease. Fortunately, I couldn't hurt the frozen orange juice, and my obliging children sat across the breakfast bar smiling at their poor, earnest father as they nibbled respectfully through my creation. Mercifully, their suffering was interrupted by the clock and we rushed down Sierra Madre Villa toward the children's schools.

At Maranatha, Erinn grabbed her pack, kissed me on the cheek, and rushed out to meet her friends. When we stopped in the line of cars unloading children near Poly's administration building, Michael packed his book bag slowly, opened the front door, and stood for a moment looking at me from the curb. He didn't say anything. As I remember, he didn't even smile. But the look in his eyes, among many mixed messages, seemed to be saying, "It's going to be all right, Dad. You'll see."

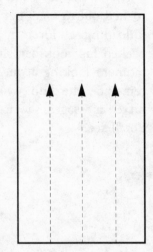

Chapter *11*

1984–90,

Giving Up the Ghost

*S*ticky, *wet snow had fallen steadily for most of that long winter day.*
Wind gusts, measured at more than forty miles an hour, were piling
up the fresh snow in giant, sculpted drifts. From my frost-framed,
double-plastic window, I could see snowplows hurrying up and down
the runways at Newark's International Airport even as our United
Airlines 727 was finally cleared for takeoff. Just as the flight attendant
asked us to fasten our seat belts, something bumped against the back
of the plane. No one seemed to notice.

The pilot taxied us into the long, impatient line of airplanes
hunkered down against the blizzard, lurching slowly along the icy
runway, anxious to fly above the storm. I rang my call button and
informed an irritated stewardess that something had bumped our

plane and that the crew should be told. She smiled patronizingly, assured me that the crew knew exactly what they were doing, and turned to rush away. I called her back, insisting that she take me seriously.

By then, people on both sides of the aisle, already impatient from our long delay, began to focus their anxiety and their anger on me. In thirty seconds, the flight attendant reappeared with the aircraft's navigator in tow. I told him that something had hit our airplane. He forced a grim smile, assured me that it was just a gust of wind, and explained that up front they had a whole array of warning lights and gauges to notify them of any danger. Then both of them turned to rush away. I called them back.

Sick of my complaints, nearby passengers were groaning audibly. In spite of the growing tension, I told the navigator that if he didn't take my warning seriously, I would "file a formal complaint with the FAA." He stared down at me in furious silence while I sat there staring back, wondering secretly if I had made a serious, embarrassing mistake.

The navigator blinked first and stalked away. The plane stopped taxiing. While my fellow passengers conspired noisily to throw me Jonah-like from the plane, the navigator in his fur-lined, hooded jacket stormed down the plane's rear ramp and out into the freezing blizzard. After five or ten minutes, he hurried back up the aisle, brushing snow from his hair.

Moments later, I heard the captain's voice say, "Will Dr. White please come forward to the cockpit!" Feeling sheepish and wondering what it felt like to be swallowed by a whale, I obeyed. As I walked through the open cockpit door, the captain turned, smiled, and held out his hand. He confirmed my fears. In the chaos of that stormy afternoon, a snowplow had hit and damaged the tail of our aircraft. The driver had either not noticed or, in fear, rushed away. The plane had been seriously disabled and needed immediate repairs. We would be returning to the airport momentarily. The crew thanked me for my warning and offered to buy me drinks.

That incident in 1984 signaled a kind of personal turning point. After years of trusting the people "in charge" to know what was right for me and for my life, I began to realize that I was the only one who could know for certain what was really best for me. And though I still believed in making and keeping commitments, even when costly, I finally understood that I had made some commitments in innocence and ignorance that could not be kept. In my eagerness to please others, I had not listened to my heart. After decades of anxiety and self-hatred, the truth dawned. I had to do what was right for me.

I had just completed my first interview in Brooklyn for the book *David* with Marie Rothenberg, the mother of a six-year-old child who had been burned and left for dead by his father, Charles. The doctors and nurses had urged Marie to wait at home while they cared for her beloved son. Marie refused. She insisted on staying with little David, day and night, while he healed from those hideous burns and suffered through the painful skin grafts that followed.

During our interviews, Marie told me endless hospital stories that illustrated why she had been right *not* to turn David's future over to the medical authorities in their life. Early on, she learned to trust herself to guarantee the quality and the consistency of her son's care. She listened carefully to the advice of doctors, nurses, and specialists. She asked for second and third opinions. She prayed diligently for God's direction in her life, but Marie knew that in the end she had to have the courage to face the tough choices and make the hard decisions on her own. So did Lyla and so did I.

In August 1984, Lyla began work on our separation agreement. Rather than hiring two lawyers, we hired one, Maureen Carlson. We sat down with Maureen and told her that we wanted to end our marriage as gracefully as possible, without recrimination or warfare. She helped us resolve quickly and amicably the matters of spousal and child support, child custody, and the division of our property. Lyla would live with the children in our home on Sierra Madre Villa. I would stay in my apartment at the bottom of the hill. We would continue to coparent our children. There would be no custody struggle. We would both have equal access, guided by what was best for the children.

In March 1985, we began the separation process that would lead to our divorce. Even though we were both emotionally torn by the process, we tried our best not to let our children be unnecessarily affected by our grief and fear. Obviously, they suffered from our separation and divorce. I would never minimize their suffering. After all, they loved us. They didn't want to see us divorced. Too many of their friends at school were going through separations and divorces of their own. They wanted us to beat the odds. It broke their hearts, as it broke ours, to see our "perfect" Christian family threatened. But even in their suffering, they, too, tried to understand.

Three years earlier, when he was just twelve, Michael had found a tape recording of our conversation with the psychologists from Fuller Seminary. "What does *gay* mean?" he asked his mother. She explained it simply. Michael continued to probe. Erinn waited much longer to ask. From the beginning, Lyla and I answered the questions that they asked as openly and as honestly as we could. It had taken more than two decades for us to understand even partially the complex and confounding issues. We would give the children all the time they needed. We hoped that they would be confident of this: we loved each other and we loved them. It was our sincere hope that one truth would override the rest and see them safely through.

In the meantime, we tried to keep our family life as "normal" as we could. I wasn't living at home, but I was there regularly to awaken my little family to the reoccurring smell of French toast and fried bacon. That, and apple crisp, were the only things I knew how to cook. My peanut-butter, honey, and banana sandwiches were the talk of the neighborhood, but my French toast still left something to be desired.

Only later, when the children were adults, did they confess to me with hugs and broad smiles that they tolerated those early-morning breakfasts as a gift to me. In fact, now they both tease me about having a father who hung around too much. "If you hadn't felt so guilty," Erinn told me with a grin, "we could have been like other kids with normal families who never talked to their parents or even saw them much."

From the beginning of our separation, Michael resisted spending so much time together as a family when we weren't a "regular" family anymore. He may have been right. Insisting on seeing it through together cost each of us a different emotional price. Only time will tell the long-range consequences of that decision. At times the stress of being together was unbelievable. I hate the suffering that my personal dilemma cost those I love the most; but it was right for me to hang on to my beloved family. And rather than cutting and running early on, even though it might have been easier for us all, I would do it again rather than risk losing any one of them.

In 1985, we were co-room parents for Michael's tenth-grade class at Poly, and we attended every possible parent-student-teacher event during Erinn's freshman year at Maranatha Christian High. In 1986, just before the divorce decree was granted, Lyla and I used most of the free mileage points I had earned on United Airlines to take our children on a once-in-a-lifetime journey to China.

The trip to China was probably another act of overcompensation on my part. As with my gooey French toast and my greasy fried bacon, our two children, barely in their teens, endured gracefully the long flights back and forth across the Pacific, the hot, dusty tours of Beijing, Shanghai, Xian, and Canton, the restaurants where cold tripe and rice with mysterious, black flecks were served at almost every meal, and the hotel rooms where the cockroaches were large enough to ride and there was no air-conditioning in hundred-degree heat and 90 percent humidity.

"You mean we could have gone to Tahiti on these same free tickets?" Erinn muttered quietly one afternoon as we scaled the Great Wall of China and posed to have our picture taken there. Looking at that photo today, I don't know whether to laugh or cry. Our strained smiles and sweaty faces say it all. In spite of everything we were determined to be the "perfect" family: Lyla smiling sincerely, with her arms outstretched behind us all; Michael patient, understanding, but unwilling to fake a grin, even for the photo that would go out with our Christmas newsletter; Erinn, smiling broadly but secretly wishing she was on the beach in Tahiti; and me looking so earnest, determined that everyone would have fun, scared that I was failing.

Jerry Falwell entered our lives that same year. He was looking for a ghostwriter for his book *If I Should Die Before I Wake!* I flew to Nashville to meet Jerry and young Mark DeMos, Jerry's able, dollar-a-year executive assistant, media representative, and close personal friend. We sat in the conference room of Thomas Nelson Publishing and talked about abortion, the subject of his new book.

Jerry remembered clearly a 1973 press conference when a female reporter cornered him. "Is it enough to be against abortion?" she asked loudly. "What are you doing for the pregnant girls who have no other options?" Convicted by her questions, Jerry organized Liberty Godparent Ministries to do something practical to help women and girls facing an unwanted or unplanned pregnancy. That was the story he wanted to tell.

I talked to Jerry frankly about my feelings on abortion. Though I had serious concerns about its misuse as a contraceptive and growing alarm at the number of abortions being performed every year, I believed that, living in a democracy, we couldn't take away a woman's right to make her own decision on such a personal matter. But I loved his plan to help women who were facing unwanted pregnancies to avoid abortion. I told him about our daughter, Erinn, and how glad Lyla and I were that Erinn's biological mother had chosen life for our future adopted daughter, how our lives had been enriched by the joy that Erinn brought to us. Jerry and I liked each other from the start, and I knew that I could write convincingly about his Liberty Godparent Ministries without compromising my integrity.

After signing contracts, I traveled to Lynchburg on Jerry's small private jet. He had a little refrigerator near his reclining, leather seat with a private supply of round snowball cupcakes covered with coconut. "My one great vice," he called them, grinning his trademark grin and holding out one of his calorie-rich concoctions to me.

As we approached Lynchburg, Jerry pointed proudly at the sprawling campus of his Liberty University on Liberty Mountain. After lunch, we drove through town in Jerry's shiny black van. Every place we went, people waved and shouted greetings to Lynchburg's leading citizen. Jerry grinned, waved, and honked back. We parked in front of a huge, old Victorian mansion on tree-lined Eldon Street. Once one of the Florence Crittenden Homes for Teenagers, this historic house had been transformed into the first full-service Liberty Godparent Home, certified by the Commonwealth of Virginia, for girls and young women awaiting delivery of their unwanted or unplanned babies. On our tour, the staff and the young female residents greeted Jerry with genuine gratitude and respect.

It was easy to see that abortion was *not* an issue that Jerry was using just to raise money and mobilize support. He really cared about the 1.5 million unborn babies that he believed were "being slaughtered every year in this country." He genuinely opposed *Roe v. Wade,* the 1973 Supreme Court decision ruling unconstitutional all state laws that "prohibited voluntary abortions before the third month."

According to Jerry, that Supreme Court decision helped revolutionize his life. From a pastor interested only in "spiritual matters," Jerry became a conservative political activist. Five years later he organized his Moral Majority. His opposition to abortion became one of Jerry's two main issues. His opposition to homosexuality was the other.

One evening when we had finished interviewing and touring for the day, I asked Jerry how he felt about homosexuality. Jerry based his antigay and antilesbian stand on those six short passages in the Bible. He used the story of Sodom as his ultimate proof text. When I asked Jerry if he knew any homosexuals personally, he answered without a moment's hesitation, "Yes, of course."

He knew that closeted gay and lesbian Christians worshiped in his church, attended his university, and watched his television program faithfully. And though he now denies it, Jerry even admitted that one of his staff members was a gay man who had lived in a committed, though closeted relationship with another gay man for almost twenty years. "If he doesn't force me into a corner," Jerry said, "I won't force him either."

As with the ban on homosexuals in the military that Jerry later supported so enthusiastically, gays and lesbians could fight and die for their country, or assist in Jerry's ministry, as long as they lived by the rules of the closet. If they didn't "come out," Jerry wouldn't "go in" after them. "Don't ask. Don't tell." It was, and it is, a dangerous and misleading double standard.

Initially, I was naive enough to be impressed that in spite of Jerry's antigay position, he had at least one gay man as an important member of his team. I didn't understand then why it was so wrong for Jerry to hold one standard in public and another standard in private. I do now. If Jerry had even preached what little compassion he practiced, imagine the hope he could have brought to thousands of Christian families and their gay sons and lesbian daughters. I flew back to California confused about this friendly fundamentalist, but glad and grateful to be employed.

During those long months of separation and divorce, almost every Sunday I sat with my family in the third-row, left-center pew of the All Saints Episcopal Church, blinking back my tears when the trumpet fanfares sounded and the choral anthems called us to praise. I shared the printed order of worship with Lyla and the children—the people I loved most in all the world. Sitting proudly beside my family, I listened to the Old and New Testament stories, joined in the collects and responsive readings, heard the prophetic voice of our rector, George Regas, knelt at the altar to receive communion.

One of the other reasons I liked to sit near the front of the church was my occasional view of a tall, handsome baritone who sang in the All Saints choir. I'm still a bit embarrassed to confess that memory.

After all, I was a forty-four-year-old man, sitting in church with my family, in the midst of our separation and divorce, stealing quick, furtive glances at a singer who was obviously younger than I, attracted to his sensual smile, his dazzling blue eyes, and his thick, blond hair. I felt guilty even when I looked at him.

Guilt had become a serious problem. I knew in my head that if it were left unresolved, this growing load of guilt would eventually cripple me, but my heart went on blaming myself for everyone's distress. I knew in my head that I should not continue grieving for what might have been, but I fought back tears every time I thought about my wife or children. I knew in my head that certain things had been decided, that my wife and children would survive, that I needed to get on with my life, but I longed to end everyone's suffering and to make things right again.

The same old tunes played over and over in my head. "You should have tried harder to 'overcome' being gay." "You should have had more 'ex-gay' counseling or electric-shock therapy." "You should have prayed and fasted longer." "You should have trusted God more." "Thirty years of struggle is not enough. You should have gone on disciplining and denying yourself for a lifetime."

One special refrain rang out louder than the rest: "You could have had it all if you had just stayed in the closet, enjoyed gay sex on the side, and made some kind of deal with your wife or kept her in the dark altogether. Nobody cares what you do in private, not really, not even Jerry Falwell. Now, by trying to live with what you call 'integrity,' you're going to lose it all!"

On Sunday mornings, sitting with my family in our favorite pew, when I glanced at the young baritone with his broad smile and magnetic eyes, I wondered if I had made a terrible mistake. What would it cost me to pursue him or any other responsible gay man? What price would I have to pay to enter into a loving, long-term gay relationship that had integrity? It seemed so much easier to have remained where I was, in the closet, with my wife and children, my vocation protected, but with a secret sensual life on the side.

Whenever that temptation reoccurred, I thought of three gay men whom I had known personally who had bet their lives on that "stay in the closet/keep your family" option and the tragic consequences of their decisions. Each happened to be a distinguished Christian leader. One served as senior pastor of a well-known church in New York City before becoming a tenured professor in an East Coast seminary. The second was an executive in a major denominational publishing house in southern California. The third was a Youth for Christ director in the Northwest who had been elected to serve two terms on his state board of health.

I met all three men during my fourteen-year tenure at Fuller Theological Seminary. Because they saw in my eyes the same longing they had known from childhood, each man felt comfortable about sharing his story with me. Their stories were so like my own. To protect the memories of these men, I am disguising their identities. Each had struggled against his homosexual orientation from earliest adolescence. Each had married and raised a family hoping in that way to end the struggle. Each had managed to discipline and deny himself through the first few years of marriage, and each had seriously considered suicide before "giving in."

Rather than ruining the ministries to which they had been called, rather than dragging their wives and children through the pain of divorce and the humiliation of coming out, each man had tried to meet his homosexual needs in secret sexual encounters, usually with strangers in a distant city or in dark, isolated places around their hometowns. During our long conversations, each man told me how unfulfilling those furtive sexual acts had been, and though he still loved his wife and family, how he longed to live his life over again, this time with a partner of his own sexual orientation.

It was too late for them, however. The decisions had been made long before we met. They would remain in the closet, and the consequences of those decisions were fatal. The senior pastor turned seminary professor was murdered in Laguna Beach by a young man he picked up at a gay bar. The publishing executive and the Youth for Christ director each died of AIDS, surrounded by their loving but devastated families.

I knew these men well. Each was a responsible man who loved his wife and children, who loved Christ and was committed to Christ's church. But each died before his time in agony and humiliation because he would not accept, because his community would not accept, because his nation would not accept these facts: Homosexual orientation is a permanent human condition. To live with integrity, a homosexual person must eventually accept that reality and get on with his or her life. And misinformation and bigotry, ancient or modern, should not prevent gay or lesbian Americans from sharing in the rights and protections granted every citizen of this land by the U.S. Constitution and its Bill of Rights.

At long last, I was beginning to realize that gays and lesbians, like our heterosexual friends and neighbors, have the God-given right to life, liberty, and the pursuit of happiness; the right to live open lives, to develop long-term loving relationships, and to have those relationships honored and recognized officially by their community; the right to raise families, to build networks of friends, to work, play, and worship without fear or discrimination; the right to come out of the closet, into the light, no longer pretending to be what they can never be; the right to be loved and accepted exactly as they are.

And this right applied to me as well, even though I knew it would mean disrupting my life. For a year, David and I had continued our part-time relationship, hurrying back and forth between our two different worlds. David was content to go on living in the closet, but I felt trapped.

I loved David, but it was getting more and more clear that our lives were headed in two very different directions. Our cultural, financial, and spiritual traditions were radically different. The only real thing we had in common was passion, and I began to wonder what would hold us together when our passion cooled.

In truth, David and I had never really gotten to know each other. Because I had been desperate, frightened, and lonely, I had committed myself too quickly. David was a thoughtful, loving, sensual person, but after a year living together in our different closets, I began to realize that we weren't compatible for the long haul.

Given his cultural roots, David needed to stay in the closet. I was feeling more and more the need to be "out." He was comfortable living two different lives, one in public, one in private. I was feeling more and more desperate to pull my two contradictory lives together. I don't believe David ever did understand my decision, but he accepted the end of our relationship with amazing grace.

As time passed, I became more and more certain that leaving the closet was my first step in the direction of real maturity. Because my sexual orientation affected every dimension of my life, I was determined to find the right man "to marry." Same-sex marriages were not legal then, as they are not legal now, but I grew up believing that genuine, satisfying, life-sustaining intimacy happens between two people in a committed, loving relationship. Entering into that kind of gay relationship became my goal.

Occasional, casual sex with a gay friend or even an attractive stranger seemed the only way to survive when I was hiding in a closet. And while those sudden, sensual encounters were exciting to be sure, I invariably felt more frustrated and more lonely when they were over. The part-time, closet "marriage" to David had been an important and life-giving transitional step, but I could not live in that kind of closet forever. I wanted a long-term, loyal, loving relationship with one man in the open where we didn't need to hide our love or feel embarrassed or ashamed by our commitment to each other.

I just didn't know how to find that man. I thought myself too old to start the dating game again. I felt threatened and silly in all those smoky, noisy, flashing-light places where young, single gay men go to get acquainted, but then, there was no time for a long-term, hearts-and-flowers courtship in my life either.

I was still traveling across the country and around the world at breakneck speed, writing, directing, speaking, consulting, and over-achieving generally in order to support two different households, to supply us all with food, clothing, and endless incidentals, to buy and maintain cars and insurance, to pay private-school bills, to save a few dollars for university tuitions, to tithe to All Saints, and to give offerings to the causes we cared about deeply. And though coming out of the closet would cost me most, if not all, my old clients, for the years ahead I still had spousal support, child support, university tuitions, and endless bills to pay. Because of my ambivalence, I had put Tom and David through endless frustration and eventual grief. Now they were gone. What other gay man would risk being involved with me?

Every time I stole a glance at the handsome, blond baritone, the same question rattled around in my brain. Assuming he was gay, why would he be interested in me? I'm too old. I'm too encumbered. I'm too tired to play the game. Then, one Sunday morning at a break in the service when I looked up to see if my favorite baritone was in his place, I thought I saw him looking back at me.

After a year of furtive Sunday-morning glances, I finally decided to act on my instincts. On Palm Sunday, when the choir formed a procession moving up and down the church aisles waving palm branches, I looked directly into the sparkling blue eyes of that handsome baritone as he passed by my pew. To my surprise, once again he looked directly back at me, and in that wonderful split second of secret intimacy, I decided to take the next step in developing a possible relationship.

After church that Sunday, thirty-three-year-old Gary Nixon accepted my invitation to join me the next evening at Beckham Place, an English pub and restaurant in Pasadena with a blazing fire and soft, oversize leather chairs. Gary felt right at home. As a child he had migrated from Canada to southern California with his family. His Anglo-Saxon roots were planted deep in English soil. His mother, a devout Anglican, insisted that for Gary's baptism as a child the family return to the little church in Bolton, England, where she had been baptized and where she and Gary's father had been married.

Gary had graduated from college with a music degree, but liked working with inanimate objects such as steel, concrete, fabric, paints, and soil far more than he liked working with animate objects such as children, who run amok and sing off-key. He was a skilled property manager overseeing the development and maintenance of a major corporation's property portfolio in southern California.

The English-pub setting had seemed a perfect idea, but Gary didn't drink and was allergic to cigarette smoke. So we escaped into the early-evening darkness and walked around the Spanish fountain and through the arched and tiled plaza and the rose gardens of Pasadena's City Hall. Gary didn't talk much, but I chattered on for both of us. His relaxed, even temperament made my pace and style feel exhausting. He tossed his head back and laughed easily. I was charmed and excited by his laughter.

Gary enjoyed hard work and had spent his lifetime working, if not at his vocation, on his craftsman home in Altadena. I liked projects best when they were over. I delighted in studying the Bible, talking theology, and reading the lives of martyrs and saints. Gary loved Christian choral music, especially the great requiems by Fauré, Bach, and Brahms. I liked preaching. He liked listening from the pew. We were perfect opposites. But as we walked together in the moonlight, I felt excited and at the same time comforted by his strong, sensual presence. A relationship between us began that evening that has lasted to this day.

In 1985, shortly after finishing work on Jerry Falwell's book *If I*

Should Die Before I Wake! the same publisher, Thomas Nelson, called me back to Nashville to meet Pat Robertson. Pat wanted a ghostwriter who could work with him to complete a book in time to help shape the issues of the 1988 presidential elections. He wanted to title the book *America's Date With Destiny.* And though he wasn't officially a candidate at the time, Pat wanted a political treatise that outlined his dreams for the nation in clear black-and-white-terms.

Knowing at least a little about Pat's political agenda from my occasional viewings of his "700 Club," I knew that I could never write such a book, especially if he spoke out against my gay brothers and lesbian sisters. Like Jerry, Pat wasn't bashing homosexuals at the time, at least not very often; but it was clear that he held to the party line of the religious right, using those six biblical passages, especially the story of Sodom, to condemn homosexuality and "self-avowed" homosexuals.

In spite of my political differences with Pat, I still had respect for his spiritual commitments. Besides, I needed another client desperately to pay the family's bills. In an informal discussion shortly after we met, I told Pat how dangerous it would be to position himself in print on a whole array of subjects even before the campaign began. Having already committed himself, Pat would find it difficult in the heat of an election to compromise or alter a position, let alone to change his mind. Of all the presidential candidates that I had studied, only two were elected who had autobiographies in print before election day.

Pat agreed. I suggested further that we call the book *America's Dates With Destiny* and bring to life the stories behind the most important dates in American history as he saw them. Again, he agreed. "Only you choose the dates," he added, and with those brief instructions, he was gone. Right or wrong, Pat Robertson could make a decision on his feet faster than any man I'd ever met. He walked into a room, filled it with his energy, asked a few questions, made his decision, and moved on again. He had no time for looking back.

Meeting two powerful religious television personalities such as Jerry Falwell and Pat Robertson and working closely with them during an intense two-year span was very revealing. Jerry's airplane was smaller but faster than Pat's, but Falwell's jet had a "secret" compartment for coconut-covered snowballs, a calorie-loaded treat that Pat wouldn't eat on a bet. Jerry didn't seem to take his growing political power or his growing waistline very seriously, while Pat watched his weight as carefully as he watched his ratings.

Jerry Falwell enjoyed playing practical, physical jokes, even on me. During our second meeting, as I stepped out of an elevator with him in Washington, D.C., he shoved me with his elbow just hard enough that I was trapped behind the door and watched it close as he and the rest of his entourage walked away laughing.

Several times, Jerry's pranks seemed a bit thoughtless, if not downright cruel. The baby alligator that he left in his wife's bathtub, for example, really frightened her. And being stranded in the elevator while everyone walked away laughing made me angry and defensive. Like others, I took offense at Jerry's muscular schoolboy pranks, but only at first. Eventually, I learned that Jerry's practical jokes were just a part of Jerry's personality, and after a while, everyone forgave him, even when he went too far.

Pat Robertson, on the other hand, was almost always polite, but distant, totally self-absorbed in his ambitious plans, and certainly not much fun. On a flight from California to Virginia, Pat got a call from Oklahoma City from the owner-editor of the *Saturday Evening Post*. Anticipating an interview and a positive article, Pat instructed his pilot to land at that city. He dropped me off, put the influential lady in my place, and took off again. I ended up in a strange airport, feeling abandoned, hoping to catch a commercial flight home.

Jerry minimized the risk of his new celebrity. He refused bodyguards and didn't pay much attention to security measures. In fact, he used the growing fear for his safety to play a classic prank on his secretarial staff. As Jerry tells it, as he approached his offices at the Thomas Road Baptist Church one morning, he called his secretary on the car phone, disguised his voice, and warned her of rumors of "a terrorist threat to Mr. Falwell's life."

By the time Jerry arrived at the church, his entire staff was buzzing with the rumor. With the stage perfectly set, Jerry sneaked up to his open window, tossed a cherry bomb into his office, waited for it to go off with a loud pop and a puff of smoke, and was smiling and applauding as his staff poured out into the parking lot.

Almost immediately, the staff struck back. They planted a loud but harmless car bomb under their pastor's hood. When Jerry left the next week's staff meeting early, without the faintest suspicion of their plot to get revenge, he jumped into his van and turned the key. When the smoke bomb went off with a loud explosion, Jerry practically fell out of the front seat, to the delight of the entire staff leaning out of church windows, laughing and applauding gleefully.

Pat Robertson, on the other hand, took his personal security very seriously. After I finished *America's Dates With Destiny,* Pat invited me to New Orleans for a private dinner at the Commodore's Palace, a wonderful old plantation-house restaurant where elegant Southern meals were served by liveried waiters. After dinner we took a short walk in the moonlight through the old streets nearby, shaded with huge magnolia trees and lined with antebellum mansions.

On a particularly dark block, two watchdogs suddenly began to bark at us furiously. We were both startled. I stumbled away from the fence, directly into Pat. Before I knew what was happening, his security driver pulled up beside us, tires squealing. I didn't even realize we were being followed. Pat was pulled into the car and rushed away. I was left standing in the darkness with two half-crazed Dobermans barking fiercely and pawing at the fence. Eventually, I found a taxi to take me back to my hotel.

Both Pat and Jerry loved to be surrounded by the press. For the first time in history, the media cared about what two fundamentalist Christians had to say, and they both took advantage of their newfound celebrity, Pat to run for president, Jerry to raise funds and mobilize support for Liberty University. Pat's presidential campaign kept him in the news. Jerry had to work harder at it.

I was present in his office in 1986 when a reporter called to ask Jerry about a rumor circulating in Washington, D.C. Jerry took the message on his speakerphone: "Were you actually the mysterious third person to accompany Ollie North and another White House aide to Iran to trade arms for hostages?"

Jerry cupped the phone and laughed heartily. "That's a national-security matter," he said in all seriousness. "I'll have to get back to you with the answer tomorrow morning at a press conference in my office."

The next day, when representatives from the world's press had gathered again in Lynchburg to meet with Jerry, he entered the room, greeted his visitors, and with cameras rolling made a long introductory statement covering the latest news about Liberty University. Finally, a reporter forced Jerry to answer directly the question they had come to ask. "No, I didn't go with Ollie to Iran," Jerry answered with a grin. "That was just a rumor." The reporters grinned to each other, put down their notebooks and cameras, and headed for the door, knowing they had been conned again.

Immediately upon completing Pat Robertson's *America's Dates With Destiny,* I was summoned by G. R. Welch, a Canadian publisher, to Heritage USA on the border between North and South Carolina to ghostwrite Jim and Tammy Bakker's autobiography. This constant travel, working away from home on book or film locations while trying to be a responsible parent, was especially hard on my new relationship with Gary. To give us more time together, he had agreed to move into my little apartment in Sierra Madre. Even there, we seldom had any quality time together. In spite of the frenetic pace, Gary honored my commitments to Lyla and the children and showed endless patience and understanding as I rushed up and down Sierra Madre Villa to see the family, and to and fro across the face of the earth to earn a living.

On the rare free day, we drove to Laguna to scuba dive the kelp beds at Diver's Beach or to explore the underwater caves and caverns at Shaw's Cove. These rare days off weren't enough. Before I began rushing to begin the interviews with Jim and Tammy, Gary suggested that we take a full week off, just the two of us together, to be really alone at last. I had earned enough mileage points to get free tickets to Cozumel, an island off Mexico's Yucatan Peninsula. Jacques Cousteau called the waters off Cozumel "one of the seven dive wonders of the world." Gary knew I could not resist his offer. We flew south to Mexico City and east to Cozumel, found our oceanfront room overlooking the harbor, slipped into bathing suits, and just before checking into the dive shop, stood side by side watching a giant cruise ship docking at the wharf nearby.

Both the sky and the sea were a deep azure blue. It was difficult to tell where the sky ended and the blue Caribbean waters began. The sun was hot, but the gentle, tropical breezes cooled and refreshed us. Suddenly, for the first time in all those stressful years, I felt that great black storm cloud of guilt and fear begin to lift. As I felt the sun's warming and relaxing rays, tears of exhaustion and relief began to roll down my cheeks. Gary put his arm around me and led me from the balcony to our king-size bed.

He held me in his arms while I cried, and as he stroked my shoulders and kissed away my tears, the sense of exhaustion and relief turned to passion. With our bodies pressed tightly together, our hearts beat as one heart. All those decades I had dreamed of making love without fear or guilt to a man I loved. All those lonely nights I had wanted to love a man genuinely and to be loved by him genuinely in return. Finally, miraculously, it was happening. Lying together on those cool, fresh sheets, with the island sun shining through the open windows and the tropical breezes caressing us, I made love as I had never made love before. There was no need that day for fantasies to launch and sustain the effort. In Gary's arms, making love was effortless, and before we slept, every old fantasy had blazed to life.

All week long, deep below the surface of the sea, I drifted behind Gary through subterranean caverns and great open gardens of red, green, and yellow growing coral. I could see his almost naked body just ahead of me gliding through the warm, clear waters surrounded by schools of fish wearing every color of the rainbow. Occasionally, when the dive master was just out of sight, I reached out to stroke Gary's arm or rest my hand on his slim lower back. Embarrassed by any show of affection in public, even at eighty feet under, Gary pulled away, but even at the bottom of the sea I could see his sheepish grin and know exactly what he was thinking. In darker, deeper waters, when he looked back over his shoulder to be sure that I was following, when I signaled him okay, I could see relief and pleasure in his eyes.

"Make a joyful noise unto the Lord, all ye lands." My heart was running over with gratitude. "Serve the Lord with gladness: come before his presence with singing." Though there were times when I'd wondered, God had been with me every step of the way. "Know ye that the Lord is God: it is He that hath made us, and not we ourselves." My sexuality, like the sea and the earth and the sky above, was all God's doing. "We are his people, and the sheep of his pasture. . . . Be thankful unto him, and bless his name." Swimming behind Gary just above the reef off the island of Cozumel, the words of Psalm 100 echoed in my grateful heart: "For the Lord is good; his mercy is everlasting; and his truth endureth to all generations."

During the summer of 1987, Gary and I flew to Washington, D.C., to join 50,000 lesbians, gays, bisexuals, and transgendered people in our first major civil rights demonstration. Two of our best heterosexual friends volunteered to march with us that day. Philip Yancey, the Christian writer and columnist, had been my closest male confidant during the trauma of the past several years. He didn't come to support the march, but to experience it with me. Even when Philip disagreed with me about homosexuality or my own personal decisions, he remained my friend. In his honest, penetrating questions, I never felt judgment or prejudice. Even when I couldn't or didn't heed his advice, I knew that he and his equally loving wife, Janet, would not give up on me.

Jay Jarman, my old Fuller Seminary student and friend from Hawaii also walked with us. Jay had become a powerful preacher in the United Church of Christ and planter of home churches in the islands. Like Philip, Jay was a heterosexual Christian who had come to show his personal support for me as I took my first feeble steps toward activism.

We marched for several hours, listened to inspiring speeches near the Washington Monument, and then heard a concert by massed gay and lesbian choirs and bands from across America. Looking about me, I wished all my friends from the church could be there with us. The hundreds of thousands of homosexuals I saw on the march were so unlike the ugly caricature presented by the religious right. We were from the American mainstream. We were doctors and lawyers, blue collar workers and students. We were old and young, rich and poor. We came from every possible race, religious, and ethnic background. We were parents and grandparents, children and grandchildren.

As Gary and I walked back to our hotel, I realized that I would never be the same. For years I had half believed the lies that my old clients were telling about gay and lesbian people, and had lived in dread of being a part of them. Now, I had seen hundreds of thousands of my brothers and sisters first hand. I had met and talked to dozens of new friends from across America. We were not a menace to this country. Quite to the countrary, we were a powerful, loving, gifted, creative presence. And though there were millions of Americans who didn't understand what it meant to be gay or lesbian, all across this country there were enough people like Philip and Jay who were open and loving and determined to understand. Out of that kind of honest discussion would come new understanding for both sides. I went to sleep that night, proud to be gay, grateful for my heterosexual friends, and excited and hopeful about the future.

On August 14, 1987, Gary and I read the story of Hank Koehn, fifty-four, a nationally known futurist and former Vice President of Security Pacific Bank. A gay man infected by the HIV virus, Mr. Koehn had written courageously for the *Los Angeles Times* about "My Passage Through AIDS." We were both deeply moved by this frank and eloquent account of the terrible physical and psychological suffering Hank and his lover, Jim Hill, had endured together. After finding their names in the phone book, we called Jim and introduced ourselves. He invited us over for a visit.

During those next months before Hank's death, these two loving men gave Gary and me a graduate course in courage and in caring. "If there is one thing worse than AIDS," Hank wrote, "it is watching and caring for the person who has it. . . . It is difficult to say who is the victim and who hurts the most. Joy seems to slowly vanish in the eyes of both."

Along with a handful of their loving and faithful friends, we adopted Hank and Jim, visiting them regularly, helping Jim change Hank's soiled sheets or gently maneuver Hank's thin, painful body into a more comfortable position after another terrifying seizure. It was our first hands-on experience with this terrible disease. By watching these two men live through their anguish and grief, we understood for the first time that the most painful suffering of all comes to a person with AIDS when he or she is rejected by family, by friends, by neighbors and coworkers, and even by the church. But we also learned that the greatest healing of all comes when someone, even a stranger, reaches out a hand of mercy or whispers a word of love.

During one late night vigil, I learned of Hank's two not-so-secret obsessions. He loved Esther Williams and had a complete collection of her old movies on video. He was also a fan of the Bolshoi Ballet and had always wanted to see them perform live. The Bolshoi Ballet was making one of their rare appearances in Los Angeles that weekend and Hank was sorry that he was too ill and too weak to attend.

After getting Jim's permission, Gary and I found a ticket scalper with four good seats. Jim managed to convince Hank that with the aid of a wheelchair and our six strong arms we could get him safely to and from the Dorothy Chandler Pavilion. I saw tears in Hank's eyes as we sat watching that great company of dancers, but a real miracle occurred as I wheeled Hank through the lobby at intermission.

Suddenly, out of the crowd came a beautiful older woman, looking regal in a white turban and white silk dress. She walked directly to Hank's wheelchair and knelt down before him. She placed her hands over his thin, wrinkled fingers and looked directly into his eyes before she spoke. "Your story in the *Times* moved me deeply," she said. "Thank you for your courage." For a moment, she just knelt there looking at Hank. Her eyes were filled with honest concern and genuine appreciation for his story. Without saying another word, she stood up, kissed Hank on his cheek, and walked away.

"Who was that lady?" Hank said, looking up at me in total disbelief.

"It was Esther Williams," I answered, hardly able to believe it myself.

"How did she know?" Hank said, wondering if this too had been arranged by us.

"I have no idea," I said honestly, but in my heart I believed then as I believe today that Hank's loving Creator arranged that meeting and gave his dying child the gift of caring from a stranger when so many of his old friends had turned away.

Late in 1989, feeling incredible grief and loss, Lyla sold our family home in Sierra Madre. We used the proceeds to put down payments on two high-rise condominiums in Glendale's Park Towers. Although both Erinn and Michael were away at college, they used Lyla's larger condo on the ninth floor of the west tower for a home-away-from-dorm, while Gary and I lived in the smaller condo on the first floor of the east tower.

This living arrangement seemed "absolutely insane" to many of our gay and nongay friends alike. They thought it would be easier for both of us to make "a clean break" no matter how painful and to "start fresh" in our new lives; but living in close proximity allowed Lyla and me to maintain our personal friendship and our close family ties and to continue those final years of hands-on parenting while beginning the painful and complicated separation of our two lives.

Often, one or both of us flew to Wesleyan University in Connecticut to visit our son and see the plays he had written, directed, and performed. We also attended special events to celebrate Erinn's progress toward her degree at Azusa Pacific University. One year, I was even asked to deliver that school's commencement address. We valued our family and celebrated holidays and special occasions together with family members and friends in Park Tower's spacious entertainment areas. My brother, Marshall, his wife, Bunny, and their children along with Lyla's sister, Sharon, her husband, Grant Meredith, and their children, all supported Lyla and me with their visits, their calls and cards of concern. My mother-in-law, Marjorie Smith, never stopped loving me or caring about my future. My own parents called or wrote regularly. Lyla and the whole family without exception reached out to include Gary in their concern. Erinn even asked Gary to assist her and a group of her mother's closest friends in producing an elaborate party with a spectacular buffet and a live band to celebrate Lyla's fiftieth birthday.

During those most difficult years, Lyla showed amazing wisdom and considerable spunk. When publishers or film distributors who didn't know that we were separated or divorced asked to take us out to dinner, Lyla was always game. When she received calls or letters asking about "the rumor," she answered simply, "Mel and I love each other more than ever." If anybody asked if I was gay, we always answered truthfully. I never lied or tried to cover the facts when specific questions were asked. We just didn't tell people anything we knew they couldn't handle. "We aren't deceiving them," Lyla said to me one day. "We're simply helping them avoid their prejudice."

When two old friends and primary leaders in the evangelical community outed me to Billy Graham, Lyla heard it first. We had served each of these powerful Christian executives faithfully and effectively and yet each had condemned me without bothering to speak to me first. Worse, they had accused me in public and in private of being both "immoral and irresponsible." Lyla made appointments to see both men personally. After confronting them for their "unbiblical behavior," she assured them that through it all, I had "acted in the Spirit of Christ" and had been to her and to our children "a responsible and loving husband and father."

We were all on our best behavior, trying (perhaps too hard) to make a loving transition from one life to another. It wasn't easy for anyone, but it seemed especially painful for Lyla. The children were growing up and would soon have homes and families of their own.

She pictured herself spending her last years of productivity and retirement alone, and the studies of single women over fifty or women after divorce provided no consolation. Lyla went through understandable anger, disappointment, fear, and grief, but after each siege she bounced back, resilient, hopeful, certain we had done our best, determined to see it through.

Over our twenty-five years of struggle, it had become terribly clear that in most cases a heterosexual should not be married to a homosexual. We had done everything in our power to make our marriage work. "If he had any other choice," Lyla told our friends repeatedly, "I would know it." She knew in her mind that we had done our best. Still, her heart was broken.

Regularly, at sunrise, Lyla and I would walk to Foxy's Cafe for breakfast. Often, when I was traveling on book or film business, we would call each other at night. Almost every day we talked, as we had always talked, about everything. Because we had experienced a forty-year friendship, we shared each other's pain and disappointment. Sometimes, after those long, heart-wrenching conversations, I would be consumed with guilt and grief. I was helpless to intervene on Lyla's behalf. She wasn't blaming me for our agony, but it felt like it when we talked.

In fact, because we had been friends for so many more years than we had been married, Lyla was surprised when I got defensive, angry, or depressed after our conversations. And though we both carried our pain uneasily at first, with the help of God and of our loving family and friends, we managed to laugh, argue, and cry our way through those first difficult years of separation and divorce.

One of my primary sources of emotional and spiritual support during that time was the Metropolitan Community Church in the San Fernando Valley. Gary and I both loved All Saints Episcopal, but we were anxious to meet and know more gay and lesbian couples with spiritual interests similar to our own. One fateful Sunday morning, I found a brief ad in a gay newspaper for the nearest congregation in the Universal Fellowship of Metropolitan Community Churches, the only denomination with a primary ministry to gay and lesbian people.

Gary and I looked up the location of the MCC congregation on a map of Los Angeles County. We drove to Cahuenga Boulevard, and after riding up and down that long, busy street through the heart of North Hollywood, we finally found the old, run-down American Legion Hall serving as the congregation's temporary sanctuary. Coming from All Saints Pasadena, with its nineteenth-century, stone and stained-glass building, we were disappointed to say the least. We circled the parking lot several times before getting up our courage to go inside.

Folding chairs in narrow rows faced a wooden cross hanging on the front wall decorated with red, plastic flowers. An organist was belting out a gospel tune on a loud electronic organ. The service hadn't begun, but already the place was packed, and the people were spontaneously singing with the prelude. Gary and I squeezed into place just as the choir entered to the sounds of a trumpet fanfare.

At the end of the enthusiastic processional, the congregation burst into applause. We soon learned that the people in this church responded to every musical number, almost every sermon, and even an occasional offering appeal with loud and enthusiastic praise. There was something deeply moving about the way these people loved and encouraged each other. Almost from the first hymn, Gary and I found ourselves choking back involuntary tears.

When pastor Ken Martin stood to speak, his gifts as a preacher and teacher were immediately apparent. When his associate, Wendy Foxworth, prayed or read the Scriptures, we were equally inspired. Over the next few years, in that strange, ugly, wonderful little place, every time Ken or Wendy stood to call the congregation to worship, I noticed the same mysterious lump forming in my throat. Invariably, when they read the lesson or prayed the pastoral prayer, I felt my stomach tighten with excitement and my hands begin to tremble. By the time Leroy Dyssart, at the piano, led the choir and the congregation in his moving arrangement of the Lord's Prayer, tears were flowing down my cheeks. And during the sermon or the Communion that followed, almost invariably the tears would flow again.

It was strange how the services never failed to move me. Every Sunday, when Ken or Wendy looked out over that little crowd and dared to proclaim that God loved gay and lesbian people without reservation, I always cried. I didn't understand it. Then one morning, at the door, when I asked Ken why he never preached about sin or judgment, but only about God's love and grace, he smiled and answered without hesitation, "The people who come to this church have heard enough about sin and judgment. It's time they heard about love for a change."

From that day, I understood. Although there are a few wonderful exceptions, such as All Saints Episcopal in Pasadena, in almost every heterosexual congregation, a homosexual feels condemned by God, by the pastor, and by most of the members of the church. All my life, I had felt condemned everywhere, but especially in church. At the UFMCC congregations, I felt safe, accepted, and at home at last.

While we were worshiping with Ken and Wendy in the Valley, Gary and I met the Reverend Elder Troy Perry, the founder of UFMCC, the first Christian denomination ministering primarily to gay, lesbian, bisexual, and transgendered people. Troy was a gentle bear of a man with intense, flashing eyes and the fiery gifts of a charismatic evangelist. In his clerical robes, he looked more like a Greek Orthodox archbishop than a gay, evangelical pastor, and when he stood to preach, scientists at Caltech could measure the results on their seismic instruments.

After being rejected by his own Christian denomination in 1968, the Reverend Mr. Perry, a pastor already known for his courageous mix of piety and gay activism, invited a handful of his homosexual friends to his home in Los Angeles for an evening of Bible study and prayer. We were surprised to learn that the first little congregation in his living room had grown to be the Universal Fellowship of Metropolitan Community Churches, the largest and one of the oldest gay and lesbian organization in the world. The congregation that Gary and I were attending in the Valley proved to be only one of more than three hundred UFMCC churches in North and South America, Europe, Africa, Indonesia, Australia, and New Zealand.

Several weeks after this first visit to the Valley MCC congregation, I got a final contract to write the Jim and Tammy Bakker story. Gary had a few weeks of vacation time available, so I asked him to go with me to Heritage USA on the border between North and South Carolina to help me gather the boxes of data we would need to write a first-rate Bakker autobiography. We lived in the Effram Zimbalist, Jr., Suite at the Heritage Grand Hotel with complete freedom to wander around the first major religious theme park and television studio in history, to visit offices and interview staff, and to sprint backstage behind Jim and Tammy as they rushed from one live television appearance to the other.

Few people outside the PTL television family took the Bakkers seriously, but after months of research and weeks of on-site observation, I stood in awe of what they had accomplished in their short, productive lives. Jim and Tammy were born and reared "dirt poor." Until she lived in a college dorm, Tammy never even had regular, indoor plumbing. Neither Bakker had any formal education, and they were kicked out of an unaccredited Bible college for getting married toward the end of their freshman year. Jim knew nothing about television before he, Tammy, and their puppets had their own live show. The Bakkers learned television the hard way: writing their own scripts, building their own sets, broadcasting live from primitive, cramped studios with borrowed lights and secondhand cameras, and begging for support from their ever-growing audience of loyal, loving fans.

One day, history will tell the real story of Jim and Tammy Bakker's considerable influence on religious television. In fact, they were not only the energy and the genius behind their own once-powerful PTL broadcast network, but they also contributed greatly to the early stages of the media empires built by Jan and Paul Crouch, and Pat Robertson as well. In fact, Jim Bakker was the original host of the program that would become Pat's "700 Club."

The production and administrative demands that Jim and Tammy put on themselves were unfathomable. When I last visited Heritage USA, just before the Bakkers' dreams collapsed, Jim and Tammy alone were producing as many live and videotaped programs as most networks. Their live audiences were larger and more enthusiastic than any audiences in Los Angeles or in New York. And their loyal viewers, from across North America and around the world, were glad to pay the bills.

Both Bakkers arrived at their television studios before dawn and stayed until late into the night. Tammy cohosted the early-morning live PTL telecast in Studio A, interviewing authors and celebrity guests, singing with the orchestra, bantering with the huge audience, and moving through elaborate production routines without rehearsal. When the final titles rolled, Tammy rushed to Studio B where her live cooking show was about to begin with Tammy hosting, cooking, interviewing, giving advice, singing, sharing news, making appeals, and offering premiums. With that show done, she rushed to Studio C to videotape special songs she had no time to practice, interview authors about books she had no time to read, and share "from her heart" moving stories set to music she had no time to rehearse.

It's no wonder that occasionally Tammy burst into spontaneous tears. It's also no wonder that Jim lost track of what he had promised or never quite figured out in advance how he would deliver on those same promises. I am not excusing the Bakkers for their serious mistakes in judgment, but I am convinced that most of Jim and Tammy's loyal viewers would have sent in their pledges even if the Bakkers hadn't offered those ill-fated time-share schemes. In fact, the Bakkers should have taken a lesson from Jerry Falwell and Pat Robertson, who seldom offered anything real for the donations they solicited. You can measure hotel space. You can't measure "upholding America's family values."

Gary and I were both relieved and grateful when the appeals court reduced Jim Bakker's forty-five-year prison term. He may have been dishonest, but it was cruel and unjust punishment to sentence Jimmy to serve more years than a rapist, a Wall Street junk-bond salesman who robbed billions from his clients, or even some cold-blooded killers. Jim's original prison term was three times longer than Charles Rothenberg's sentence for pouring kerosene on his son and setting him ablaze.

We didn't watch Jim and Tammy's PTL program regularly before I met them, but Noni did as did millions like her. Without raising political issues, their heart-felt music and their moving testimonials to faith brought inspiration and comfort to people across the nation. The Bakkers had not joined with the religious right in their crusade to superimpose their vision of morality on the rest of us. In fact, they risked their own success to reach out to gay and lesbian people across the barriers the religious right had built.

Their courageous interview of the Reverend Steve Pieters was just one example. Steve was a gay clergyman and the director of the national HIV-AIDS program sponsored by the UFMCC. He had lived with AIDS for more than a decade. Throughout the terrible plague, Steve had struggled to mobilize Christian churches across America on behalf of those with HIV and AIDS. It had been a long, frustrating task. Most pastors and their congregations showed no interest or concern as more than eighty thousand gay Americans up to that time had died from this disease.

Of all the religious television celebrities, only Jim and Tammy Bakker invited Steve to share his desperate message with their viewers. With genuine tears of concern in her eyes, Tammy interviewed Steve, turned to her audience, and begged them in Jesus' name to be sensitive and generous with those who suffered. Even when it meant risking their viewers' disapproval and losing their viewers' support, Jim and Tammy reached out to gay and lesbian people, not to endorse or approve, but to demonstrate Christian love in a time of terrible crises. I, for one, am grateful for their courage and sorry for their suffering.

The Bakker autobiography was never released. Their true story is waiting to be told. After returning to Lynchburg in 1987 to ghostwrite a second time for Jerry Falwell, this time his autobiography, *Strength for the Journey,* I was hired to write the story of Demos Shakarian, the founder of the Full Gospel Business Men's Fellowship International. Demos was considered one of the pillars in the modern charismatic movement, committed to the renewal of the first-century gifts of the Holy Spirit, among them physical healing and speaking in tongues.

Demos died recently and I'm sorry that I didn't have a chance to say good-bye. I loved the old man and admired his grace and grit. A California dairyman of Armenian ancestry, Demos and his wife traveled across the nation and around the world sharing their enthusiasm for the Christian faith and demonstrating in their way the Holy Spirit's gifts.

But when I met Demos in 1988, he had suffered a near-fatal stroke. Seriously paralyzed on one side, the old man struggled bravely for more than a year to recover his powers of speech and movement. Day after day, as I interviewed this Christian pioneer, he dragged himself around the exercise railings mounted in his backyard or walked with his cane up and down the sidewalk in front of his home in southern California.

When Demos finally returned to address his cheering followers from the platform of the Anaheim Convention Center, he hobbled bravely across the stage without his cane and slurred his barely understandable greetings to the crowd. Everyone in the huge arena cried, including me. Our proposed title for the book was perfect: *Another Kind of Miracle.* Although God had not granted Demos an instant cure for his pain and his paralysis, God's Spirit had been with him every difficult, demanding day of recovery.

Apparently, that kind of miracle was not good enough. People close to Demos decided that it might show "lack of faith." Demos's wife told me in their kitchen, "We can't let the people down." Fearing a demise in Demos's influence if the truth were known about his long, difficult, and still partial recovery, and sincerely concerned about the effect his struggle would have upon the simple believer, they sent a powerful lawyer to collect the finished manuscript, warned me not to question their decision, and walked away without even considering my losses in time and money.

It was a rather painful and expensive lesson. Demos had told me his real story, and that real story was so much more inspiring and so much more helpful than all the hollow, misleading talk of miracles that followed his brief return to ministry before his death. But apparently, to someone powerful in Demos's family or in his organization, keeping up the image was much more important than dealing openly with the truth.

They had made claims about God's healing power. They had built an international movement on those claims. That movement and its various bureaucracies and bureaucrats required faithful, generous support. So when their founder and leader didn't get the kind of miracle he had promised them, they buried the truth. In spite of Demos's own experience, they were unwilling to reexamine the original claim about God's healing power. It is the same principle upon which the religious right builds their opposition to homosexuality: when your claims are proven false, refuse to examine the evidence, and for "the greater good" stand by your old claims even if it means burying the truth and wasting lives.

In 1989, shortly after *Another Kind of Miracle* was postponed indefinitely, Word Books sent me to Manila to write *Aquino*, the dramatic, true story of President Corazon Aquino and the Aquino family's three-generation saga of political leadership in the Philippines. While I was commuting back and forth to that beautiful island nation, the communist empire began to unravel. Even as we watched in shock and disbelief, Marxist socialism collapsed and the cold war came crashing to a close.

In May 1989 a million Chinese youths crowded into Tiananmen Square to say "No!" to communism and "Yes!" to freedom. Tanks crushed many of those courageous young people, but their cries for freedom had been heard and soon echoed across Asia and Eastern Europe.

On June 4, 1989, the people of Lech Walesa's Solidarity party scored an overwhelming victory over communism at the ballot box in their first free parliamentary elections.

In Hungary, on September 10, 1989, in one day, 57,000 people walked across the border into Austria, saying with their lives, "The communist system has failed us. We want no more of it."

In East Berlin, on October 18, 1989, East Germans united to force their communist bosses out of power. A million hands reached out to tear down the Berlin Wall.

In December 1989, the people of Czechoslovakia elected Václav Havel their first noncommunist head of state in forty years.

And on October 6, 1990, with the Soviet Union in economic and political chaos, Soviet president Mikhail Gorbachev and Boris Yeltsin, president of the Russian Republic, began a joint "500-Day Plan" ending Marxist socialism in the USSR and moving that nation decisively toward democracy and free enterprise.

With all the celebrating, no one even dreamed that the end of communism would mean the beginning of a whole new era in the history of gay bashing by the religious right. Their television and radio ministries had been financed in large part by using the communist threat to raise funds and recruit volunteers. Without communism, Jerry, Pat, and James had only two issues hot enough to mobilize their forces: abortion and homosexuality. In 1990, the religious right launched a campaign against us that still shocks and terrifies me with its painful and deadly long-range consequences.

After *Aquino* was published, Word Books sent me back to Manila for one last conversation with President Corazon Aquino. Across the world, tyrants, communists and noncommunists alike, were being chased out of power. "And it all began in the Philippines," Cory said, smiling. We were sitting together in her presidential office in the guesthouse of the Malacanang Palace, once the home of Ferdinand and Imelda Marcos, tyrants who had been deposed by the almost bloodless People Power revolution in 1986.

"Ninoy really believed that the Filipino people were worth dying for," she said slowly, looking at her husband's picture on her desk. Ninoy had been the youngest mayor, the youngest governor, and the youngest senator in the history of the Philippines. When his popularity threatened Marcos's hold on power, Ferdinand, with U.S. consent, declared martial law and had Ninoy arrested on trumped-up charges and imprisoned in Fort Bonifacio for almost eight years, most of them in solitary confinement. When Ninoy needed heart surgery, Marcos exiled Ninoy to the U.S. hoping he would die there. Instead,

Ninoy recovered his health, taught at Harvard University, and plotted his return to Manila.

"We all urged him to stay in America," Cory recalled. "We were afraid that he would be imprisoned again or even killed upon his return to the Philippines. But Ninoy wouldn't listen." When asked what kind of revolution he would lead to free his people, Ninoy quoted these ancient words from the prophet Zechariah: "Not by might, nor by power, but by my spirit, says the Lord."

On Sunday, August 21, 1983, Ninoy's plane landed at Manila's International Airport. He came in peace without one single weapon, hoping to topple a regime that stayed in power with bullets, bombs, and bayonets. As Ninoy walked down the boarding ramp, one of Marcos's men shot and killed him just a few hundred yards away from where masses of Filipinos were waiting to welcome him home. The shock and the anger raised by Ninoy's death brought millions of Filipinos into the streets to mourn his death, to protest the Marcos' tyranny, and in three short years to elect Ninoy's wife, Cory, president of the Philippines.

Cory and I talked a long time that day about Ninoy and her memories of his love and courage. She accepted a first-edition copy of *Aquino,* thanked me graciously, and posed patiently for the obligatory presidential photo.

As I flew back across the Pacific that same evening, I remembered these words from one of Ninoy Aquino's prison dairies. "A time comes in a man's life when he must prefer a meaningful death to a meaningless life." I was flying back to my beloved country where gay and lesbian people were under a merciless media attack from the religious right. Their lies were killing us. In every generation, people like Ninoy Aquino or Martin Luther King or Dietrich Bonhoeffer had to decide between standing against the lies or risking their lives to oppose them. As the day ended and the world below me balanced on the edge of darkness, I wondered if my years as a ghost would ever end or if somehow, in the time I had left on this magnificent planet, I would ever find my own voice and speak my own truth?

chapter 12

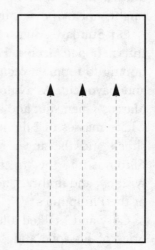

1990–91,

One Last Year of Silence

$\mathcal{E}$arly *in 1990, Gary and I moved to an apartment in Laguna Beach,* California. Lyla had been appointed director of developments and stewardship at All Saints Episcopal Church in Pasadena. Erinn was working on her elementary-school teaching credential at Azusa Pacific. Michael was at Wesleyan University in Connecticut, thinking seriously about becoming a writer like his dad (only better). Gary's work kept him in Los Angeles during the week, but we spent Wednesday nights and weekends together at Laguna Beach.

Over the years, I had researched and written many of my books and films in Laguna. That quaint, gay-friendly village on the sea, just fifty miles south of Los Angeles, with its community of artists and writers, had always felt like home to me. For twenty years, Lyla and I had taken the children on weekend and summer vacations to the Laguna Riviera, a rustic, inexpensive hotel on the beach with a welcome sign that reads: "Ye can't be both grand and comfortable." I taught the children to swim in the Riviera pool when they were still infants.

In the restaurants and cafés of Laguna, Lyla and I had talked, argued, and cried our way through the best and worst of times. Gary and I liked to browse in Laguna's antique mall and swap underwater adventure stories with scuba divers at Diver's Cove. And for more than a quarter of a century, it was during walks on the beaches or the bluffs of Laguna Beach that I had felt closest to God.

During one of our daylong visits to Laguna shortly after our divorce seemed inevitable, Lyla gave me a beautiful ring made from a five-dollar American gold piece. "On the front is Lady Liberty," Lyla said as she slipped it on my finger. "You are free now to do what you need to do. But remember," she added with a kind of mischievous grin, "this coin, like your life, has two sides." Immediately, I took off the ring and looked at the other face of the gold piece. Below the words *In God We Trust* had been engraved a beautiful family of eagles: a father, a mother, and their two young. Every day that ring reminded me of Lyla's incredible love and understanding.

The struggle was over. Stressful, anxious days, tearful days, were still ahead. Certain issues remained to be settled, but the decision had been made. I was a gay man, and with God's help I would do my best to live my new life with integrity. Now, after almost thirty years of "ex-gay" therapy and tens of thousands of dollars down the drain, that new life had begun. And though I was committed to love and care for Lyla and the children for the rest of our lives, I was also free to make choices about my own future that I had never made before.

I was standing at another crossroads in my life, and once again I had come to Laguna to write and research, but above all to think and pray. Almost every morning, before sunrise, I walked alone to Shaw's Cove and climbed my favorite cliff above the sea to watch the sun rise upon the Pacific. Almost every evening as the sun set, I hiked Cliff Drive along the Heisler Park trail north from Las Brisas to Seal Rock.

Every day, morning until night, even while I was writing, I thought, prayed, and struggled with my decision to remain silent and in the closet or to come out and tell the truth about homosexuality as I had experienced it from my childhood. I was free, but would I content myself to enjoy my new freedom in privacy and silence, or did I have an obligation to God and to myself to go public, to take a stand that might be painful and costly on behalf of those who were still suffering, as I had suffered, lives of confusion, repression, guilt, loneliness, and fear?

While I wrestled with my future, I continued ghostwriting to make a living. In 1990, while in Laguna, I finished *Standing on the Promises,* the autobiography of W. A. Criswell, for forty-five years the senior pastor of Dallas's First Baptist Church, the largest Baptist congregation in America. Criswell was Billy Graham's old pastor and one of the patriarchs of modern Christian fundamentalism. In 1991, I was ghostwriting speeches for Ollie North and other lay leaders of the religious right and ghostwriting articles for the *Reader's Digest,* including the Reverend Edward Victor Hill's tribute to his wife, "The Unforgettable Jane Edna Hill."

Criswell, North, and even E. V. Hill, the pastor of the Mount Zion Missionary Baptist Church in Los Angeles, were all leaders of the religious right. And though they weren't bashing gays to support their various enterprises at the time, I heard each of them make untrue claims and misleading comments against us on radio or on television while I was monitoring their broadcasts in Laguna. Even though I was dependent on ghostwriting for the religious right to pay our living expenses and my children's school bills, I knew it was long past time for me to take my stand against the fictions they were spreading about gay and lesbian people.

During the 1990s, when the religious right shifted the focus of their fund-raising appeals from the "evil communist empire" to "the homosexual agenda for the destruction of America," I began collecting samples of their terrible lies against us. One of my early hate-mail "treasures" was an emergency Jerry Falwell fund-raiser sent in an oversize envelope (five by fourteen inches) with a bold red banner across its face stating simply: "Declaration of War . . . Official Notice."

Jerry Falwell was officially declaring war against gay and lesbian people. Why? Because, according to Jerry, homosexuals "have a godless, humanistic scheme for our nation—a plan which will destroy America's traditional moral values." He went on to claim that our "goal" as gays and lesbians was the "complete elimination of God and Christianity from American society [and] is being designed right now!"

It was the same tired, old lie that Adolf Hitler and Heinrich

Himmler had used in 1936 when they created a Reich Central Office for the Combating of Homosexuality and Abortion. The Nazis, like the religious right, stirred up that ancient pool of misinformation and hatred against homosexuals to recruit new volunteers and mobilize their troops. In a February 18, 1937, speech to the officer corps of Hitler's storm troopers, Himmler warned "that if we continue to have this burden [of homosexuality] in Germany, without being able to fight it, then that is the end of Germany, and the end of the Germanic world."

Without knowing it, Jerry was using a page right out of Hitler's book to take advantage of people's fear and confusion about homosexuality to raise funds and recruit volunteer "soldiers" for his cause. In that fund-raising letter to an estimated 5 million people on Jerry's old Moral Majority mailing list, there was a "Declaration of War" form asking Christian Americans to sign up in Jerry's battle against gay and lesbian Americans. Those who donated $35 or more to "keep the Old Time Gospel Hour on the air" would get an antigay videotape as well.

Pat Robertson quickly followed Jerry's lead. In my little apartment at Laguna Beach, I watched Jerry and Pat on television with my VCR tape recorder running constantly. Almost daily on his "700 Club," Pat was warning faithful viewers like my mother and father about the imaginary "gay agenda" that would "bring ruin to the American family." Invariably, those antigay warnings ended with an appeal for donations to help Pat stop the homosexual "menace."

While in Laguna, I joined the 700 Club and sent small donations to dozens of other antigay organizations on the religious right so that I would be able to receive and collect their mailings. Pat and the others were sending out millions of letters loaded with half-truths, hyperboles, and lies about gay people and our so called "threat" to the nation.

James Dobson's "Focus on the Family" broadcasts, newsletters, and fund-raising appeals also featured antihomosexual attacks on an almost daily basis. Dobson and I had been neighbors in Sierra Madre. We sat side by side in the bleachers at Maranatha High School football games with his son on the field and my daughter leading cheers. In his attacks on gay people, he seemed obsessed with such false and vicious claims that homosexuals "threatened family values," were out to "recruit the young," and that Christian churches would be required to hire practicing gays in spite of the danger we "pose to their children."

Dobson, and his Washington lobbyist, Gary Bauer, were the source of some of the most vicious antigay propaganda that I collected.

A fund-raising letter for Lou Sheldon's Traditional Values Coalition, written by his daughter, Andrea, went even further. She claimed that a large gay/lesbian march on Washington was attended mostly by "militant and angry homosexuals demanding the right to sodomize 16 year old boys." In fact, I attended that march of more than half a million loyal gay and lesbian Americans with more than two thousand gay and lesbian Christians from UFMCC churches alone.

Sheldon's ugly, inflammatory lie sent out to raise funds from millions of people, including the twenty-five thousand fundamentalist churches on his mailing list, was inexcusable. While collecting and analyzing data about hate crimes in America, I began to realize that the long-range consequences of those lies by Sheldon and the others lead directly to the suffering and death of God's homosexual children.

James Kennedy's Coral Ridge Ministries had practically funded its television outreach on similar disgusting, inflammatory antigay propaganda. "Honestly," Kennedy sneered cynically in one of his typically blatant fund-raising letters, "would you want your son, daughter, or grandchild sharing a shower, foxhole, or blood with a homosexual?"

In a "Homosexuality Survey" Kennedy asked the same misleading, rhetorical questions that Hitler and Himmler used in speeches to inflame and recruit the German people: "Do you believe homosexuals should be given special privileges under the law that would force employers—including schools and churches—to hire them?" (Implying quite falsely that such laws were being considered.) "Should employers and landlords who disapprove of homosexual behavior on biblical grounds be allowed to refuse employment and tenancy to openly practicing homosexuals?" (Once again implying that gays and lesbians should lose their jobs or apartments simply because we are gay.) "Do you believe our government and health agencies should treat AIDS as they do any other deadly disease, such as pox or tuberculosis?" (Raising again an idea that has been rejected by the entire medical community that people with AIDS should be treated like lepers, that separation and quarantine would help end this terrible HIV plague.)

I wrote Jim Kennedy's most popular film, *Like a Mighty Army*. We had known each other and worked together on various projects for many years. Surely he knew that hundreds of gay and lesbian people were connected with his church in Coral Ridge and with his TV and film ministries. He knew better than to condemn us with the avalanche of insinuations, innuendos, and lies that he was using to raise money, but he needed an easy target to raise quick cash, and gay and lesbian people seemed the easiest target in sight.

By sending out similar inflammatory antigay fund-raising appeals, Concerned Women for America's founder, Beverly LaHaye, was raising millions of dollars to support her six-hundred-thousand-member organization, the largest women's organization in this country. In 1991, she asked for donations to cover the cost of bodyguards because "gay activist groups . . . have targeted me. They would love to silence me," she claims, "and shut down CWA."

The boldness of these antihomosexual exaggerations amazed and frightened me. Beverly LaHaye, for example, quoting a supporter, claimed that gay activists "will outlast you. They have shut down almost every evangelical voice in America because of their threats. They have long memories. They will haunt you everywhere you go. They are hooked up by computers. They have time and money to go after you. You better count the cost." The flagrant absurdity of her charges stunned me and left me wondering how far my old friends and acquaintances would go in their war against gay and lesbian people.

And yet, when confronted by the press, leaders of the religious right insisted they had no desire to discriminate against us. To confuse the issue further, they declared that gay and lesbian Americans were demanding "special rights," and though they never made clear what "special rights" we were supposedly demanding, they began to organize a nationwide, precinct-by-precinct campaign against us. In fact, with their campaign to end our "special rights" they launched a movement that still threatens the very democratic foundations on which this country is built.

In Laguna, for the first time in my life, I took out the U.S. Constitution and began to read it seriously. In the First Amendment of the Bill of Rights, for example, our forefathers insisted that the "Congress shall make no laws to establish religion." Yet my old clients on the religious right were claiming that we were "a Christian nation with moral absolutes built on biblical truth. " They were plainly working toward that day when Christian fundamentalism, their version and its ideology, would prevail. It had become apparent that they don't believe in democracy, not really, but in some kind of theocracy, with them, of course, as God's representatives. They also don't believe in the separation of church and state, but long for the day when the power of government will be in their "trustworthy" hands.

They were organizing across the country to gain political and not just spiritual power. School board by school board, precinct by precinct, voter by voter, they were determined to gain control of the nation's political process, promising their supporters that, once in power, they would "cleanse the nation" of sin and of sinners. And the more I watched and listened, the more it was for certain that gays and lesbians were at the top of their purge list.

The Bill of Rights guaranteed that the Congress will pass no laws "to abridge the freedom of speech." And yet the religious right wanted gay and lesbian voices silenced. They even worked to quiet those who would speak or write on our behalf. When educators dared to suggest that gays and lesbians could be competent, loving, responsible parents, the religious right organized to get their voices silenced. When the school superintendent in New York City approved a curriculum that even mentioned gay and lesbian young people, he was run out of office by the religious right.

The Bill of Rights guaranteed that Congress will do nothing "to abridge the freedom of the press." Yet the religious right wanted the "liberal media" closed down because so many educated and informed reporters and columnists disagreed with their position on such issues as homosexuality. My old clients were also demanding that the shelves of the nation's libraries be stripped of gay and lesbian periodicals, of our authors, our poetry and fiction, even our biographies. They even wanted books and authors removed who said anything positive about us.

The Bill of Rights guaranteed that Congress will do nothing to abridge the right "of the people peaceably to assemble." And yet the religious right wanted our parades canceled, our rallies shouted down, our community centers, schools, and even our churches closed.

Pat Robertson and the others weren't satisfied to defame and malign us in order to raise money with their barrage of antihomosexual propaganda. Early in 1990, as I monitored their progress from Laguna Beach, it was clear that the religious right was launching a massive campaign against the civil rights of gay and lesbian people. Faster than I could believe, Pat Robertson's Christian Coalition mobilized more than 250,000 members and 550 chapters in 50 states. They were moving quickly to organize at least 1 million Americans, representing every precinct and every school district in America. And it was painfully clear that one of the Christian Coalition's central goals was to oppose civil rights legislation that would protect gay and lesbian people from discrimination.

In Laguna, reading once again the fascinating and frightening history of Europe just before World War II, I became intrigued by the similarities of the tactics of the religious right to those of Hitler, Himmler, Goebbels, and the Nazi Third Reich. I know there will be those who think me an alarmist when I draw any comparisons of the tactics used by my old clients with those of Hitler and his henchmen. I hope my critics are right and I am wrong. I still remember seeing the words of George Santayana hanging above the bodies in Jonestown: "Those who cannot remember the past are condemned to repeat it."

Although I feel strongly that the lessons of history must be relearned by every generation, Jim Jones misused history to terrify, isolate, and control people. I don't want to be an alarmist, using stories about Hitler and Germany's gays to create fear and suspicion. I want to bring hope and understanding to this discussion. Chicken Little is *not* my hero. I don't want to be perceived as a bitter, angry man running frantically about, yelling "the sky is falling" at the top of my voice. In fact, I am positive in my outlook for the future of lesbians and gays in this country. Look how far we have come already.

When I began my journey toward self-acceptance in the early 1970s, there were forty-nine states with anti-sodomy laws. Now, thanks to the amazing courage and commitment of lesbian and gay activists and their allies over the past decades, there is less than half that number. Slowly, civil right and hate crime laws are being changed in cities, counties, and states across the nation to guarantee the Constitutional rights granted all Americans in spite of their sexual orientation. A handful of great American corporations and even a few local governments are beginning to grant the partners of lesbian and gay workers the same benefits granted the partners of their heterosexual employees. Case by case, the courts are declaring that lesbians and gays can no longer be hunted down and hounded out of the military.

More local police departments are acting quickly to recognize hate crimes against us and more local courts and judges are prosecuting gay-bashers to the full extent of the law. Wise and courageous educators are beginning to recognize and help meet the needs of lesbian and gay students. Everyday, more print, radio and television reporters and talk-show hosts are telling our side of the story and making our issues clear at last. And one by one, thoughtful Americans are beginning to realize that the religious right is wrong to stir up again in this generation the old anti-homosexual superstitions, hatreds, and fears.

Nevertheless, in spite of all the progress in understanding and acceptance we have made, leaders on the religious right continue to mount an ever more hysterical campaign against us. Finding it more and more difficult to raise enough money and to recruit enough volunteers, their claims against lesbians and gays grow more lurid and more far-fetched every day. You cannot listen to a religious radio or television station very long without hearing another evangelist or talk show host or radio counselor warn this nation about the "threat of the gay agenda." With every print or media warning comes the suggestion that lesbians and gays have too much power in this country, that their immoral presence should be purged, and that their civil rights should be withdrawn.

The similarities between those tactics of Hitler's Third Reich are unmistakable. The terrible suffering of European Jews under Hitler has long been documented, but early in his campaign to "liberate Germany," Hitler, as a fund-raising, manpower mobilizing technique, also promised to end civil rights for homosexuals.

Although most German states had decriminalized homosexuality during the Enlightenment, Hitler found and threatened to enforce Paragraph 175 from the 1871 Prussian criminal code punishing by imprisonment "a male who indulges in criminally indecent activity with another male." In the beginning, it appeared that the law would just be used to frighten homosexuals back into their closets and to gain support for Hitler's grab for total power, but soon after its adoption, Heinrich Himmler insisted that the law be enforced.

At first, I was confident that my old clients were just using their anti-gay propaganda to raise money and gain power. But as their claims against us began to reach a kind of hysterical, feverish pitch, I thought again of Hitler's advice to his propagandists: "The great masses of people," he said, "will more easily fall victims to a big lie than a small one." As I continued to collect the bigger and bigger lies being told against us by my old clients, I began to wonder what would happen if, in fact, our nation's economy continued on its downward spiral. Whom would they blame for the nation's "drift towards immorality"? How far would they go to stop that "drift"? What would happen to the human rights of gay and lesbian people if a zealous member or even a close friend of the religious right was elected president? Would he actually follow through on their threats to "purge" gay and lesbian people from this nation?

Up until 1933, Germany, too, had provided a fairly safe and enlightened home for its gay and lesbian citizens. Berlin especially was a world center, not just for gay bars, restaurants, cabarets, and theater, but for all kinds of gay and lesbian organizations, informal groups and special interest clubs, gay community centers, gay-friendly libraries, gay books, magazines, films, even gay religious groups and gay-friendly churches.

Dr. Magnus Hirschfeld's Institute of Sexual Science in Berlin was the world center for enlightened research about homosexuality, conducting studies, offering seminars and discussion groups, and providing scholars and the public a library of more than ten thousand priceless volumes covering the history, psychology, physiology, spirituality, and biographies of gay and lesbian people. Gays and lesbians began to feel fully accepted, and though there were plenty of clues that storm clouds were gathering, few of them took Adolf Hitler or his brownshirts very seriously.

Then on January 30, 1933, Hitler was named chancellor of Germany. Just a few weeks later, on February 23, Hitler used one of his first major decrees to ban all homosexual-rights organizations. Still, few Germans believed that Hitler would actually use the seldom-enforced Paragraph 175 to arrest or imprison, let alone slaughter, homosexuals. Parliament was in place and the gays and lesbians of that great, enlightened country assumed that German law and German courts would protect them.

On February 27, 1933, Hitler burned the Reichstag (parliament), blamed the communists, and seized absolute power in Germany. In a sudden, unthinkable turn of events, the nation's gay and lesbian citizens had no one left to protect them. On May 6, 1933, Magnus Hirschfeld's prestigious Institute for Sexual Science was demolished by a mob of chanting pro-Nazi students. The irreplaceable library Hirschfeld had assembled was thrown book by book to the streets below and burned in a huge bonfire on the Opernplatz. During the same summer of 1933, Hitler's SA troops began to raid gay bars. Almost immediately, the arrests began.

Using Paragraph 175 as their excuse, Hitler's police broke into the offices of homosexual organizations and gay or gay-friendly periodicals, confiscated mailing lists, broke into the homes of the men whose names appeared on those lists, and demanded their address books to expand their ever-increasing cycle of terror, arrest, and imprisonment. In 1934, 766 male German citizens were convicted and imprisoned for "indecent activity with another male."

In 1935, Nazi law banned all gay gathering places and outlawed homosexuals as "sexual vagrants." By 1936, the annual number of gay men arrested and imprisoned exceeded four thousand. In 1938 alone, more than eight thousand German gay men (or suspected gay men) fell victim to Paragraph 175. Before the Third Reich ended, more than fifty thousand gay men were convicted on charges of "sexual deviation"; more than half of them were arrested between 1937 and 1939, those years when Hitler needed an easy target to gain support and mobilize his power.

Once gay (or suspected gay) Germans had served their prison terms under Paragraph 175, Himmler had them thrown into concentration camps where they were used as slaves or summarily shot. "That wasn't a punishment," Himmler claimed, "but simply the extinguishing of abnormal life. It had to be got rid of, just as we pull out weeds, throw them on a heap, and burn them." When Allied armies liberated Nazi concentration camps they freed Jews, other ethnic minorities, gypsies and most political prisoners. But they kept the gays in prison. In fact, Paragraph 175 was not repealed in Germany until 1968.

After a year in Laguna, reading and rereading the data, I began to see awful similarities between Germany in the early 1930s and the U.S. in 1990 and 1991. With all our progress, state laws, similar to Paragraph 175, outlawing "sodomy" (even between consenting adults in private) were on the books in twenty-four states (including nine states that prohibit only homosexual sodomy). And in 1986, the U.S. Supreme Court had gone on record in the *Bowers v. Hardwick* case, officially supporting state-court decisions against consenting "sodomy."

But would these laws ever be enforced? Would gay men or lesbians ever be imprisoned or even executed for the "crime" of loving one another? How far would the religious right go in their campaign against gay and lesbian Americans?

The answer that I discovered during that last year of my silence was terrifying, not just for homosexuals like myself, but for all Americans who believed in freedom and in democracy. During my employment as a ghostwriter for the religious right, many of my clients, especially Pat Robertson, spoke of R. J. Rushdoony with respect and admiration. Rushdoony, a prolific author and student of the Bible, was the president of the Chalcedon Foundation, called by the *Los Angeles Times* "an influential religious think tank that has given rise to much of the religious right's political activism in recent years."

Rushdoony was the father of Christian "Reconstructionism," which holds that believers should actively remake America's declining, secular, humanistic society through strict adherence to biblical commands. "Resurgent Christianity," according to Rushdoony, demands that Christians obey *literally* both Old and New Testament law. I still have a handwritten letter from Rushdoony himself making clear how far the religious right should go in their war against homosexuals. "God in His law," Rushdoony wrote, "requires the death penalty for homosexuals."

It wasn't a new idea. Death had been the penalty for homosexual acts during most of the medieval and early modern periods of European history, a policy Heinrich Himmler had endorsed. In Germany in May 1935, one Professor Eckhardt had published an article entitled "Unnatural Indecency Deserves Death" in which he declared it the responsibility of the new right to purge the nation of the "homosexual threat."

Sitting in Laguna's public library, reading all that frightening recent history, I began to see the terrible connection between the resolve of Hitler, Himmler, and Eckhardt to kill all homosexuals, and the similar feelings of R. J. Rushdoony and his disciples on the religious right, who were determined to take the Bible literally in resolving the "homosexual question." They hadn't invented the evil spirit of homophobia and homohatred that was stalking our land, but they were stirring up that ancient ghost once again without asking themselves where their antihomosexual campaign might lead this nation.

My old clients on the religious right were misleading millions of Americans to fear and to hate gay and lesbian people, to discriminate and legislate against us, and inadvertently motivating extremists and crazies to terrorize, abuse, and even kill us. In Laguna, I began to see firsthand the immediate and long-term damage of those antihomosexual broadcasts and sermons, books, magazines, and videos in terms of ruined lives, broken families, and murdered souls.

In 1989, there had been seven thousand reported and documented incidents of violence and harassment against lesbians and gay men in the United States. Bias crimes against homosexuals rose by 122 percent in New York City in the first five months of 1990. A study of five major American cities concluded that violence against lesbians and gays had increased 172 percent over the past five years. In 1991, reported hate crimes against gays and lesbians were at runaway levels. And it was happening all around me, even in Laguna Beach.

Before I arrived in Laguna in 1990, two gay men had been killed in separate incidents in Heisler Park, blocks from our apartment, by gay bashers out looking for "queers." Before I left Laguna, Jeff Michael Raines, a former high school football player, and at least eight juveniles, most of them students at San Clemente High School, attacked and almost killed Loc Minh Truong, a Vietnamese-American out walking in the evening on the sands of Laguna Beach. One of Raines's friends admitted, "We went looking for fags." Raines and his young friends didn't even ask the Vietnamese-American about his sexual orientation. They just beat and kicked him until his face disappeared in a mass of bashed and bloody tissue. The relatives of that terrible hate-crime victim couldn't even identify Mr. Truong at the South Coast Medical Center where he lay in a coma.

At the end of our first year in Laguna, our landlord refused to renew our lease. We didn't lose our little cottage because we didn't keep it spotless, planted, and cared for, but because we were gay. Seldom did we walk the streets of that "gay-friendly" beach city that visitors passing by on Coast Highway didn't yell "faggots" or "fairies" at us from their passing cars. Twice we dodged full beer bottles that exploded on the sidewalk at our feet. Several of our gay neighbors were victims of serious antigay vandalism; two suffered violent hate crimes against them. And the Christian gays I met in Laguna told me stories of rejection and adversity that left me with a growing sense of anger, shame, and frustration.

Every Tuesday night, I drove into South Laguna for our weekly EC Bible study with forty to fifty other Christian gays and lesbians. Evangelicals Concerned was founded by Dr. Ralph Blair, a New York psychologist, Bible scholar, and evangelical historian, as a safe place for gay Christians to meet, talk, pray, study, and retreat. From the earliest years of my adult struggle, I had been inspired and informed by Dr. Blair's carefully researched booklets, articles, and newsletters. Several times when I was nearly overcome by ambivalence and guilt, I visited Dr. Blair in New York and found great wisdom and comfort in his words.

After Ralph Blair began Evangelicals Concerned as a Friday-night Bible study for his patients and friends in New York, similar EC chapters began to spring up across the country. In a few short years our membership rolls in Los Angeles and Orange County alone included at least five hundred gay and lesbian Christians. In Laguna we had moved from home to home, searching for living rooms large enough to accommodate our growing membership.

Night after night at these EC meetings, I heard true stories from dozens of gay men and lesbians who had grown up in Christian homes and churches just like mine. Their stories left me weak with anger and grief. Each of them had been rejected by pastors, parents, and/or Christian friends. Though they were clergy and lay leaders, though they had served Christ and the church skillfully, faithfully, generously, though they had lived lives of integrity, they had been asked to leave their churches once they told the truth. Many had lost jobs, apartments, friendships, just because they were honest. Others remained in the closet suffering from loneliness and fear.

"This is difficult for me," a young man said during one Tuesday-night discussion. "I have never told anyone why I was sent to the hospital last year. And I'm ashamed to tell it now."

The man began to cry. Several EC guys nearby reached out to comfort him. For a moment, we sat and waited as we had so many times before. Each of us had cried while our friends in the circle had waited, understanding our pain, knowing that in time it would subside.

"When I told my parents that I was gay," he began again softly, "they told me that I was no longer welcome in their home."

Again he paused, shaken by the memory of that terrible moment when his own mom and dad had turned him away for just admitting who he was and who he had always been.

"I went to the garage," he whispered between sobs, "got a bottle of paint thinner, and drank it."

By then, we were all crying with him.

"They had taught me about sharing Jesus' love since I was a child," he said angrily, "and then when I needed a little love of my own, they sent me away."

In Laguna, for the first time, Gary and I began to realize that the Christian church had become our enemy and the enemy of our gay brothers and lesbian sisters. And it wasn't just their rejection that we found to be despicable. For the first time in our lives, we began to see the direct connection between hate crimes and the Christian church. The religious right was banging away at us constantly, but our own denominations, even mainline Protestant denominations, had created such an antigay spirit in the land that it was bringing about psychological violence and physical suffering and even death.

There are churches like All Saints Episcopal in Pasadena and the UFMCC and other independent and mainline gay-friendly congregations across the nation who are demonstrating love to God's gay and lesbian children. But they are the exception. As a rule, the Christian churches of this country, especially the conservative Christian churches associated with the religious right, have become the nation's primary source of antigay bigotry and discrimination. And by default, in their silence and their endless ambivalence, the more liberal, mainline churches approve and support the current campaign of hatred and even violence against us.

It is a staggering notion, but recent studies illustrate that Americans hate gays and lesbians in direct proportion to the number of times they attend their local church. While preparing to write her moving novel *The Drowning of Stephan Jones,* author Bette Green interviewed dozens of young men who had been found guilty of hate crimes against gay and lesbian people. In far too many cases, those young haters came from Christian homes and families.

In his important study *Violence Against Lesbians and Gay Men,* author Gary David Comstock reported that "available studies show that those who attend church regularly and are more 'orthodox,' 'devout,' or 'fundamentalist' tend to be more disapproving [of gay and lesbian people]." He quotes a study by Kinsey, Pomeroy, and Martin concluding that the "ancient religious codes [especially the prohibitions in Leviticus] are still the prime sources of the attitudes, the ideas, the ideals, and the rationalization by which most individuals pattern their sexual lives."

Comstock used two recent examples to illustrate how the ancient words of Moses in the book of Leviticus was still the major source "used to shape and justify social policy and practice toward lesbians and gay men." In 1986, Pope John Paul II wrote, "In Leviticus 18:22 and 20:13, in the course of describing the conditions necessary for belonging to the Chosen people, the author excludes from the People of God those who behave in a homosexual fashion." And in that same year, when the U.S. Supreme Court upheld the constitutionality of the state of Georgia's antisodomy law, the majority opinion stated that "proscriptions against [homosexual] conduct have ancient roots . . . firmly rooted in Judeo-Christian moral and ethical standards." A dissenting opinion objected to this "invocation of Leviticus and Romans."

To make his case for the religious right that "God requires the death penalty for homosexuals," R. J. Rushdoony also quoted Leviticus 20:13. Two thousand years before Christ, the author of that passage wrote these words: "If a man also lie with mankind, as he lieth with a woman, both of them have committed an abomination: they shall surely be put to death." Throughout the ages, this biblical passage had been used as the primary reason to hate and kill homosexuals as it was being used again.

However, in Laguna, when I studied the passage in its context, I could see that the death penalty was also demanded for a variety of other sins as well: A child (or an adult) who curses his father or his mother shall be put to death (Lev. 20:9). If a man commits adultery with another man's wife, both shall be put to death (Lev. 20:10). If a man sleeps with his mother or with his daughter-in-law or his mother-in-law or with his sisters or with an animal, they shall all be put to death (Lev. 20:11, 12, 14, 15, 17). A medium or a wizard shall be put to death (Lev. 20:27). If a priest's daughter becomes a prostitute, she shall be burned with fire (Lev. 21:9). One who works on the Sabbath shall be put to death (Lev. 23:30). One who curses or blasphemes the name of God will also be put to death (Lev. 24:16). If a man even has sex with his wife while she is having her period, both of them shall be cut off from among their people (Lev. 20:18).

Not one legitimate biblical scholar that I could find supported a literal translation of these passages in our modern times. Imagine killing a child for cursing her parents or putting someone to death for working on Sunday or executing a neighbor for using God's name in vain. Even conservative Christian scholars seemed to agree that the warnings were not about ethical or moral issues so much as they were a "Holiness Code" describing acts that caused a Jewish man to be unclean and therefore unable to enter the courtyard of the temple for worship. According to EC founder Ralph Blair, "even the *Fundamentalist Journal* admits that this Code condemns 'idolatrous practices' and 'ceremonial uncleanness,' " and concludes: "We are not bound by these commands today."

And yet R. J. Rushdoony, a Bible "expert" admired and quoted by leaders of the religious right, is clearly on record that Leviticus should be taken literally, at least when it condemns men who lie with other men. Rushdoony is not a literalist. He is a selective literalist, choosing to interpret literally only those texts that suit his predetermined purposes, in this case honoring the ancient, evil, ignorant spirit of superstition and hatred against gay and lesbian people. "God in His law," Rushdoony writes, "requires the death penalty for homosexuals." And leaders of the religious right, though maintaining a thin veneer of civility, follow blindly in his tracks.

I have spent my lifetime reading, memorizing, studying, and teaching the Bible. I have tried my best to conform my life to its moral and spiritual teachings. Even though that magnificent collection of sixty-six ancient books was written over a period of more than one thousand years by at least one hundred different authors, even though they wrote in Hebrew or in Greek in times and cultures far different from our own, even though they wrote in forms often unfamiliar to contemporary readers, I still believe that the Bible is inspired by God and a trustworthy guide for matters of Christian faith and practice.

In fact, I learned Greek to study the New Testament and Hebrew to study the Old. I have a master's degree in divinity and a doctorate in ministry with a major emphasis in biblical studies from Fuller Theological Seminary, the largest independent evangelical seminary in the world. I have spent my lifetime studying, memorizing, quoting, preaching, teaching, and filming from the Bible, all of it, including those controversial texts.

If you know anything about those six biblical passages used to attack and condemn us, you will admit that the authors never once speak of "sexual orientation." The fact that some people are shaped at conception, at birth, or conditioned in earliest childhood to a lifetime of same-sex intimacy is a scientific discovery less than a century old. And yet Moses lived approximately thirteen hundred years before Christ, and the Apostle Paul wrote his letters to the churches in Rome and Galatia almost two thousand years ago. The ancient prophet and the fiery missionary-preacher were fighting pagan idolatry, temple prostitution, child molestation, and irresponsible sexuality, hetero- sexual and homosexual alike. They didn't know about today's gay and lesbian people living in committed relationships who lead normal, productive lives, who love God and cherish and honor their families.

My old friends from the religious right say they take the Bible seriously, and I believe them. But I must ask, why do they go on denying the historic, cultural, and linguistic evidence (and modern scientific discoveries) that would help them understand the meanings of those passages for our times?

Through the centuries, those selective literalists, such as R. J. Rush- doony, who have chosen to put their brains and their hearts in neutral while reading the biblical texts used to condemn us have left a trail of blood and suffering in their wake. They and their predecessors, an- cient and modern, have misused God's Word to insist that the world was created in seven actual days and that it was created flat with a heaven above and a hell below. They have misused it to support slavery, child abuse, ethnic and racial cleansing. They have misused it to discriminate against women and children, the physically handi- capped, and lepers, to launch inquisitions, to burn their enemies at the stake, to create gulags and concentration camps, to murder 6 million Jews, and now to hound and harass my gay brothers and lesbian sisters.

Misusing the Bible to support old prejudice is not a new phenom- enon. When Copernicus claimed that the sun, not the earth, was the center of our universe, Martin Luther misused the Biblical text to condemn this "upstart astrologer." He wrote, "This fool wishes to reverse the entire science of astronomy; but sacred Scripture tells us that Joshua commanded the sun to stand still, and not the earth, (Joshua 10:13)."

Melanchthon condemned Copernicus by quoting Ecclesiastes 1:4-5, "The sun also ariseth, and the sun goeth down, and hasteth to his place where he arose." He suggested that severe measures be taken to silence those who agreed with Copernicus. "It is the part of a good mind to accept the truth as revealed by God," Melanchthon warned, "and to acquiesce in it."

After quoting from the Ninety-third Psalm—"The earth also is es- tablished, that it cannot be moved"—John Calvin attacked the scientist directly. "Who will venture to place the authority of Copernicus above that of the Holy Spirit?" [See Thomas S. Kuhn's, *The Copernican Revolution,* Harvard University Press, 1957, pp 191-192.]

Catholics who dared to teach the new discovery were called "infidels" and "atheists." And in 1632, when Galileo argued the Copernican position, the pope responded by backing the Biblical view of the universe with "the heavens above and the earth below." He condemned Galileo as a heretic, and sentenced him to house arrest for the remainder of his life.

Ironically, Galileo was a devout Catholic and found "no conflict between his scientific and religious beliefs. He upheld the importance of scripture but claimed that it reveals not scientific facts but spiritual knowledge for our salvation, truths that are above reason and could not be discovered by observation." [See Ian G. Barbour's *Issues in Science and Religion,* Harper and Row, New York, pp. 29-30.]

Luther, Melanchthon, Calvin, and the Vatican all insisted that the Bible be taken literally in its poetic description of the universe, even when scientific evidence proved them wrong. Instead of seeing this ancient book as a trustworthy and inspired source of spiritual truth, they fell into the same error that has misled Robertson, Falwell, Dobson and the others. It wasn't until 1992, more than three centuries later, that Pope John Paul II finally admitted that the church had misused the Bible to condemn Copernicus and Galileo and to support a view of the universe that has been proven incorrect.

I wonder if gay and lesbian people will have to wait three hundred years for the religious right to reexamine their false claims and confess their misuse of Scriptures against gay and lesbian people. Meanwhile, God's homosexual children continue to face outrageous lies from the religious right and a mounting campaign of discrimination and terror from those who believe them.

While living in Laguna, I began to compile case studies of gay and lesbian people who had become victims of the growing antihomosexual climate fueled by Christian leaders, especially the voices of the religious right. In so many cases, those men guilty of hate crimes against gays or lesbians could defend themselves by quoting Christians who had used the Bible to condemn gay people in the past. These young men who are sent to prison for their crimes feel as if they have been given a license to kill homosexuals by the biblical teachings of their antigay Christian parents, pastors, and Sunday-school teachers, or by their favorite antigay televangelist or Christian talk show host.

Airman Terry Helvey followed Seaman Allen Schindler into a public rest room in Yokosuka, Japan. Without provocation, Helvey attacked his shipmate and kicked and beat him to death for just one reason: Schindler was gay. An autopsy showed that his skull had been bashed in, his ribs broken, every one of his vital organs damaged, and his genitals mutilated. The courts sentenced Helvey to life imprisonment for his hate crime.

Rebecca White and Claudia Brenner were hiking on the Appalachian Trail in Adams County, Pennsylvania. Stephen Roy Carr, a stranger to both women, followed them awhile and then, totally unprovoked, began firing with a high-powered rifle. Claudia was hit first in the upper arm, twice in the neck, in the head and face. One of the bullets that hit Rebecca exploded in her liver. Bleeding from her gaping wounds, Claudia dragged her friend behind a tree and then, unable to stop the bleeding, ran for help. While she was gone, Rebecca died. "We never had a chance to say good-bye," Claudia says.

And though Carr's lawyer implied that the two women had provoked the attack by teasing their killer sexually, it became clear in the trial that Carr had killed for one reason only. He thought the two young women might be lesbians. Carr was convicted of first-degree murder and sentenced to life in prison without parole.

Another kind of hate crime I had not associated with the religious right are the hate crimes gay and lesbian people, especially young people, commit against themselves. In January 1989, Bob W., a seventeen-year-old high school senior from a suburb of Chicago, Illinois, climbed up on a chair in the family's two-car garage, tied a rope around his neck, fastened it to a beam in the ceiling, and kicked the chair away. The coroner doesn't know how long the gay teenager hung there before he suffocated and died. His parents found a short note describing Bob's "struggle with homosexuality," a letter of acceptance from his denominational seminary, and a page torn out of the seminary's catalog clearly forbidding homosexuals from enrollment.

Who is to blame for that innocent teenager's death? In 1990, the U.S. Department of Health and Human Services issued *Report of the Secretary's Task Force on Youth Suicide*. The secretary under President

Bush, Dr. Louis Sullivan, acted quickly to downplay the report. Its message was clear: "Gay youth are 2–3 times more likely to attempt suicide than other young people," and gay and lesbian youths account for "nearly one-third of all suicide attempts among adolescents in this country" (pp. 3–110). When the authors of the report were asked to explain how religion contributes to these suicides, they answered: "They [gay teens] may feel wicked and condemned to hell and attempt suicide in despair of ever obtaining redemption" (pp. 3–128).

There it is again. Rejected by their Christian homes and churches, they feel rejected by God as well. How well I remembered those terrible days from my own childhood! Everything I read in Laguna pointed to this one grim fact: by stirring up the ancient pool of hatred and bigotry against gay and lesbian people, the religious right was directly or indirectly responsible for the suffering and death that followed.

Early in 1990, I met the "Angel of Death." At least that's what 60 Minutes called Marty James during their television documentary of his work with AIDS patients. In the past seven years, Marty had assisted in the "self-delivery" (suicide) of more than a dozen gay men suffering through the last, painful, impoverishing stages of that disease. I first read about his work in a moving *Los Angeles Times* article. "Marty's story," wrote reporter Stephen Braun, "illuminates the heart-breaking frustration of men who wanted to recapture the last shreds of dignity from a disease that allowed none and their reliance on a helper who tried to navigate the fine line between suicide and murder while blinded by compassion."

Long before Dr. Jack Kervorkian was in the headlines, Marty James had risked his own freedom to help gay men with AIDS to "die with dignity." Although Gary and I both came from the Christian tradition that sees life as a gift that God gives and that only God should take away, we both understood why Marty would break the laws of God and man to help a needlessly suffering friend to die. In our short time together, Gary and I had seen enough friends and acquaintances with AIDS forced to endure an endless plague of painful, crippling, bankrupting diseases and opportunistic infections. For months at a time many of them lay helplessly connected to dripping tubes and bleeping monitors while their bodies writhed and atrophied, their friends and families disappeared, and their resources drained away. "How much physical, emotional and financial suffering must the system demand," Marty asked me, "before a man is allowed the right to die?"

My own struggle with sexual orientation was nothing in comparison to the struggle endured by people with AIDS. I couldn't believe that in the face of this national tragedy, most leaders of the government and the church remained silent and uncaring. It was so obvious that once again bigotry was leading to the suffering and death of gay people. If this plague had not at first affected gay men primarily, the entire nation would have mobilized to end it. I was determined to write a book or produce a film that would help in some small way to confront this terrible injustice and to raise a few more dollars for AIDS research and to provide more services for those who suffered. Marty James seemed the perfect subject, but when I presented my idea to him, he smiled, took my hand, and said quietly, "But you have to take one more step before we could begin."

That same day, Marty introduced Gary and me to Michael S., an AIDS patient who was close to death. His body was covered with Kaposi Sarcoma lesions. He had been hospitalized three times by nearly-fatal bouts with Pneumastis Pneumonia. The list of painful, ugly diseases and opportunistic infections that had plagued him seemed endless. The bottles and boxes filled with medicines that Michael consumed each day covered a large dining room table. Recently, he had been terrified by the early signs of dimentia. Michael had seen too many friends lose control of their minds and bodies, only to spend their last days in a vegetative state, attached to hospital life-support systems. He had suffered enough. He wanted to die with some kind of dignity before they took that decision out of his hands and locked him away in the terminal ward of the county hospital.

After our first meeting, Marty asked point blank if I would help Michael die. "Of course," I answered, all too quickly. Marty was smarter than that. He urged me to consider the possible consequences of my decision. I didn't sleep that night. I paced my home, thinking about Michael and praying for wisdom and for courage. The next week, I spent with Michael S. He told me his story. I told him mine.

After establishing a rather deep friendship in a very short time, Michael finally asked me himself if I would help him die. By then, I had seen his suffering first hand. I knew what would happen to this single man, living alone, when dimentia struck full force and the medics came to take him away. I assured him of my support and tried to guarantee to my own satisfaction that he really was ready to die.

Because I believe in the soul's life after death, I was most concerned about Michael's spiritual condition. But I didn't want to raise the issue for fear he would think me proselytizing or standing in judgment. Finally, on Saturday night Michael asked if I would go with him that next Sunday to Dignity, the Catholic gay/lesbian support group. At Dignity, we knelt side by side, prayed together, and took communion. With tears streaming down his face and a radiant, confident smile, Michael stood up from the altar, embraced me, and said, "Now, I'm ready to go home."

On Monday afternoon, we assembled the anti-nausea drugs and sedatives that Michael had been collecting. About noon, Marty James came by to see that we had taken every precaution and to ask Michael one last time if he was absolutely certain that this was his day to die. Michael was serious but totally sure that he was ready. Together, we prepared Michael's room for his "self delivery." Pictures of his family and his lover who had died from AIDS were positioned on a nightstand in easy view. I brought a bouquet of flowers and placed it on the dresser. We lit fragrant candles. A selection of Michael's favorite quiet classical music was already playing on the stereo. I read Michael's favorite passages of hope and comfort from the Old and New Testament. We held hands and prayed together.

About 1:00 P.M., Michael ate a bowl of warm soup to prepare his stomach for the anti-nausea drugs. When he was comfortable, we opened the sedative capsules, poured their contents into a mixture of fresh yogurt and honey which Michael consumed. As the sedatives took hold, he talked quietly about the friends he wanted to see in heaven. When he grew sleepy, Michael climbed under the covers and asked me to hand him the large Teddy Bear with the bright pink ribbon his lover had given him on their tenth anniversary. As Michael drifted off to sleep, Marty and I lay down beside him on the bed. Even while he slept, we continued talking to him, assuring him of our presence and of God's love. Occasionally, one of us would stroke his face or squeeze his hand. In less than two hours, Michael just stopped breathing. His suffering had ended at last.

While Marty stayed with Michael's body, I took a short walk around the block, thanking God for being with us, praying that God would understand and forgive me if I had made a terrible mistake. When I returned, the medics had arrived. Marty James had been sure that Michael's physician had examined him during the previous week. By knowing the extent of Michael's illness, the doctor could grant a death certificate immediately. Marty had let sixty minutes pass before he called the medics, or they would have been compelled by law to do their mechanical best to resuscitate him, adding one more indignity to his suffering and death. They knew immediately what had happened, thanked us for our obvious concern, and took Michael's body to the morgue.

Later that day, his mother sat in Michael's kitchen, weeping her loss, celebrating Michael's gain. "Thank you for helping my son to die," she told me. "I wish I had had the courage. He has suffered so long." Michael's friends and neighbors assembled quickly. One by one they thanked me. I knew in my heart that we had done the right thing.

Over the years, I have seen conservative Christians, clergy and laity alike, work hard and sacrifice much to help end suffering of various kinds across the nation and around the world. So, it amazed me when I saw how slow those same Christians were to reach out a hand to help end the suffering of lesbians and gays, especially those with AIDS, even when those Christians have contributed to that suffering.

One of my old friends and clients from the religious right appointed his own committee to investigate the HIV-AIDS disaster. He was trying to determine for himself how responsible he should be to use his ample resources to help end the suffering caused by that terrible virus. My old friend was a well-known, conservative Christian businessman whom I had assisted with various writing projects over the years. I loved and respected him and his family. They were loyal, committed members of their church. They had supported Christian charities across the nation and around the world. They had been generous and loving to me, to Lyla, and the children.

Then one afternoon, during my last year of silence, while interviewing my friend for an article I was ghostwriting, I asked him casually why after his study he hadn't donated anything to help discover a cure for AIDS or to help people who are suffering from the virus. "During our research on the HIV epidemic," he replied, "I met a lot of men with AIDS. Not one of them apologized for what he had done to contract the virus. If they're not sorry, why should I help them?"

I was stunned by his reply. That same wealthy Christian had gone through open-heart surgery to bypass a clogged vein. "Why was it clogged?" I should have asked.

"From not being careful about diet or exercise," he would have answered.

"To whom did you apologize for your neglect that lead to your heart disease?"

"No one."

"Then what is the difference between you and people with AIDS? Is their 'sin' of loving one another any worse than yours? And since when did the followers of Christ begin asking for apologies before we ministered to the sick and dying in His name?"

Immediately, I returned to my hotel room and sat by myself in angry silence, almost overwhelmed by my guilt. While flying home from the Philippines after meeting with President Aquino, I had decided to end my silence, to confront my clients on the religious right who were misinformed about God's homosexual children. I knew I should confront this man. I knew I should tell him the stories of my friends who had died or who were living in noble agony with AIDS. I knew I should ask him what he was doing about his loyal employees who were sick and disabled by the disease.

But I was his ghostwriter. Ghostwriters don't talk back. And worse, I was a ghost hiding in a closet. To speak honestly would have revealed my secret. That would have cost me my job. I know that now for certain. Out of real fear and out of growing financial need, I let the opportunity pass. Instead of speaking the truth, I remained silent. And as I sat in my hotel room brooding, I thought about my friends at ACT-UP who were putting their bodies on the line because they knew for certain that "Silence = Death." My silence that day helped continue the suffering of my gay brothers! What difference might I have made if I had only mustered up enough courage to speak?

The clock was ticking. My final days in the suffocating closet were coming to an end. It had been bad enough working for wealthy business people who supported the religious right's campaign against us. It was even worse that I had been ghostwriting books, films, articles, and speeches for the leaders of that movement who were at that very moment waging a propaganda war against gay and lesbian people that was leading directly and indirectly to discrimination, suffering, and death.

Then, in August 1991, my first gay love, Thomas Montgomery, called from Portland, Oregon. Gary and I had visited Thomas and his partner earlier in the year. He had seemed perfectly well. But on the phone, I could tell that Thomas was terribly sick. I flew immediately to Portland and was surprised and pleased to find Tom waiting for me at the airport. On the drive home, he told me about his long bout with AIDS and the various crippling opportunistic infections he had battled. In the master bedroom of the home they had remodeled and furnished together, Thomas showed me the mass of Kaposi's cancer that covered at least a fourth of his body with ugly, crusty, purple, lesions.

While his lover fixed dinner, I sat on the bed beside Thomas, still a young man, facing imminent death. For a long time, he didn't speak. We just sat there in the silence, remembering. "I love you, Mel," he finally said quietly. "And I'm grateful that you helped me find my way back to God." He paused again and then laughed. "I guess I'll be seeing Him pretty soon now."

Thomas had suffered all the indignities of this terrible plague. As his immune system gave way to the virus, he had been wracked with pain by so many different maladies that he had stopped counting. Tom knew more about rare diseases and their various symptoms and treatments than most doctors, but his real suffering had come from the discrimination and isolation he had felt from so many people. And so much of that prejudice suffered by so many of the more than 250,000 who have died from this disease in the U.S. alone stems directly from the hateful propaganda of the religious right. After my first year in Laguna, after seeing for myself the suffering and death caused directly and indirectly by the religious right, I knew my silence had to end.

The next morning, Thomas drove me back to the airport. We said one last good-bye. After checking my suitcase at the curb, I hugged Tom awkwardly through the window. When he drove away, we both were crying. On September 6, just a few weeks later, he died. His lover spread Tom's ashes on a lonely walk along their favorite trail on the north side of Mount Hood. A little of my own heart is buried there.

Chapter 13

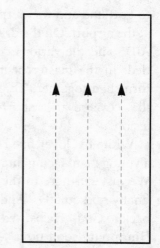

1991–93,

A Ghost No More!

O_n *October 23, 1991, I received a fund-raising letter from Jerry* Falwell that pushed me to the brink. Across the top of his six-page, single-spaced appeal, Jerry had printed in his own hand, "Last Wednesday, I was threatened by a mob of homosexuals. This convinced me that our nation has become a modern day Sodom and Gomorra," signed, "J.F."

My former client on the religious right went on to describe how he had been "rescued" from a dangerous "homosexual mob" by his son Jonathan and the Los Angeles police. After declaring "it is truly a miracle that I am alive today and able to write you this letter," Jerry continued:

Unless we act now, America—like Sodom and Gomorra—may face the wrath of God's judgment. These
two Old Testament cities were so filled with homosexuality and perversion that they were utterly destroyed. God wiped them clean from the face of the
earth! Will our nation—founded on Christian princi-
ples—face a similar fate because God-fearing moral
people failed to stop homosexuality from becoming an
accepted lifestyle in our churches, schools and public
places?

With Jerry's fund-raising letter in my hand, I rushed to the Laguna
Beach library and pulled out back issues of the *Los Angeles Times* to
see if there was any mention of this "assassination attempt" on Jerry
Falwell's life. I found his name on the front page of a recent *Time's*
article responding to the charges in Jerry's fund-raising letter. Eyewitnesses denied Jerry's allegations. Apparently, the demonstrators
stayed well within their designated area. No potential acts of violence
against property or people were seen or reported. Nothing was
thrown. No one rushed the hotel. No backup was required. No emergency declared. Police inside and outside the building testified that
neither Jerry nor any member of his party needed to be rescued nor
had they ever been in any kind of danger.

After declaring in his fund-raising letter that "certain persons fully
intended to take my life last Wednesday," once again Jerry used the
imaginary gay threat to raise money. "It seems only a few are willing
to speak out publicly and declare homosexuality a sin," Jerry concluded. "Many times I feel that I am out there alone . . . please send me
today a gift of $35 or even $25 to help me educate the American
people regarding this crucial matter. . . .

"We have a faithful staff who help me daily to speak out to America," Jerry explained further. "They must be financially cared for. We
have tremendous printing bills to pay. Our postage costs are high. We
must pay our editors and writers. Please help me. . . . Send your $35
or even $25 gift today. I have never needed your help more. Please
pray also that God will protect me as I serve Christ."

Though eyewitnesses told a different story, Jerry may honestly have
been frightened by the crowd that day. Whatever really happened, it

is certain that once again he had used gay people in another desperate attempt to raise money. And in the process, once again, he had stirred up the dangerous feelings of suspicion and hatred against us.

"Night after night," Jerry wrote in that same fund-raising letter, "we are bombarded on TV news with scenes of homosexual rampage and violence. Using their influence in Hollywood, homosexuals have succeeded in having their deviant behavior portrayed positively as a legitimate alternative lifestyle. They have lost all fear of condemnation. They speak openly and proudly of their sordid sexual acts and unashamedly flaunt their perversion. They carry no shame whatsoever for their actions. It is time the moral majority in this country stood up to join with me in saying—THIS IS ENOUGH."

That latest Jerry Falwell antigay fund-raising letter was the last straw. My silence had to end. On Christmas Eve day, December 24, 1991, I sent my first "coming out" letter by Federal Express to Jerry Falwell's home in Lynchburg, Virginia, telling him I was a gay, warning him that his fund-raising campaign against gay and lesbian people was leading to the suffering and death of my brothers and sisters, and begging him to meet with me to discuss this urgent, life-and-death matter in Christian love.

After all, we were Christian brothers, and in Matthew 18:15, Jesus makes it perfectly clear how Christian brothers and sisters should resolve a conflict. "If your brother sins against you," Jesus said, "go and show him his fault, just between the two of you. If he listens to you, you have won your brother over. But if he will not listen, take one or two others along, so that every matter may be established by the testimony of two or three witnesses. If he refuses to listen to them, tell it to the church; and if he refuses to listen even to the church, treat him as you would a pagan or a tax collector."

In the spirit of Jesus' advice, I wrote, faxed, and phoned Jerry Falwell, hoping to discuss these matters with him in person and in private. I wasn't "grandstanding," as he later claimed to the press. I wasn't looking for publicity. My goal was to meet and talk with Jerry in prayerful privacy. For more than twelve months I waited for an answer. He refused to reply.

In the meantime, Jerry's lie that we "have a godless, humanistic scheme to destroy America's traditional moral values" and Andrea Sheldon's lie that we "were militant and angry homosexuals demanding the right to sodomize 16 year old boys" were only the beginning.

My old friends and clients on the religious right seemed to be racing each other to see who could tell the biggest lie about gay and lesbian people, all to raise donations.

Pat Robertson lied when he said there was some kind of evil gay agenda, that we demanded special rights, that we threatened to undermine the spiritual traditions of this nation. Jim Dobson lied when he said we were a menace to America's children, that we recruit, that we abuse, that we can't be trusted to parent, to teach, or to pastor. Jim Kennedy lied when he said that gays and lesbians are unworthy to fight and die for their country, that if we are not banned from military service our heterosexual boys in uniform will be raped, sexually harassed, and exposed to HIV infection.

Charles Stanley, Chuck Colson, Tim and Beverly LaHaye, Phylis Schlafly, Gary Bauer, and the others all lied when they talked about a corrupt gay and lesbian lifestyle, as though there were one lifestyle for all lesbians and gays. In fact, we are church organists and choir directors, deacons and members of the board, pastors, priests, and rabbis. We pray to the same God. We read the same Scriptures. We are responsible parents, pastors, teachers, and lay leaders. Gay people are at the core, not at the fringe, of this great nation. Our only desire is to be seen and accepted as we really are.

In the midst of their avalanche of lies, I began to write letters to all of them, protesting their lies and offering to meet with them on behalf of truth. I wrote Jerry first. He didn't answer. Then, I wrote Billy Graham, and he, too, opted not to reply. I wrote Pat Robertson, James Kennedy, and James Dobson. No one would accept my request to sit down as brothers in Christ to discuss the new biblical, theological, pastoral, and scientific data about homosexuality that might help inform my old friends on the religious right. (I've included copies of my key letters in the appendix.)

Early in 1992, while we were still in Laguna Beach, the lies against gay and lesbian people reached a new critical mass. No longer was the religious right just telling lies to raise money or to mobilize volunteers. They tried to use their lies against us to convince the people of Oregon to amend their state constitution to classify homosexuality as "abnormal, wrong, unnatural and perverse."

Once again the ancient story of Sodom was told incorrectly in pulpits across the state. Once again the words of Leviticus were misused and misquoted in Sunday school classrooms, Bible studies, and prayer meetings across Oregon. Sincere Christians marched directly from their churches to shopping malls and gas stations, to offices and parking lots, collecting signatures from their fellow Oregonians on their petitions supporting Ballot Measure Nine.

Thousands of sincere but misinformed voters believed the religious right's tired old lies that gays and lesbians were looking for "special rights"; that we had a "gay agenda" that "threatened the moral standards of the nation" and even "undermined the Christian faith"; that we "recruited and molested children"; that we were "unfit to teach or preach, even to worship, work or live beside them."

Families were divided by the heated debate. Cruel words were spoken on both sides. Accusations were hurled back and forth. Ugly graffiti, both pro and con, appeared across the state. Rocks were thrown. Fires were set. Several conservative churches and the Oregon Citizens Alliance offices were damaged. Pro-gay organizations had their leaders threatened, their mailing lists stolen, their offices trashed and firebombed. A gay man and his lesbian friend were burned to death in their home by an unidentified arsonist.

And though almost every major elected official in the state, including the governor, senators, and most congresspeople took a stand against the measure, and though major Catholic and mainline Protestant church leaders joined their voices in opposition, and though gays and lesbians and our wonderful friends and families all across the state organized to stand against the lies being told by the religious right, the antigay petitions were signed and Measure Nine was placed on the ballot.

Once again, leaders from the religious right were ignoring the U.S. Constitution in their determined effort to force their version of morality on the rest of the American people. In 1868, the Fourteenth Amendment to the Constitution was passed declaring that "no state shall make or enforce a law that shall abridge the privileges of citizens . . . nor deny them equal protection under the law." And yet under the leadership of the religious right, the people of Oregon were encouraged to do just that.

If Measure Nine passed, Oregonians who happened to be gay or lesbian (or those *perceived* to be gay or lesbian) could be fired from their jobs and evicted from their homes. Public libraries and TV and radio stations could be required to remove books or to censor programs that discussed homosexuality. Doctors, lawyers, and other professionals who are gay or lesbian could have their state licenses revoked. Harassment and even physical violence against gay and lesbian people (or those *perceived* to be gay or lesbian) would be inadvertently condoned.

I knew the people of Oregon. It was sad to see the people of that beautiful state divided by hatred and violence. Like so many others across the nation, they were being misled by the inflammatory voices of the religious right. As a result, my gay brothers and lesbian sisters in Oregon, their families and friends, were suffering.

Wanting to do something to help, I called Linda Welch, a leader of the No on Nine Campaign and Dan Stutesman, an official of Oregon's People of Faith Against Bigotry, volunteering to write a letter against the measure and send it at my own expense to five thousand Oregon pastors and church leaders. I had spent seven productive years in Oregon. I had earned my baccalaureate degree at Warner Pacific College in Portland and my master's in communications at the University of Portland. From 1958 until 1965, I had emceed the Saturday-night Youth for Christ rallies in Portland's Civic Auditorium and hosted KGW-TV's "The World of Youth." I had preached and taught in Oregon schools and churches. Oregonian pastors, youth directors, and Sunday-school teachers had used my films, read my books and articles, and taught from curricula I had written for their denominations.

The leaders of the campaign against Measure Nine encouraged me to write and send my letter immediately. I tried to write without anger or bitterness, sharing my personal journey, stating my homosexual orientation, explaining to my fellow pastors and church leaders how they had been led astray by the inflammatory rhetoric of Jerry Falwell, Pat Robertson, Lon Mabon, and the others. I begged them to speak even a word of tolerance on behalf of those who suffered.

"You and I have spent our lives seeking to be true to the Scriptures," I concluded. "And though we may disagree on the subject of homosexuality, surely we agree on this: the Bible should not be used to rob any of our fellow Americans of their basic human rights. . . . As the Bible itself clearly shows, political and prophetic issues cannot always be torn apart. This measure is also a prophetic issue, calling our nation to justice, to mercy, and to truth. When we are silent, we also take a stand. Now, the Gospel is at stake. A single word of wisdom from you could make a momentous difference and even save lives, not just in Oregon, but across the nation."

On November 3, 1992, Measure Nine was defeated. However, more than five hundred thousand Oregonians had voted for it. Misled by the voices of the religious right, and by their copycat, gay basher in Oregon, Lon Mabon and his Oregon Citizens Alliance, thousands of churches and hundreds of thousands of Oregonians had been convinced that their gay and lesbian neighbors were, as the ballot claimed, "abnormal, wrong, unnatural and perverse."

During the next few weeks, I received eighty written replies from pastors who had received my letter in Oregon. Only two were positive. Several others calmly and lovingly disagreed. Almost every letter quoted the same six biblical passages used to condemn gays and lesbians, especially the story of Sodom and the Leviticus passage warning of "death" to men who lie down with other men. Many promised sincerely that they would pray for me, but most of their letters surprised and frightened me with their underlying spirit of ignorance, anger, and hatred.

"Your letter is written by the devil and comes straight out of hell!" wrote Pastor D. from Hermiston, Oregon. "Please, God," he concluded, "don't delay punishment." Pastor B. wrote from Corbett, Oregon, condemning my "sad, sterile, and unnatural lifestyle," suggesting all gay men "sodomize little boys." Pastor H., from Grants Pass, warned me about my "life-controlling problem" and predicted that if I had my way, "America would become a lawless, depraved, and murderous society." Pastor B. in Gresham condemned me for "leading others astray." Again using Scriptures to condemn me, Pastor M. in Sweet Home claimed I was "cursed by God." Pastor P. in Coos Bay, quoting Leviticus, warned that I would be "put to death" for my "sinfulness." Pastor S. in Rainier, Oregon, said simply, "May God have mercy on you!"

The letters were written by pastors and lay leaders from Baptist, Free Methodist, Nazarene, Presbyterian, Mennonite, Assembly of God, Church of God, Churches of Christ, Christian, independent, Bible, and community churches. It didn't take long to learn that antihomosexual teachings know no ecclesiastical barriers. With a few heroic exceptions, the leaders of almost every organized religious group seem to delight in bashing gays. But the religious right has turned gay bashing into an art form. They didn't invent the hatred of gay and lesbian people. Nor do they have an exclusive franchise on its practice. They just tapped into that deep, dark, primitive pool of blind superstition and unreasonable fear to mobilize their troops and fill their treasuries.

In my Laguna diaries I wrote: "Wherever the lies about gay and lesbian people come from, those lies are accepted almost universally these days by clergy and laity alike. From their pulpits and lecterns, through their radio and television programs, their books, magazines, and tracts and their avalanche of direct mail, the hateful rhetoric trickles down into local homes and churches with devastating results.

"Misunderstood, rejected, beaten, and even discarded, gay children commit suicide or end up as runaways on the mean streets of our cities. Unless they stay safely in the closet, gay and lesbian adults risk losing their jobs, their apartments, their families, and their children. Now, thanks to precinct-by-precinct, antigay hate campaigns by the religious right, in the cities, counties, and states of this nation, legislation is in place or pending to take away even our most basic civil and human rights. Only the courts, God bless them, are keeping hatred at bay. But on a typical day, gays and lesbians who dare to speak the name are harassed and hunted at home, at work, at school, at play, and in the military. Hate crimes against us are increasing at a frightening rate. We can't even find sanctuary in our churches."

After I wrote to five thousand pastors in Oregon (and to five thousand other pastors in Colorado where a similar antigay amendment was pending), copies of my letters were circulated by fax machine among my old ghostwriting clients and friends on the religious right. Word that I was gay spread quickly among those who hadn't heard it directly from me. Contracts and unwritten agreements we had made to do a book or film together were canceled. My letters and faxes were ignored. My phone calls went unanswered.

Because I had been honest about my sexual orientation, it was becoming painfully clear that I could no longer serve the very people who had heaped honors and awards on me for my lifetime of contributions to Christ and His church. In spite of my graduate degrees in ministry and twenty-five years of Christian service as a pastor, a seminary professor, a writer of best-selling religious books, and a producer of prizewinning religious films, admitting I was gay ended all chances of continued service. For the first time in my life, I began to wonder seriously how I would support my family, but even more important, I began to wonder what I should do to help turn back this growing avalanche of bigotry, discrimination, and violence the religious right had loosed against us.

About that time, the Reverend Michael Piazza, pastor of the largest gay/lesbian church in the world, called to ask if he could drop by our cottage on the beach at Laguna for a visit. I knew Michael and his amazing congregation. A year earlier, they had invited me to preach a spiritual-emphasis weekend in Dallas while their church was still meeting on the ground floor of an embarrassingly pink office building they had rented when they outgrew their four-hundred-seat sanctuary on Reagan Street.

Michael parked his rental car near our cottage, hugged me cheerfully, and suggested immediately that we take a long walk on the beach. He didn't even take time to change his shoes before we were in the wet sand, walking through the tide pools. I pointed out a peregrine falcon that lived in a magnificent wind-twisted pine high on the cliffs above Shaw's Cove. I picked up sea slugs stranded by the high tide and showed him Nun's Cove with its fresh assortment of shells and driftwood. We walked along Crescent Beach and passed by a series of fascinating caves en route to Seal Island. I was chatting about the wonders of Laguna. Michael was polite, but anxious to get on with business.

When I paused on my typically frenetic walk just long enough to watch a large flock of pelicans flying by, Michael took advantage of the pause to ask what he had come to ask. "I want you to be the dean of our new cathedral in Dallas," he said directly. "I don't have any money to pay you, at least not yet. We've spent all our funds building the cathedral, but we want you to seriously consider coming anyway."

I was genuinely surprised by Michael's offer. Quickly, he explained that his commitment as senior pastor to preaching, teaching, and administering the largest lesbian/gay church in the world required his full-time attention. He needed someone to help develop the cathedral's national ministry as a spiritual center for the gay and lesbian community. He had dozens of speaking and writing opportunities he couldn't accept. Michael also wanted to establish a national television ministry and to launch nationwide Circles of Hope, small, informal study and action groups that would help gays and lesbians in towns and villages across the country where there was currently no proactive, pro-spiritual gay or lesbian presence.

In 1970, just two years after the Reverend Troy Perry founded the Universal Fellowship of Metropolitan Community Churches, one of the earliest sister congregations was founded in Dallas, Texas. Under the leadership of the Reverend Don Eastman, and now, the Reverend Michael Piazza, that congregation—the Cathedral of Hope UFMCC—has grown to be the largest Christian church in the world with a primary ministry to lesbians and gays, their friends and families.

I was looking for a safe, supportive place to come out against my old clients on the religious right, to help alleviate the suffering caused by their homophobic rhetoric to my gay brothers and lesbian sisters, to write my own coming-out story, and to see where God would lead. All my life I had felt called to Christian ministry. At this moment when my old opportunities to minister were dying, it seemed that God was using Michael and the Cathedral of Hope to bring new ones to life.

No actual job description was agreed upon. "If you'll just come to Dallas and do your thing here," Michael told me, "something will happen that will honor Christ and help extend the Cathedral's ministry to the nation." Little did we know how prophetic Michael's words would be. Michael didn't even spend the night. He rushed back to the airport and left me alone on the beach considering the implications of the move from California and my beloved family to Dallas, Texas, the place Michael called "the buckle of the Bible Belt."

The first consideration was my family. Lyla was working sixty and more hours a week with her army of volunteers at All Saints Church, where she had become the director of stewardship and was being invited to conduct seminars in fund-raising all across the country. Lyla was staffing two major campaigns a year to support the ministry of this influential parish, including model programs for the homeless, people with AIDS and their caregivers, health care for Pasadena's uninsured school children, pre-school child care, substance abuse, and low cost housing. On those rare occasions when she could take a day off, she came to Laguna and we walked the beach together, talking about everything, but especially about our children and the ways that God had blessed them. Not only had they survived those difficult days of our struggle and stress, but they had grown into creative, responsible, loving adults who shared our values and enjoyed our presence.

Everything was changing so fast. Erinn had graduated from Azusa Pacific with her teaching credential in elementary education. When she and her classmate, Bob Harriman, were married, they had asked me to conduct the service. Bob had then gone on to earn his master's degree in student administration and had later accepted a position in a nearby Christian university. Erinn remained busy caring for our granddaughter, Katie, who was just a few months old.

When Michael graduated from Wesleyan with honors, Lyla and I sat drenched and proud in a rainstorm with a plastic raincoat held over our heads watching him cross the platform to receive his diploma. Protesting that he didn't want to cost us "any more money," we finally managed to convince him to let us underwrite his first year of writing. Halfway through that year, Michael was hired to write a film script for Twentieth Century–Fox. Already, he had an impressive little office on the lot at Fox Studios near Century City. In my files I had a collection of the plays my son had written, directed, and performed at Wesleyan, and his posters and other memorabilia were tacked proudly to my office walls.

When I told my family about the offer to move to Dallas, Lyla looked sad for a moment, and then after a few honest words of warning and a genuine smile of support, she encouraged me to accept the Cathedral's offer. Erinn was immediately happy that I would be working in a church again, but insisted that I return for Katie's first birthday party. Michael was genuinely glad that my ghostwriting days were over. "Go for it, Dad," he said, grinning. One by one they hugged me. I didn't even try to hide my tears.

I loved my family and wanted always to be near them. Besides, I had a brand-new granddaughter and I wanted to see her pass through each of those delightful stages from infancy to maturity. I wanted to carry her around on my back in the old pack that I had used to carry Erinn and Michael. I wanted to pass on to her my love for the sea as we walked hand in hand on Laguna Beach. I wanted to teach Katie to swim in the Laguna Riviera pool. I didn't want to hear her first "I love you, Grampa," over the telephone long distance. For all those years my family and I had been together, if not in residence, only a few minutes away. Moving to Dallas would be painful in personal losses. And in all probability, the move would be a financial disaster as well.

Becoming dean of the largest gay and lesbian congregation in the world would end my closet days forever. Once the word was out, there would be no turning back. In all likelihood, my network of conservative Christian friends, clients, producers, and publishers that had taken a lifetime to build would vanish. There would be no salary at the Cathedral. They couldn't even help us with our move. How would I pay the bills if I couldn't go on ghostwriting, producing films and TV specials for my old clients? And though I felt called to preach and teach, I would no longer be asked to speak in conservative Christian universities, seminaries, or churches. I even worried about the national press, especially the sensation-seeking tabloid papers and what they might do with my story, and the embarrassment it might bring my family.

How Gary's life would be changed by the move was of equal concern to me. I wasn't even sure that he would go along with the idea. He had a responsible position in Los Angeles, managing commercial properties for a major corporation. He had been honored as employee of the year in 1991. He had excellent work benefits, generous health and life insurance, and, in a plunging economy, total job security. I was asking him to leave all that to begin the journey into a brand-new life for both of us.

I wanted to accept Michael Piazza's offer to join him and his people at the Cathedral in Dallas, but I didn't want to go alone. My romance and friendship with Gary had evolved into a long-term, committed relationship, but could I ask him to sacrifice his career to go with me? When I finally got up my courage to ask, he didn't even pause to consider. The night I told him about Michael Piazza's offer, Gary just hugged me and said, "Let's go!"

There was a war being waged by the religious right against homosexual people across this country. Because of my old clients' strident antigay campaign, my lesbian sisters and gay brothers were suffering bigotry, discrimination, violence, and death. It was past time for me to do something to help those who suffered and, at the same time, by taking a stand against the lies my clients were telling, to help cut off that suffering at its source. I had prayed, worried, and fussed long enough. With Gary's vote, the decision was unanimous. It would be a risk, but we would take that risk together. I remembered Naomi's famous words to Ruth: "Where you go, I will go. And what you do, I will do also. Your people shall be my people. And your God, my God."

When there were difficult decisions to make, such as the move to Dallas, or when Gary could see that I was perplexed, fearful, or stressed, just before we turned out the lights on another day, he would climb into bed, prop up the pillows, and pat gently on the sheets. "Get up here," he would say quietly, and I would sit between his knees and lean back against his chest. "Talk," he whispered, and as I began to rehearse the options one more time, Gary would massage my neck and shoulders, ask important questions, and let me ruminate until the decision was made, the conflict was resolved, or I just fell asleep in his arms.

Those moments with Gary were comforting to be sure, but over the years, they had proven to be far more than just a source of comfort. They had become a source of truth as well. Accepting my sexual orientation and entering into a loving, committed gay relationship had proven to me once and for all times that my homosexuality was another of God's gifts. Many of my old friends and counselors on the religious right had told me that homosexuality was a sin and that God would abandon me if I "gave in" to that sinfulness. Others thought I was just crazy or misled.

"You're somewhere in the middle of Freud's sexual-identity scale," one of my many counselors informed me. "You are clearly a bisexual," another exclaimed. "You're AC-DC," one of my friends said with a sly grin. "You flow both ways." "You're just confused," a supporter of the "ex-gay" movement once warned me with an unctuous smile. "You never had an effective male role model so you never really grew up." Then before praying for me one last time, he added, "You're suffering from a kind of retarded adolescence that God will help you overcome with time."

Since childhood, I had been a victim of those conflicting voices. In their noisy cloud of misinformation and judgment, I had doubted, feared, and questioned my sexual orientation. In Gary's arms, that painful debate ended. For me, the ultimate test of sexual orientation had not been the test of passion but the test of time. In his wonderful book *Memories, Dreams, Reflections,* Carl Jung writes, "A man who has not passed through the inferno of his passions has never overcome them."

The real test of sexual orientation came when romantic feelings died, when those first few months or years of fiery sexual passion burned down to a warm glow (or even burned out altogether), when there was no urgent desire, as I heard a young friend say recently, "to jump on each other's bones," when we were content to lie beside each other in bed reading, watching television, talking and holding hands, or when we just slept side by side.

The fires of passion were a test of sexual orientation to be sure. It had been important to ask myself whom did I cast in my sexual fantasies, a woman or a man? At the beach or swimming pool, was it a male body that excited me and demanded my attention, or was it a female body that "turned me on"? When I glanced through those full-page ads for tight-fitting jeans or underwear in newspapers and magazines, was it the male model or the female model who caught my eye? I tried to ignore these involuntary, physiological responses far too long when I should have trusted myself to heed them, but there had been other tests of sexual orientation when passions cooled that I had found equally trustworthy.

Was it a man I wanted to come home to after a hard day's work, or was it a woman I needed to greet me at the door with a smile and a hug? Was it a man who brought me comfort by his very presence in the kitchen, at the fireplace, and in the bedroom; or was it a woman's company that made me feel safe, comfortable, and *at home* at last? Was it a man I wanted to sit beside at church, at a coffee shop, and in the movies; or was it a woman I liked to see in candlelight across the restaurant table?

In the early years of our friendship, passion drew me to Gary like a bee to honey. But after almost ten years, though passion still flared between us, other, equally compelling forces drew me to him. Finally, after all those years, in my relationship with Gary, I knew who I really was, a gay Christian man in a committed relationship with another gay Christian man. Was it right for my relationship with Gary to be demeaned, dishonored, and declared sinful and disgusting on Jerry Falwell's "Old Time Gospel Hour," Pat Robertson's "700 Club," or Jim Dobson's "Focus on the Family" simply because it was a homosexual rather than a heterosexual relationship? Should my human rights be threatened and my civil rights be denied by the Christian Coalition because I felt more compatible with a man than with a woman?

At that moment, my old clients and friends from the religious right were raising tens of millions of dollars supposedly to support antigay legislation already pending in fourteen states and more than one hundred counties and cities across America. Loving, private sexual acts between consenting adult homosexuals were illegal in twenty-four states, and the religious right was mobilizing to put antigay volunteer workers in every one of America's fifty thousand voting precincts to pass legislation that might end our rights forever.

Even worse, good people such as my parents were being confused by the avalanche of lies. They watched Pat Robertson faithfully. They heard Jim Dobson on the radio. Almost every day another antigay fund-raising letter appeared in their mailbox with the disgusting and untrue charges against gay people underlined in red. My parents didn't want my civil rights curtailed. They liked and respected Gary and could see we loved each other, but like millions of other religious and political conservatives in this country, my parents were being swept away by the lies against us being told by the religious right. They knew me and Gary and they loved us. They knew our beliefs and lifestyles and knew they were similar to their own. But they believed that we were the exception. In their minds, everyone else who is gay must be just as Pat Robertson and all the others depicted them.

If only Pat, Jerry, and the others could understand the great good they *could* do in helping their faithful listeners to understand the truth. My mom and dad need to know that gay and lesbian people are just like everybody else. I know I'm beginning to sound like a scratched record, caught in one groove, playing the same old track over and over again. But this truth cannot be repeated enough. Gay and lesbian people do not want or need "special rights." We are for not against "family values." We have no "agenda" that threatens the spiritual or moral standards of this nation. We just want the right to love and to be loved without fear, ridicule, or discrimination.

We are not the enemy. The real enemies are those who teach hate instead of love, those who use misinformation and fear tactics to raise money and mobilize volunteers, those who play on ancient superstitions to destroy lives and ruin families. All we want is our God-given right to live and to love with integrity and to take our place in the community as responsible neighbors and faithful friends.

Back as far as 1980, while I still cowered in my closet, two gay teenagers in Anaheim, California, refused to be intimidated by those who hate. With the whole world watching, Andrew Exler, nineteen, and his boyfriend, Shawn Elliott, seventeen, demonstrated courage and conviction that astounded me. After dating regularly for just two months, Andrew and Shawn headed for "Date Night" at Disneyland. Hand in hand, they rode the Matterhorn. Then on Space Mountain, they placed their arms around each other as the young heterosexual couples were doing. After watching "Great Moments with Mr. Lincoln" and hearing Abe speak of individual liberties and rights, they headed for the outdoor disco.

Eyewitnesses reported to the *Los Angeles Times* that the dance floor was jammed with teenage couples when Andrew and Shawn walked to the center of the floor, directly in front of the bandstand, and began to dance. For a moment, no one noticed. Then, one by one, the teenage couples dancing near Andrew and Shawn began to whisper and point in their direction. Security personnel monitoring the dance through television cameras saw the two boys dancing proudly. Tall men in white uniforms carrying walkie-talkies with small headsets in their left ears rushed to the scene. A few couples left the floor. Others stood to stare at Andrew and Shawn. Finally, the young bandleader noticed the confusion and stopped the music, but the courageous gay men danced on, refusing to be intimidated.

Looking back now, I wish Jerry Falwell had been there to see those two young gay men doing exactly what God intended them to do. I wish Pat Robertson could have been a witness to their courage as they danced their way into their place of honor in the history of our liberation movement. I wish Jim Dobson had been in the crowd to see what two of our gay kids were willing to pay to enforce the values of families who have learned to love instead of hate.

In the legal battle that followed, Andrew and Shawn refused to settle until the courts declared their victory. The religious right suffered a terrible defeat four years later, in 1985, when the verdict was announced. Disneyland was instructed by the courts to let Andrew and Shawn dance. While the leaders from the religious right jumped up and down in rage, a growing number of Americans, even those who didn't understand homosexuality, were wondering to themselves, "Don't these preachers have anything better to do than pick on two young gays who just want to dance?" In a *USA Today* poll, more than 50 percent of this nation's people said, "Let 'em dance."

As I walked the beaches of Laguna and thought, prayed, and worried about moving to Dallas, I remembered Darrel, the Boy Scout in his loincloth and feathers who forty years before had reached out his hand and led me in my first dance. This time, Michael Piazza was holding out his hand to me. To join him in the dance would be a terrible risk, but how awful it would feel to plug my ears to the music and walk away. Over those next few weeks, it became more and more clear that it was time for me to take Gary by the hand, walk out into the middle of that floor, and begin the dance. And just perhaps, if we had half the courage and the grace that Andrew and Shawn had shown, others would come dance with us.

Chapter 14

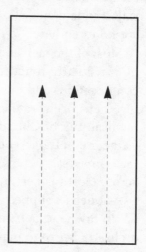

1993–94,

Time for Doing Justice!

O*n Gay/Lesbian Pride Sunday, June 27, 1993, the Cathedral of Hope* in Dallas, Texas, was jammed at two services by more than two thousand happy communicants. Michael Piazza, our senior pastor, helped me fasten the hidden Velcro strips on the brand-new, white alb he had given me as a gift on my birthday, just twenty-four hours earlier. If you don't know what an alb is, don't be embarrassed. Neither did I. It is that basic white garment worn by priests and high-church Protestant ministers under their stoles and chausubles when they lead in formal worship.

"Looking good," Michael said, grinning his most impish grin, knowing how silly I felt making my debut as dean of the Cathedral in my first white dress. My low-church worship tradition frowned on pomp and pageantry. In the congregations of my childhood, we sat on hard wooden pews, sang simple choruses, and passed aluminum Communion trays with little plastic cups up and down the aisles. I am an unrepentant, low-church yuppie, at home in suit and tie. But because homophobia runs rampant in most American churches, there are as many gay and lesbian Christians from Catholic and high-church Protestant traditions who have joined the Cathedral as there are evangelicals, fundamentalists, and charismatics. Their worship traditions, too, are honored here.

Most of the men and women who make up the nearly ten thousand lives regularly touched by the Cathedral have been rejected by the congregations and the denominations of their childhood. So we come together to celebrate our faith with our own wonderful eclectic, ecumenical mix of Christian and even Jewish liturgical traditions at the Cathedral in Dallas and in hundreds of other churches associated with the Universal Fellowship of Metropolitan Community Churches across North America and in sixteen countries around the world.

As Michael slipped a stole around my shoulders and placed a hymnal in my hand, a trumpet fanfare sounded, the organ and Cathedral orchestra began to play, and the choir and congregation stood to join their voices in an enthusiastic hymn of praise. Michael took my arm and suddenly we were walking together down the Cathedral's long center aisle, my heart nearly bursting with excitement.

"We are a people coming home," they sang, "coming to our own." I tried to join in the singing, but my voice choked with emotion and my eyes filled with tears. As I moved slowly through that huge crowd of gay and lesbian Christians, dozens of new friends and strangers smiled at me from both sides of the aisle. Many of them, too, were crying.

It's easy to understand why tears flow so freely at the Cathedral. When you've been a victim of the teachings of the religious right, when you've been kicked out of your homes and churches, condemned by your pastor, priest, or rabbi, and your Sunday- or Sabbath-school teachers, rejected by your family and friends, you feel condemned and rejected by God as well.

Then, you wander into the Cathedral and hope begins to stir to life again. Morning sunlight streams through stained-glass windows that retell the ancient Hebrew-Christian stories but include in great chunks of colored glass, images of a pink triangle and barbed wire from the concentration camps where our German gay brothers died, of the AIDS quilt, and of the Greek lambda of liberation.

As the people gather, you feel excitement and joy. You hear trumpets, bell choirs, and great musical ensembles. In each Sunday service, you see close to a thousand gays and lesbians standing side by side to sing and pray and share their discovery that the religious right is wrong to condemn and reject us. God loves gays and lesbians, too. And at the Cathedral of Hope, you feel the Spirit of our loving Creator, Redeemer, and Sustainer present in the crowd giving hope and healing to all those present.

For almost forty years I had been plagued by guilt and fear. Finally, after decades of "ex-gay" therapy, needless guilt, and growing despair, I had learned to celebrate my sexual orientation as another of God's gracious gifts and to take my place in the world as a responsible and productive gay Christian. In my lowest moments, I wanted to die. I never dreamed that one day I would be happy or hopeful again. That is the biggest lie of all. There is light at the end of the tunnel. Closet doors can be opened and gays and lesbians can emerge blinking into the light of a brand-new day. Families can be reunited. Gays and lesbians can live healthy, happy, productive lives. We can love and be loved as we always dreamed. I have seen it happen in my life and in the lives of countless friends and acquaintances.

For all those years, I was certain that my family would be destroyed by my struggle. Now, in spite of the suffering they have endured, my family has triumphed individually over my worst fears. We see each other often and love each other still. Today, I can be grateful to my wife and family for their patience and their understanding. Then, I could only worry and hope. They couldn't really understand why I was putting them through those long, painful years. Now they understand better, but even then, when they were most angry, disappointed, confused, or afraid, they went on loving, trusting, and forgiving me.

As I walked down that aisle en route to my installation as dean of the Cathedral, I knew there would be some changes in my life, but I had no idea how radical those changes might be. After the processional, as Michael Piazza and I stood together looking out across the congregation, he nudged me and pointed up at the balcony. A television cameraman and several still photographers were aiming their telephoto lenses at us.

After forty years in the closet, the last dozen hidden even deeper in the shadows as a ghostwriter to leaders on the religious right, it was rather unnerving to find myself a kind of gay celebrity. That Sunday's edition of the *Dallas Morning News* featured my picture in living color on the front page with a long, sympathetic story by religion writer Dan Cattau, describing my friendship with leaders from the religious right.

From that next Monday, the phones in the Cathedral have not stopped ringing. Calls came in immediately from Connie Chung, Tom Brokaw and Katie Couric, Barbara Walters and Sam Donaldson, from Fox's "Front Page" and ABC's "Good Morning America." Larry King requested an immediate Friday-night appearance on his "Larry King Live" telecast from Washington, D.C. Both National Public Radio and the British Broadcast Company did interviews in those first few weeks. Not long after, Morley Safer, his producer, Patti Hassler, and their crew arrived to do a documentary for "60-Minutes."

As Michael Piazza introduced me to my new Christian family on that installation Sunday, I knew for certain that the old struggle was over. I was free at last to begin a new life. I was a ghost no more. I had found my own voice at last. All those years I had not dared to dream that the struggle would end. All that time I was afraid that God had abandoned me. I was wrong. God had been with me each step of the journey. I stepped to the Cathedral's pulpit shaped in a triangle of pink marble, looked out across my new Christian family, swallowed back the waves of emotion that I felt, and began to speak.

"You may think that you are looking at another overeducated, overprivileged, slightly balding—okay, more than slightly balding—member of the white, male patriarchy. But you're wrong. Now, thank God, after thirty years of struggle, I can say at last who I really am. I am gay. I am proud. And God loves me without reservation."

Before my opening words were finished, the crowd began to cheer. Suddenly, they were standing on their feet applauding and shouting their support. I joined in that standing ovation because it was not really for me, but for the God who created each of us, the God who loved us and gave us strength to survive the false warnings, the false cures, and the false promises we had all endured.

Toward the end of my installation sermon, I spoke directly to my old employers. "To Jerry Falwell, Pat Robertson, and my other old clients on the religious right whose antigay rhetoric is killing us, and to Billy Graham and my other old friends whose silence helps but not all that much, I say this. I will not hate you, for Jesus said, 'Love your enemies.' I will not plot revenge against you, for Jesus said, 'Do good to those who despitefully use you and persecute you for my name's sake.' And I will not stoop to using your techniques: half-truths, hyperbole, and lies, for Jesus said, 'The truth will set you free.'

"But this, too, I promise. I will not remain silent any longer. The religious right is wrong: wrong about the Bible, wrong about Jesus, wrong about God, wrong about the church, wrong about the family, and seriously wrong about gay and lesbian people. On this Lesbian/ Gay Pride Sunday, I pledge myself to do my best to prove you wrong with all the courage, wisdom, and love I can muster.

"Be confident," I concluded hopefully. "The victory will be ours. Falwell, Robertson, and the others have gone too far. They are blaming gay people for everything bad that's happening in this country, and one by one thoughtful Americans are beginning to wonder if this antigay rhetoric isn't getting out of hand. They're beginning to realize that the religious right isn't right at all.

"Those TV and radio gurus who condemn us are not interested in truth, not really. They're more interested in raising money, in building their mailing lists, and in rallying their constituencies around an easy, helpless target . . . us. Well, we aren't so easy or helpless as they think. Jesus, the Spirit of Truth, is on our side. We will proclaim the truth in love, but we will proclaim it."

When I declared war on the religious right that day, I was responding to the war they had already declared against us. Two thousand years ago a young Jewish prophet confronted his own generation of Pharisees on the religious right. He had the audacity to suggest that love is the only way to conquer them. I have hope that one day even Jerry Falwell and the others who claim quite falsely that they "love the sinner but hate the sin" will understand the terrible damage that they are doing. Until that day, we must confront them, debate them, outorganize, outvote, and outlove them whenever and wherever we can. Whatever they do, we must try our hardest not to succumb to the lovely temptation of hating them back.

Before Gary and I were even settled into our home in Texas, we met with more than one hundred volunteers from the Cathedral of Hope who wanted to join our Truth in Love campaign to help confront the lies being told against us. Individual monitors were assigned to video- or audiotape every antigay remark by each of the homophobic radio or television personalities. The books, articles, and mailings of each of the homophobic leaders and their organizations were monitored by individual volunteers as well.

By now, you know who they are, these men and women who want gays and lesbians silent, back in the closet, stripped of their civil rights, and in some of the most extreme cases, even dead. Here are a few of my favorites: Jerry Falwell, Pat Robertson, Jim Dobson, D. James Kennedy, Chuck Colson, Tim LaHaye (Capital Report), Beverly LaHaye (Concerned Women for America), Gary Bauer (Family Research Council), Ralph Reed (and the Christian Coalition), R. J. Rushdoony, the Christian Action Network, American Security Council, Christian Life Coalition, Rutherford Institute, American Family Association, Operation Rescue, Eagle Forum, Citizens for Excellence in Education, Free Congress Foundation, and of course their copycats in each state, such as the Oregon Citizens Alliance led by Lon Mabon.

In order to confront the lies these people tell, we began to gather other kinds of data as well. A medical/scientific committee was appointed to research every latest bit of data on such related issues as the origins of sexual orientation and recent findings on HIV and AIDS. Another committee met to study the Bible and to collect the latest biblical studies regarding the passages used against us. A legal committee met to help us get a clearer picture of the rash of antigay legislation that was breaking out in more than 170 different cities, states, and counties across the country.

Within weeks, antigay propaganda from the religious right began pouring into our Cathedral offices. Almost immediately we had to find other volunteers to catalog and file the mountain of homophobic lies we were collecting. Other volunteers began to search for stories of members and friends of the Cathedral who had been affected by those lies in tragic ways. (We are still collecting. Send us what you have.)

The claim made by the religious right that if you have enough faith, God can make you an "ex-gay" quickly proved to be one of the deadliest and most damaging lies of all. Pat Robertson, the only one who bothered to answer the letter I had written him earlier, invited me to join the 700 Club for a $35 contribution and suggested that I call his 800 counseling line for help and healing.

Although he didn't even try to prove it, Pat informed me that thousands of homosexuals were being "healed" through his prayer lines every month. How sad that Pat is so self-deceived, and worse, how ludicrous that he would try to pass that serious self-deception off on me after I spent more than one-quarter of a century trying desperately to be an "ex-gay" myself.

Needless to say, Pat and the others cannot support their claims that there are thousands of homosexuals who have experienced "miraculous sexual reorientation" after calling their "ex-gay" hot lines or visiting their "ex-gay" counseling centers. Every generation, the religious right trots out another well-meaning batch of "ex-gay" testimonials to support their false promises of a "cure," but no real follow-up records are kept, no serious studies undertaken. There is no evidence that "reparative therapy" has permanent success in the lives of most of those who claim a cure, and weeks, months, or years later most realize the temporary nature of that "cure."

Any "ex-gay" or former "ex-gay" can tell you how it *is* possible to repress your natural sexual orientation for a while, especially when you have a new Christian community surrounding you with love and prayers. It isn't so difficult, at least not at first, when you have a new husband or wife or special Christian friends watching you like a hawk and pastors, teachers, and counselors confronting and caring for you each step of the way.

Nevertheless, the verdict is in. The facts are certain. We don't need another scientific study or another pathetic story of long-term failure and loss from the "ex-gay" movement to prove that homosexuality, like heterosexuality, is a permanent condition. Some few homosexuals, like some few heterosexuals, manage to live celibate lives. Another small percentage, though lesbian or gay, manage somehow to pretend to be heterosexuals for a lifetime.

But most gay men and lesbian women who survive the terrible, wasted years of "ex-gay" repression and denial eventually have to make a decision. Will they finally accept their sexual orientation as another of God's gifts and go on to live responsible gay or lesbian lives, or will they go on struggling against this gift forever?

Pat Robertson, since you will not talk to me directly, I might as well address you here. With every new generation, there are hundreds of lonely, desperate gay and lesbian people who find temporary comfort in your well-meaning but deadly "ex-gay" counseling programs. You film and videotape their testimonies. You marvel and applaud as they share the stories of their "healings" on the "700 Club." You ask for large donations to support your program and people respond lovingly and generously to your request. But neither you nor they ever bother to find out for themselves how most of these sad stories end. We do know how they end because by the thousands they come to the Cathedral of Hope for healing that is based on acceptance, not denial.

After years, decades, and even lifetimes wasted struggling to be "ex-gay," they finally come through our doors, and the doors of other gay/lesbian friendly congregations and organizations like ours all across the country. They come to us broken, embarrassed, guilty, angry at you, and angry at the God you serve; while you continue to deny the evidence that reparative therapy is short-lived at best and you go on denying the tragic, long-term consequences of the false hopes and counterfeit cures you offer.

While still living in Laguna Beach, I met Michael Bussee—one of the founders of the "ex-gay" movement— at an EC Connection (retreat) in San Francisco. Michael is a gifted writer with a poet's heart. I'm still urging him to publish an account of his moving journey of faith and courage. Among so many other things, Michael's story (featured in the prize-winning film, *One Nation Under God*) illustrates again the long-range failure of the "ex-gay" movement and its leaders.

After years of manning an "ex-gay" hot line, after writing and recording "ex-gay" materials, after teaching "ex-gay" seminars and sharing his "ex-gay" testimonial in churches and on religious broadcasts across the country, after founding Exit, the "ex-gay" ministry at Melodyland and helping cofound Exodus, the national organization of "ex-gay" ministries, Michael realized that in spite of all his genuine, prayerful efforts at faith and discipline, he hadn't changed at all. "Sexual orientation is forever," Michael told us. "I was so sincere. I tried so hard, but I wasted years of my life misleading myself and misleading others."

After finally learning to accept his homosexual orientation as a gift from God, after falling in love and beginning a lifetime relationship, Michael and his partner, Gary Cooper, another ex-"ex-gay," spent years in the closet, frightened that no one would accept them, "ex-gays" and gays alike. They seemed so surprised by the tearful, standing ovation they received from their new lesbian sisters and gay brothers at our EC retreat. They wept when we hugged them and thanked them for sharing their painful journey with us.

During our weekend together, Michael told us a story that will stick in my heart forever. Early one Sunday morning at the Melodyland church in Anaheim, Michael found Enrico S., another "ex-gay," waiting at his office, weeping. Enrico's whole body was trembling. "I hurt myself," Enrico gasped between sobs. "Why did you hurt yourself?" Michael asked. "I keep failing," the young man answered. "The feelings just keep coming back. I fight them. I honestly do, but it's no use."

Without speaking another word, the young man unzipped his pants and lowered his briefs to reveal cuts, dozens of them. Enrico's penis and scrotum were covered with fresh wounds, still seeping blood. The skin looked burned and bubbly.

"Enrico had gone over the emotional edge," Michael recalled. "He had used a razor blade, slashing at his genitals, trying to drive away his homosexual feelings. The Bible said, 'If your eye offend you, pluck it out.' Enrico had taken the Bible seriously. Then he had poured Drāno over the cuts."

Michael got Enrico to the hospital in time to save his life, but those deep emotional and psychological scars would last forever. As Michael told the story, I was remembering not just Enrico, but my friend Jeffrey, who had also emasculated himself when we were in college together thirty years earlier. As I sat there with my gay and lesbian friends, I wondered how long the people of this nation would refuse to deal honestly and lovingly with this subject and how many more innocent gay or lesbian people would have to suffer and die before that happened?

Holding out these "ex-gay" hopes that our sexual orientation can be changed is just another way of telling lies. And one day, Pat Robertson, Jerry Falwell, Jim Dobson, Jim Kennedy, Lou Sheldon, Gary Bauer, and the rest of the gay bashers who hold out these simplistic "ex-gay" solutions to desperate gays and lesbians will be held accountable by God for the terrible consequences of those lies.

Jerry Falwell, next time you send out an antihomosexual mailing to the millions of people on your mailing list, remember that you are helping to create an atmosphere of ignorance intolerance, and hatred in this nation, and that you are confusing and misleading a whole new generation of people just as Jeffrey and Enrico were misled. Before you mail out one more homophobic book or videotape ("for a small donation") remember these words of Martin Luther King. "The church at times has preserved that which is immoral and unethical. Called to combat social evils, it has remained silent behind stained-glass windows, an echo rather than a voice, a taillight behind the Supreme Court rather than a headlight guiding men progressively and decisively to higher levels of understanding."

Pat Robertson, every time you produce another "700 Club" segment of "news" against gay and lesbian people, remember that you are adding to the noise pollution that keeps the truth from being heard, contributing to the suffering and death of your gay brothers and lesbian sisters, and assuming at least partial responsibility for thousands of wasted young lives just like Jeffrey's and Enrico's. The next time you invite gay people to call your 800 line "to find how getting saved will end their struggle with homosexuality," remember these thoughtful words of Martin Luther King: "In spite of the noble affirmations of Christianity, the church has often lagged in its concern for social justice and too often has been content to mouth pious irrelevancies and sanctimonious trivialities. It has often been so absorbed in a future good 'over yonder' that it forgets the present evils 'down here.'"

James Dobson, every time you interview Gary Bauer, your antigay lobbyist in Washington, D.C., or another of your handful of false, gay-bashing "experts" with psychology degrees on your "Focus on the Family" radio program, you cloud the air, undermine the truth, and contribute to the destruction of another American family just like Jeffrey's or Enrico's families were destroyed. The next time you are tempted to condemn gay and lesbian people with your half-truths, your hyperboles, and your lies, remember these words of Dr. King: "Jesus did not seek to overcome evil with evil. He overcame evil with good. Although crucified by hate, he responded with aggressive love."

Jerry, Pat, Jim, the rest of you, how about switching from your media and print campaign of aggressive hate and disinformation to "aggressive love." It was Jesus' way. Why not try it. You say you "love us homosexual sinners, but hate our sin." If you truly loved us, you would meet with us, discuss these matters with us, consider carefully the historic, scientific, medical, psychological, biblical, and pastoral data, hear our stories, and try to understand our pain, the pain for which you are largely responsible. Instead, you go on bashing us. Reread your mailings. Play back your audiotapes and your videotapes.

Ask yourself, do these angry, sarcastic, inflammatory accusations against us sound like "aggressive love" to you?

With people like Falwell, Robertson, Dobson, Kennedy, Bauer, Sheldon, John Paul II, and now Rush Limbaugh and the rest of them on the religious and political right constantly sounding their false alarms against gay and lesbian people, there is no way to discuss the issue calmly, quietly, honestly. Jeffrey and Enrico lived in a world where one sin seemed worse than all the rest. Feeling lonely and condemned, they did desperate, terrible things.

Someday, hopefully before Jeffrey's or Enrico's tragic stories are repeated a thousand times, the people of this nation will refuse to take seriously the false warnings and the tragic misinformation of the religious right. Someday, hopefully before many more lives are wasted, the nation's parents will reach out in love and acceptance to their homosexual children. Someday, hopefully before another generation of lesbians and gays are rejected by their churches and their synagogues, the clergy and laity of this nation will realize the wrong they're doing and reaccept into full membership the gifted and generous folks they are currently turning away.

On July 19, less than thirty days after I was installed as dean of the Cathedral, President Clinton announced his "Don't ask, don't tell" "compromise" plan for "ending" the ban on gays and lesbians in the military. When the president made lifting that ban a campaign promise, the religious right mobilized their forces to force the president to change his mind.

On one day alone, the White House received more than four hundred thousand calls against lifting the ban. The mail rooms and switchboards at the White House, the State Department, the Pentagon, and the Senate and House of Representatives were inundated by millions of letters and cards, calls and faxes, most mobilized by the religious right.

One of our monitors taped Jerry Falwell's opening shot in the religious right's war against lifting the ban. "If we lift it," he claimed quite falsely, "our poor boys on the front lines will have to face two different enemies, one from the front and the other from the rear."

Jerry Falwell shamed himself with those ignorant and insulting words condemning tens of thousands of courageous and committed young gays and lesbians in the military. Those gay men and lesbian women learned as I learned in our adolescent years how to maintain decorum in the locker rooms and later in the barracks. Unlike our heterosexual counterparts, we learned from adolescence to live in close quarters, shower and sleep with the very objects of our desire, and at the same time to control our needs and to discipline our desires.

Our monitors quickly discovered that opposing the president's promise to lift the ban had become the latest in a long line of hysterical, misleading, false antigay appeals guaranteed to make more millions for the religious right. Some people don't realize that Pat Robertson, Jerry Falwell, even Jim Dobson, have to mobilize an estimated $1–3 million in donations every week, much of it just to pay their media bills. Each of these three religious right organizations has a larger annual budget than the Vatican. So, in order to help keep the donations rolling in, Pat, Jerry, Jim, and the rest of the radio and television religious personalities rushed to condemn the president. But Jim Kennedy—perhaps because he was in more desperate straits than the rest—outshamed them all.

In his August 3, 1993, "emergency" fund-raising mailing (almost every D. James Kennedy mailing is an "emergency"), he claimed the following false reasons to oppose lifting the ban on gays and lesbians in the military. "Picture your own son or grandson serving in the armed forces at risk of homosexual rape . . . sexual harassment . . . placed at serious risk for AIDS." The long, inflammatory letter, including various other false claims, complete with a pledge-of-support form begging for a donation of at least $10–$20, was printed on paper the color of U.S. Army camouflage combat fatigues.

Just three weeks after Jim Kennedy's fund-raising mailing, the Pentagon finally made public a long-delayed $1.3 million Rand Corporation study on gays in the military commissioned by the Pentagon itself. That 518-page report was quickly buried by national officials and by leaders of the religious right because it refutes all the major arguments that opponents made against lifting the ban.

Fact: In the military, as in the civilian population of this country, sexual abuse is primarily a heterosexual problem. With rare exceptions, homosexual soldiers do not seduce, harass, or sexually abuse their fellow soldiers.

Fact: The Defense Department has a strict HIV testing policy in place and bars all new recruits with any signs of HIV infection. Everyone is tested annually, and rapid-deployment forces are tested more often. Battlefield transfusions are rare.

Fact: Millions of gays and lesbians have served their country with honor. Tens of thousands are serving all four military branches today. Most do not openly admit their orientation and, according to the Rand report, "are appropriately circumspect in their behavior."

Fact: There is no credible evidence that homosexuals hurt combat effectiveness and unit cohesion. Quite to the contrary, gays and lesbians have distinguished service records.

Fact: The report dismissed as outdated fears that the presence of known homosexuals would exacerbate problems relating to privacy in showers and foxholes.

The Rand report, like at least three Pentagon studies before it, recommended completely eliminating the ban on gays in the military. But once again, facts did not prevail over the fund-raising appeals of the religious right. Instead of hearing the truth from the religious leaders they trusted, millions of innocent conservative Christians in America were misled by the broadcasts and fund-raising appeals of the religious right. Instead of raising these ancient, unfounded homophobic fears, Jerry, Pat, Jim, and the rest of them should have saluted gays and lesbians by the millions who have lived and died bravely in the front lines of every war this nation has fought.

The president's new "compromise" would allow gays and lesbians to serve in the armed forces only as long as they did not disclose their sexual orientation publicly or privately. It was a blatant command to lie, an order to return to the closet, a demeaning and dehumanizing decision that will force our brothers and sisters to live under constant fear of discovery and, in all probability, lead to another round of witch-hunts in the armed services.

Between 1980 and 1990, through those military witch-hunts, the military had discovered and dismissed 16,919 service members for homosexuality, at a cost of almost $500 million to replace them (from a GAO report, 1992). Their God-given sexual orientation was the only reason that these young men and women were sacked from the service. And though most of those discharges were honorable, the discharge papers, known as a DD214, clearly stated the reason for the individual's expulsion to future employers. Like the old ban, the new "compromise" would cause suffering and loss to thousands of gays and lesbians in the military and lead to millions of dollars in needless waste to a government already deeply in debt.

On Thursday, July 29, I read in the Dallas Morning News *that on Friday,* July 30, leaders of the gay and lesbian community were gathering in Washington, D.C., to protest the president's "compromise" in a noon-time rally in Lafayette Park. After meeting with the press corps to discuss our community's deeply felt disappointment with the president's decision, they would march across Pennsylvania Avenue, stand before the White House in silent protest, and be arrested in a symbolic act of civil disobedience.

As I read the names of our community leaders scheduled to attend the rally and protest, I realized that no one representing lesbian and gay religious or spiritual organizations was on the list. David Mixner, a gay community leader and one of Mr. Clinton's campaign advisers and fund-raisers, would attend, along with such others as Tim Mc-Feeley, executive director of the Human Rights Campaign Fund, William Waybourn, executive director of the Gay and Lesbian Victory Fund, Tanya Domi from the National Gay and Lesbian Task Force, and their allies in this campaign to lift the ban from other gay/lesbian and gay/lesbian friendly organizations including Patricia Ireland, president of the National Organization for Women.

They were gathering in the nation's capital to vent and visualize the grief and disappointment that all of us were feeling. Under Troy Perry's national leadership, the congregations of the UFMCC had mobilized to phone and write the president and members of Congress on behalf of lifting the ban. During our first weeks in Texas, I had visited my own congressman, Martin Frost, to seek his support for ending this military policy of discrimination against gay and lesbian Americans. Members of the Cathedral's Truth in Love campaign had phoned, faxed, written, lobbied, and prayed, but up against the powerful antigay lobby of the religious right, our campaign to end the ban had failed.

Once again injustice had prevailed. The suffering of our brothers and sisters in the military would continue. Frankly, I understand why the president broke his promise to end the ban. I had hoped he would

be able to stand against the avalanche of antigay propaganda un-
leashed by the religious right, but I understood it when they overwhelmed him with their homophobic media blitz. If anyone was to
blame for this new policy of discrimination against us, it was my old
clients from the religious right. Knowing that once again the nation's
conservative Christian community was the cause of our suffering, I
felt it was my responsibility as dean of the largest gay/lesbian Christian church in the nation to join with our political activists in their
symbolic protest and arrest.

Gary drove me to the Cathedral for a last-minute strategy session
with my new boss, Michael Piazza, and in less than two hours I had
boarded a plane on one of my United Frequent Flyer Award free
tickets that ironically I had earned traveling for my clients on the
religious right.

The only way to get to Washington, D.C., that day on United from
the Dallas–Fort Worth International Airport was to fly west to Denver
before flying east to the nation's capital. With so little time to spare,
you can imagine how frustrated I felt finding myself on a wrong-way
trip to Denver, but on that strange and wonderful flight, I met an
angel-messenger disguised as a blind African-American priest with the
Episcopal Church.

Actually, my wise and wonderful seatmate, the Reverend Dan H.,
assured me that he was fully human, blinded as a child, and now
happily married with a ten-month-old baby. In spite of my seatmate's
doubtful grin, I was convinced that God had assigned my seat that
day. How could it be a coincidence that on the first day of my life as
a Christian activist I would rush aboard a wrong-way plane as a
standby passenger and be seated "by chance" next to an African American who had been bitten for the first time by a police dog while
protesting injustice at the ripe old age of eight and arrested for the first
time at twelve while marching with Dr. Martin Luther King, Jr.?

God knew I needed instant training to be even moderately effective
as a Christian activist. I still believe with all my heart that Father H.
was assigned to me that day. "For lesbians and gays to win the war
against injustice and discrimination," he said quietly, "you must remember these lessons from Dr. King and the civil rights movement
that he led. First, stay vigilant. At all times, know who your enemy is
and what your enemy is doing. Second, never let up pressure. You

must never rest in your work to gain and protect your rights as American citizens. And third, don't get impatient. It will be a long, arduous struggle, but truth is on your side. You will prevail."

After flying more than eight hours that day, my gay friend Dick Sproul, an accountant with *USA Today,* met me at Dulles Airport after midnight and loaned me his sofa for a few hours of sleep. Troy Perry had told me to always wear a clerical shirt at protests "to show to the world that religious leaders, too, are in the front lines of this war against injustice." But I didn't even own a clerical collar yet. The training for that day's civil disobedience began at nine-thirty A.M., so I looked up a shop that sold liturgical clothing on a street near the White House and was standing at their front door when they opened at nine. In five minutes, I was fitted, out the door, and racing to the briefing session for my first arrest as a Christian activist.

As I rushed through the door into this company of distinguished gay and lesbian leaders, David Mixner was the first to greet me. "Aren't you Mel White?" he said, walking across the room to say hello. "We all just read your story in the *Los Angeles Times*. Thanks for your courage." I was dumbfounded that he had recognized me, let alone thanked me for my "courage." In fact, I was ashamed that I had waited so long to take a stand. After working for all those years with the men and women responsible for the suffering of gays and lesbians in America, I wanted to apologize to these activists who had fought so long and so courageously against the ancient homophobia being stirred up into bigotry and hatred in our time by the religious right.

After being trained in nonviolent civil disobedience; after discussing our individual responses to the crowd of reporters who were waiting; after learning how to respond to the National Park Service police who would arrest us, transport us to jail, and book us; and after meeting with our legal and safety monitors who would watch over us until they had secured our release, I took my first baby steps toward becoming an effective gay, Christian activist.

There is no way to describe how I felt that day as twenty-four of us walked arm in arm through the crowds toward Lafayette Park and the White House. After all those years in my closet, suddenly I was in the nation's capital representing tens of thousands of gays and lesbians in the military and millions of our brothers and sisters across the country who stood in solidarity with them. Television crews and print reporters rushed about interviewing and filming us. Government clerks and officials leaned out of windows and crowded the sidewalks. Tourists snapped pictures. A touring Boy Scout troop from Iowa stopped nearby to see what was happening. A handful of lesbian and gay AIDS activists shouted at us angrily, scorning us for "wasting our time" fighting the military ban while tens of thousands of our brothers were dying. Police were everywhere.

Somehow I managed to remain dry-eyed until our small group left the Lafayette Park rally. As we started across Pennsylvania Avenue to the White House, a few hundred friends and supporters who had gathered in the park began to sing "We Shall Overcome." When we reached the zone midway between the east and west guard gates, where it was illegal to stop or protest, I stood for a moment looking up at the White House. The American flag was flying. Secret Service agents were everywhere. I wondered if President Clinton was watching. I hoped he knew the great regard we had for his office and the awe we shared for his terrible, unenviable responsibility to serve all the people equitably.

The press had approximately ten minutes to interview us before the Park police would move in to begin their arrests. David Mixner spoke briefly. Patricia Ireland added her remarks. Next came Miriam Ben-Shalom, a lesbian decorated for her military service, and Don MacIver, a gay former Green Beret with a chestful of medals earned in Vietnam. Both spoke fervently on behalf of lifting the ban. Then, suddenly, the leaders turned to me.

"My name is Mel White," I began quietly. "I am the recently appointed dean of the Cathedral of Hope in Dallas, Texas. I speak on behalf of hundreds of thousands of gay and lesbian Christians in this nation who also wish that President Clinton had kept his promise to lift the ban. But I do not blame only the president for his failure. I blame the religious right, who used their powerful media voice to stir up the ancient, evil spirit of homophobia to pressure the president into this unacceptable 'compromise.' The lies they tell about gay and lesbian Americans lead directly to our suffering and death. This is but one example. I am here to protest those lies."

At that moment, a dozen or more police cars and paddy wagons began to arrive, sirens blaring. A policeman gave us the two-minute warning. In Lafayette Park, our supporters again began to sing, "We Shall Overcome." One by one, my new friends were arrested. As each gay or lesbian leader was led away, the crowd across the street cheered and applauded in support. Finally, two policemen came for me. They took away my belt and my shoelaces. They strapped my hands behind my back. They photographed me, wrote down my name, address, and social security number and led me to a waiting bus.

As I sat in the back of that bus with my hands strapped tightly together, I could hear our friends still singing. "Deep in my heart, I do believe. We shall overcome some day." The TV crews and reporters were wrapping up their gear. Most of the tourists had wandered away. The Boy Scouts from Iowa still looked on in wide-eyed wonder, and the AIDS activists were still shouting their anger at us for wasting time when men and women were dying.

The last man to be arrested was Don MacIver, the gay former Green Beret. I didn't know it then, but many of those Park policemen wore special badges that identified them as military veterans. Some of them had also served in the Green Berets with Don in Vietnam. They surrounded him and arrested him last perhaps to honor his service to our country and as special recognition for Don's distinguished military record. The police were forced to take off Don's belt and bootlaces, but when they started to remove the medals for courageous service that he had earned in Vietnam, the crowd began to shout in protest. "He earned those medals," they yelled. "Let him keep them."

Once again, God appointed my seatmate that day. Don and I rode side by side to the Anacostia police substation and waited together more than three hours to be booked. During that time we shared our very similar stories. From a Christian home and family, Don had spent his lifetime internalizing antigay bigotry and discrimination stirred up by conservative Christians. After experiencing so much homophobia in the churches of his past, Don had found it difficult to take an active part in any Christian congregation. As the police called me to be booked, Don grinned and said quietly, "Just coincidentally, I'm moving to Dallas in the next few weeks, and after this conversation, I'd like to talk to you about joining the Cathedral of Hope."

Today, Don MacIver is one of our valued volunteers helping us do some justice through the Cathedral's Truth in Love campaign. Once again during those twenty-four hours, on a plane and in the backseat of a bus, I was amazed by the wisdom of the Apostle Paul, who wrote, "All things work together for good, to those who love God and are called according to God's purpose."

While I was being booked, the Park police locked me in a tiny jail cell with an iron cot and a metal toilet. For a short time, I sat alone in that cell, staring at the cement floor and barred window, remembering all the men and women who had suffered in house arrest, jail cells, stockades, detention centers, penitentiaries, torture chambers, and concentration camps because they were willing to risk their lives on behalf of justice. For the first time in my life, this overprivileged, upper-middle-class, white male got a little feeling for the price of doing justice that so many others have paid. I would be released that day without any real suffering, but over the centuries, men and women who believed in doing justice had lived and died in cells just like this one.

In that tiny cell, I felt God's call to do some justice on my own. In the past, I may have disagreed with some of the tactics of Act-Up or Queer Nation, but their courageous activists have paid a terrible price to lead the way in our community's fight against discrimination, bigotry, and injustice. Now it was time for me to follow their example and to muster up a little courage of my own. When the jail door opened and I was released, I knew in my heart that the long wait was over. As dean of the Cathedral of Hope, I couldn't be content just to sing hymns, pray, and occasionally preach or teach. It was my time to heed God's voice and do some justice as well.

The Bible makes it clear. Doing justice—keeping things absolutely fair for everybody—is the work of God. When we see an individual or a group—African-American, Asian-American, Hispanic-American, old or young, male or female, citizen or illegal alien, gay or nongay— being treated unfairly, Jesus calls us to do something to help end the suffering.

In Nazi Germany most of the Christian churches—Evangelical, Protestant, and Catholic alike—supported Adolf Hitler. They went on singing hymns, praying, and preaching sermons as usual while the government of the Third Reich arrested, tortured, and murdered millions of innocent citizens. Imagine how the Jews, the Gypsies, or the young German gays who died must have felt about those hymns of praise echoing in their ears as they were forced into the trains that would carry them to their death.

But even in Nazi Germany, God had a handful, a remnant, a tiny band of faithful servants determined to do justice. The life of one of those people, Dietrich Bonhoeffer, a courageous young German pastor and theologian, has inspired me from my seminary days. Just before the war, Bonhoeffer was offered a full professorship at Union Theological Seminary in New York City, but as the last German passenger liner was loading in the New York harbor for the final trip home, Bonhoeffer rushed back to the dock.

"My best friend in Germany is another young pastor," he said. "I feel it would be an utmost disloyalty to leave him alone when the conflict comes. I must either go back to stand by him and act with him or get him out and share my life with him."

Bonhoeffer risked his life to do justice for his friend and for his nation, and just days before the war ended, the Nazis arrested, tried, and murdered him. He might have written more great books or preached more great sermons or delivered more great lectures. Instead, he gave his life for justice.

There is a war raging against gay and lesbian people in our country right now. Our civil rights are on the line. Our freedom is at stake. The homophobic lies of the religious right are murdering the souls and threatening the civil rights of gay and lesbian Americans. We must stand against those lies.

I'm not suggesting how or when anyone else should act. But for me, it begins by coming out, in appropriate ways to appropriate people who desperately need to be informed by our example. All the studies prove that people who know personally a gay man or a lesbian are the people who stand for justice on our behalf. People who do not know personally (or who don't think they know) a lesbian or gay are those who are more likely to vote against us. Coming out, stating proudly who we are to the people we know and love, has become the first and most important step we take on the road to doing justice.

Doing justice begins by walking away from the churches and the synagogues, the preachers, priests and rabbis, who use God's word to condemn us and into churches and fellowships where we are loved and respected as God's children who happen to be lesbian or gay.

It begins by withholding our tithes and offerings from homophobic churches and synagogues and by giving our money and volunteering our time to churches, synagogues, and other organizations that are working for justice on behalf of gays, lesbians, transgendered, and transsexual people.

It begins by preaching and teaching justice in our own churches and synagogues; by organizing and training our congregations to do some justice and not just to talk about it; by seeing that every precinct in our district has at least one lesbian or gay man in place to oppose the Christian Coalition and expose their lies; by writing the radio and TV stations that carry the broadcasts of these soul murderers, asking for equal time to tell the truth; by kneeling and praying and protesting on the steps of city hall or standing arm in arm on state capitol steps when our civil rights are at stake; by working with the media to help them understand our side of the story; by building networks with our friends and allies, with the NAACP, with the ACLU, with People for the American Way, with NOW; by fighting for justice wherever and however we can on behalf of all our fellow Americans who suffer.

Forgive me for speaking about doing justice before I have set any kind of real example. Forgive me for suggesting ways we might do justice in our community before I have acted with any courage of my own. However doing justice begins for you, let it begin! Let justice roll down as water, let righteousness flow like a mighty stream.

I don't know what will happen if this nation's economy gets worse and those in power need a scapegoat. They're already marginalizing gay and lesbian people exactly as Hitler marginalized the Jews. "Homosexuals are only one percent of the population," claims the religious right, "and not ten percent as in Kinsey's old report." "Gays and lesbians are richer than the average American," they charge further, "with more discretionary money to spend because they don't have wives, husbands, children, or mortgages." "They have far more privileges than the average American," they accuse. "They even fly more and earn more frequent-flier credits than heterosexual travelers." Day by day, half-truth after half-truth, lie after lie, they are setting up America's gays and lesbians as an "overprivileged," "overpowerful," and "overpromiscuous minority."

Read about Germany in the early thirties. On their way to gaining power over that great nation, see what Hitler and his henchmen did to marginalize the Jews and other helpless minorities including gays. The religious right is doing it again, this time straight out of Hitler's book. I don't think the severity of what happened in Germany will be reached here. But what might come to pass if our economy dives downward, if unemployment rises, if poverty and misery grow, if violence and crime rates increase, if our budget deficit leads to economic collapse, if the religious right wins the day and a real antihomosexual candidate gets elected in 1996 by a frightened, hungry nation?

In my lifetime, 12 million Jews, gays, and other marginalized people were killed in Germany without provocation. In the former Soviet Union, at least 50 million men, women, and children were murdered. The current "ethnic cleansing" in old Yugoslavia reminds us that holocaust is real and happens anew in every generation. Already, we are being marginalized, demeaned, discriminated against, beaten with baseball bats, and killed by those who don't even know us.

All the polls say that about 50 percent of the nation supports equal rights for lesbians and gays, while the other 50 percent wants our rights taken away. It's a close race by anyone's standards and we could lose it. What could happen next if the shrill, strident, still surging cry of the religious right wins the day? What could happen to us if their leaders take the field? Could it mean sanitariums with high walls for people with AIDS and even HIV? Could we live to see our human rights withdrawn, our churches closed, our leaders arrested, our activists martyred, and barbed-wire barricades strung around ghettos where we are forced to live?

One of my gay heroes, Dag Hammarskjöld, former secretary general of the U.N. before he was killed in a plane crash plotted by assassins from the political right, wrote these words in *Markings,* his classic diary: "Soon, we shall meet, death and I, but he shall plunge his sword into one who is wide-awake." Whatever happens, we must not wait around to be surprised.

When Michael F. Griffin shot and killed the abortion doctor David Gunn in March 1993, he did it with a prayer on his lips and the rhetoric of the religious right echoing in his heart. What must we do to keep from being next? The antigay rhetoric of the religious right leads to darkness and despair. We must be the people of the light to drive that darkness away.

Shortly after my installation, my friend Jonathan Potts reminded me that we Christians are in the business of bringing light to dark places. Jonathan and his life partner, Dan Stohler, were special friends to Gary and to me. For ten years or so, I had met Dan regularly to talk about our lives, to study the Bible, and to pray together. After Dan fell in love with Jonathan, the four of us often met for dinner or went out for snacks after EC meetings in Pasadena. Both men were HIV positive. Gary and I dreaded the awful day when we might lose one or both of our good friends. Before Jonathan got too ill to travel, the four of us spent a wonderful week vacationing in Provincetown, Massachusetts.

A few weeks after our vacation, Jonathan went to the hospital for his final courageous bout with AIDS. He had wasted away to skin and bones. Dark purple Kaposi's sarcoma lesions covered his body. His sallow skin was stretched tight across his cheekbones, and his dark, sunken eyes reminded me of prisoners discovered in Hitler's concentration camps. He still joked and ordered us around, but we knew for certain that this time Jonathan was dying.

On one of our last visits, Jonathan took my hand and pulled me down toward his bed. His eyes sparkled and his cold, thin hand trembled. "I had the weirdest experience this morning," he said softly. "While I was lying here, the room suddenly filled with darkness. You could feel it moving in like fog. I got scared. I felt like evil had entered the room and was trying, somehow, to capture me. 'Help me, Jesus,' was all I could think to say."

Jonathan paused. He was breathing hard. He struggled to clear his throat.

"At that moment," Jonathan continued, "I saw a tiny gold angel near the ceiling in the far corner of the room. It looked just like the angel my sister pinned to my pillow. See?"

I looked at the tiny golden angel on Jonathan's pillow and smiled. Jonathan grinned back.

"When I asked Jesus to help me," Jonathan whispered, his eyes beginning to fill with tears, "the little angel began to move slowly towards me. And as he moved down into the darkness, the room began to fill with light." For a moment Jonathan couldn't speak. He seemed almost overcome by the happy memory.

"As the little angel got closer," Jonathan said, "the darkness just went away."

A few days later, Jonathan moved into the light forever. Now, we continue our journey without him, but he left us with this promise. When we act in faith, there is enough light in this world to conquer the darkness. As we journey together, let that light so shine in us that the darkness will be driven away and this long, dark night will end forever.

Six Letters to the Religious Right

Jerry Falwell

5,000 Oregon Pastors

Billy Graham

Pat Robertson

Jim Kennedy

John Paul II

Letter to Jerry Falwell

(December 24, 1991)

MEL WHITE
Personal and Confidential

Jerry Falwell
Lynchburg, Virginia, 24502

Dear Jerry,

   In 1986 and 1987, when I was ghostwriting your autobiography, *Strength for the Journey*, there was no reason for us to talk about me or about my life story. Your publisher, Simon and Schuster, and your agent, Irving Lazar, had hired me to do a job and I did it. You never asked me about my political beliefs or my personal values. And though we came from two rather different worlds, I liked you immediately and I appreciated your frankness, your sense of humor, and your loyalty to friends and family. For your friendship and for the clients you have sent me, I am grateful.

But in the past few years, Jerry, it has become more and more painful for me not to share with you my own personal journey. Now, in light of your October 1991 letter against homosexuality and homosexuals, I can no longer remain silent.

I am gay. For the past eight years (which include all the time I've been in your employment) I have been in a loving, monogamous relationship with another gay man. I am a member of a Metropolitan Community Church congregation (the only Christian denomination that is truly open to gay and lesbian people) and a member of Evangelicals Concerned (a national Bible study and prayer movement of gay and lesbian evangelical Christians).

I came close to sharing this part of my own story with you one night in a hotel suite in Washington, D.C., when we were celebrating the successful release of your autobiography. During that conversation you admitted that the church needed to do much more to help those who suffered from AIDS, and you confided that one of your own close friends was a gay man in a long-term relationship with another gay man. "I'm not going to put him in a corner," you said quietly, "if he doesn't put me in one."

You seemed compassionate and understanding that night. Then, today, I received a copy of the October 1991 fund-raising letter describing me and millions of men and women like me as "perverts" who "unashamedly flaunt their perversion." The letter declares "homosexuality a sin." It warns that "our nation has become a modern day Sodom and Gomorra" and that you have decided to speak out against this "perversion" for the purpose of "moral decency and traditional family values."

Jerry, I am hoping that staff or agency "ghostwriters" wrote that letter and that you didn't have time to read it before it was signed and mailed on your behalf. Did they realize the immediate and long-term impact of its cloud of misinformation, half-truth, and hyperbole? Did they understand the confusion and the suffering that it helps cause in the lives of American families who have gay or lesbian members? Did they know that the letter's misleading statements fuel bigotry, hatred, and violence?

Closer home, did anyone consider the tragic consequences of that letter in the lives of the people who see you as their spiritual guide? Certainly you know that in the Thomas Road Baptist Church, in Liberty University, and in the audience of the "Old Time Gospel Hour," there are thousands of Christians struggling with this issue. Did anyone think about the confusion, the anguish, and the despair that the letter's simplistic, judgmental, and erroneous position creates for them and for their families?

I know personally what it means to be a victim of this uninformed and noncompassionate "Christian" position on homosexuality. I went through twenty-five years of Christian counseling and "ex-gay therapy" including electric shock to try to overcome my sexual and affectional orientation. Finally, feeling abandoned by God, by the church, and by society, I longed to end my life.

Now, looking back, I can see that God was there, all the time, in the midst of my suffering, leading me to a remnant of faithful, well-informed Christians who had the courage to speak the truth whatever it cost them.

My most helpful counselor was fired from Fuller Seminary (where I was a professor for fourteen years) because she dared to tell the truth about homosexuality and the false claims that the "ex-gay" movement makes. And though telling the truth cost her her academic position, she saved a lot of lives and ministries in the process.

If you are really trying to educate the nation about homosexuality as the letter states, you owe it to yourself to look more closely at the scientific, sociological, ethical, and biblical data that is now available to us. The letter mailed in your name was tragically uninformed and dangerously inflammatory in the process. What a wonderful thing it could be if *you* really took this issue seriously and tried to deal with it lovingly, thoughtfully, and in the spirit of Christian truth.

Jerry, we are called by Christ to bear witness to the truth, and yet the October 1991 letter is based on lies. We gay people are not "perverts" nor "degenerates" as the letter claims. My homosexuality is as much at the heart of what it means to be Mel White as your heterosexuality is at the heart of what it means to be Jerry Falwell. The wide array of intimacy and relational needs that you and your wife, Macel, meet for each other are only met for us in same-sex relationships. If you really want to help end promiscuity, tell the truth. We need you to honor and support our relationships, not oppose and condemn them.

The letter also lies when it claims that we gay and lesbian people are a menace to this nation. In fact, we are your fellow pastors, deacons, church musicians, and people in the pew. We write and arrange the songs you sing. We are your studio technicians and members of your staff. We are doctors and scientists, secretaries and clerks. We even write your books.

We are not a threat to the American family, either. We are committed to the family. Millions of us have raised wonderful families of our own. We have adopted the unwanted and the unloved and proved to be faithful, loving parents by anyone's standards.

And we certainly pose no danger to your children. Most child molestation cases are heterosexual. You know that. The truth is we have taught and nurtured your children in schools and Sunday schools without your ever knowing that we are gay.

Most of us gay and lesbian people are just normal folk who try our best to live respectable, productive lives in spite of the hatred and the condemnation heaped upon us.

We didn't choose our sexual orientation, Jerry, and no matter how hard we try, we cannot change it. There is no trustworthy, long-term evidence that sexual "reorientation" or a lifetime of celibacy is possible for tens of millions of gay and lesbian people. What brings us health is the realization that our sexuality, too, is a gift from God. And to lead a whole, productive life we have to quit struggling against God's gift and learn to lead our lives as responsible gay and lesbian Christians.

Almost every day, I speak with gays and lesbians who are struggling to survive the waves of hatred and self-hatred generated by Christians who write letters like your letter of October 1991, or who make similar statements in sermons, on talk shows, and in interviews. Is it any wonder that gays and lesbians have finally run out of patience and are taking to the streets to protest the prejudice and the bigotry?

In your recent contact with the Act-Up demonstration in Los Angeles, it must have been terrible to realize how many people felt hatred toward you and your position. With the memories still fresh in your mind of those fearful moments in the Hotel Roosevelt kitchen, let me help you understand the bigotry and the violence we face every day, not just on the streets but in our homes, on our jobs, and even in our churches.

Every year, thousands of innocent gay and lesbian people face physical and psychological assault. Dozens are murdered. Tens of thousands are rejected by their families, fired from their jobs, and kicked out of their homes or apartments. Three times I have had rocks or bottles thrown at me from passing cars simply because I was walking with friends near a gay church or restaurant. Fundamentalist Christian extremists hound and harass us, carrying hateful signs and shouting profane and demeaning accusations in the name of "Christian love."

I know that every group has its zealots, and I thank you for stating clearly in your letter that "the majority of gay persons are not violent." But Jerry, we have reasons to demonstrate. And the letter issued in your name, using the same old, tired lies to whip up more bigotry and more hatred against us makes you a primary target for our demonstrations.

Is it any wonder that we are protesting Governor Wilson's veto of AB101, a measure that would have protected gays and lesbians from being fired simply because of their sexual orientation? Think about it. Even though you have praised my Christian commitment and my writing skills, would you hire me or recommend me again now that you know I am gay? Don't you find it ironic that if I had made my sexual orientation known, I could not have served the church faithfully these thirty years as pastor, professor, author, filmmaker, and television producer?

At this moment when hysteria and misinformation about gay and lesbian people threaten our most important public and private institutions, you could become a great healing agent. Wise counsel about homosexuality could lead to reconciliation in the family, in the church, and in the nation. Telling the truth that gay and lesbian people are a responsible and productive force in the church and throughout society could lead to understanding where misunderstanding and hatred now grow.

Jerry, I am also worried about the motives behind your letter. I remember clearly in one of our interviews that you described a noisy confrontation you once had with "radical activist gays" in San Francisco. "They played right into my hands," you said to me. "Those poor, dumb fairy demonstrators gave me the best media coverage I've ever had. If they weren't out there, I'd have to invent them."

Whatever motives caused the letter to be written, antihomosexuality is not an appropriate issue for fund-raising. Too many lives are damaged or destroyed in the process. On behalf of myself and other

Christian gays and lesbians in Lynchburg and around the world, please, before you speak or write again about this issue, could we meet face-to-face to talk about the consequences?

I make this proposal, Jerry. Will you meet with me—anytime or anyplace at your convenience—so that I can share with you the other side of the story? I appeal to you as a fellow Christian believer in the name of our Lord, Jesus, who said: "If thy brother do ought against thee, go and tell him between thee and him alone" (Matthew 18:15). I am glad to volunteer my time and travel to serve you. Do what you want with the information I could bring, but please hear it!

Lyla, my wife for twenty-five years of this painful journey, is eager to join in our discussion. As a heterosexual woman, wife, and mother, Lyla knows firsthand what it costs the families and friends of gays and lesbians to go on loving and supporting them when everyone else turns away. Her wisdom and counsel would serve us both well.

Maybe Macel, too, would like to be included in our conversation. Wherever and whenever it takes place, I am confident that in a open, loving dialogue we will both grow in our understanding of the issues and in our determination to contribute to the healing of the Christian church and of the nation.

Sincerely,
Mel White

Letter to 5,000 Oregon Pastors on the Eve of the Antigay Amendment 9 Vote

(October 1, 1992)

MEL WHITE

A Personal Letter
To the Evangelical pastors and lay leaders of Oregon

Greetings, brothers and sisters in Christ:

You may know me through my books (or the books I have written with Billy Graham, Pat Robertson, and Jerry Falwell) or through my films (from the *Charlie Churchman* series through *Tested by Fire* and *Deceived: The Jonestown Tragedy*) or through my articles in *Christianity Today, Leadership, Faith at Work,* or *Eternity* magazines.

Some of you were my students at Fuller Theological Seminary during the fourteen years I served there as a professor of preaching and communications. Others heard me preach or teach at various conventions, spiritual-emphasis events, and seminars for pastors and youth workers. You might even remember my years in Portland (1958-65) emceeing the Saturday-night Youth for Christ rallies or hosting KGW-TV's "The World of Youth."

What you may not know is this: I am a homosexual. I discovered my homosexuality in my earliest childhood and have lived with it uneasily throughout the past quarter of a century of Christian ministry. Finally, after thirty years of "ex-gay" therapy, including electric shock to "overcome" my homosexuality, and decades of needless guilt and growing despair, I have learned to accept my sexual orientation and to take my place in the world as a responsible and productive gay Christian man.

I am writing you today on behalf of my homosexual Christian brothers and sisters who have also lived their lives in silence and in fear while serving Christ faithfully as members of your denomination and even as members of your local church. On November 3, the voters of Oregon will make their decision about Ballot Measure Nine. If that initiative passes, our gay brothers and sisters in Oregon will suffer a terrible injustice; and the cause of hate, fear, and intolerance will be advanced across the nation.

Ballot Measure Nine means that gay and lesbian people (or those *perceived* to be gay or lesbian) could be fired from their jobs and evicted from their homes. Public libraries and public broadcasting could be required to remove books or programs that discuss homosexuality. Doctors, lawyers, and other professionals who are gay or lesbian could have their state licenses revoked. Harassment and even physical violence against gay and lesbian people (or those *perceived* to be gay or lesbian) would be inadvertently condoned.

Ballot Measure Nine sponsors, most of them, sadly, from our own Evangelical churches, believe that the Bible condemns homosexuality as "an abomination of almighty God," that homosexuals "can be cured—sexually reoriented—through conversion," that AIDS is a "self-created misery of pleasure-addicted gays," that gay people "are a threat to family values," and that "gay activists" must be stopped "before they trample on your freedoms."

Supporters also claim quite wrongly that we gay people "recruit children to homosexuality"; that we "cannot be trusted to teach, pastor, or serve in the military"; and that our civil rights in jobs and housing don't need protection "because they are already protected by the U.S. Constitution."

I spent seven years in Oregon earning my BA degree from Warner Pacific College and my MA from the University of Portland. In my experience, Oregonians have always been an example to the nation of tolerance and fair play. I appeal to you in that spirit to consider the growing mountain of evidence discrediting and disproving the claims made by the supporters of Ballot Measure Nine against us gay and lesbian people.

First, let's review the biblical data. The authors of those six passages used to condemn us knew nothing about sexual orientation. They were fighting pagan idolatry, temple prostitution, and irresponsible sexuality. They didn't know about gays and lesbians living in committed relationships, who lead normal, productive lives, and who cherish and honor their families. Now their words are being used out of context in Oregon to whip up a frenzy against gay and lesbian Americans who, in spite of the prejudice and discrimination against them, live courageous, creative, and committed lives.

Second, there is no scientific data that gay people can be reoriented sexually with any degree of permanence. Quite to the contrary, there is accumulating scientific evidence that homosexuality is a genetic condition (or at the least, a human characteristic permanently determined in the first few years of life). Both the American Medical Association and the American Psychological Association have removed homosexuality from their list of psychological illnesses. And the testimonials that you hear or read from "ex-gays" who claim to have been sexually reoriented by conversion or by a gift of the Holy Spirit do not stand the test of time.

Third, only the most ignorant and prejudiced among us continue to claim that AIDS is a "gay disease" or "an act of God's judgment against gay people." Heterosexual women and innocent children are rapidly becoming the primary victims of this terrible virus that thrives in the climate of ignorance and fear perpetuated by Ballot Measure Nine and its backers.

Fourth, those who see gay and lesbian people as a threat to our own or to other people's children—let alone to family values—are terribly misinformed. I am just one of the millions of gays and lesbians in this country who love and support their own families while dealing realistically with their sexual orientation. It is a vicious lie to say that "we recruit children to homosexuality" when the facts prove that we are responsible and trustworthy parents and grandparents, uncles and aunts, nieces and nephews.

Fifth, to generate larger offerings from their listeners, our critics warn of some insidious "gay activist agenda." I'm a "gay activist" and a grandfather, an Evangelical Christian, and a writer-filmmaker committed to biblical truth. If we "gay activists" have any agenda at all, it is simply to protect our brothers and sisters from the kind of prejudice, hatred, and violence generated by the false warnings on religious radio and television.

Sixth, backers of this ballot measure claim that the civil rights of gays and lesbians in Oregon don't need protection. It isn't true. Hate crimes against us are increasing dramatically. We are cursed, clubbed with baseball bats, and murdered simply because we are gay. We are losing our jobs and our apartments, not because we are bad employees or irresponsible tenants, but because of our sexual orientation. We are not allowed to serve in the military when Pentagon studies prove irrefutably that gays and lesbians serve their country with skill and honor. And though we love Christ and serve His church faithfully, in most churches we cannot be ordained to ministry or even volunteer to serve as laity unless we remain in the closet.

Surely you know at least one of the many gay and lesbian Christians who serve Christ responsibly and creatively as clergy and lay leaders in your denomination. And though they may never have felt free to share their unique and difficult journeys of faith, the homosexual members of your congregation are out there, supporting your ministry with their tithes, their prayers, and their faithful service as teachers, musicians, deacons, trustees, and even members of your staff.

From the beginning, gay and lesbian Christians have served Christ's church wherever it brought hope and healing to our broken world. Now, however, religious personalities are using fear and distortion to paint us as the enemy. Their misinformation leads to prejudice, hatred, violence, and Ballot Measure Nine. As a result, all across the country our gay Christian brothers and sisters are suffering in silence, leaving the church in anger and disappointment, and even taking their own lives because too few Christian leaders have the courage to tell that truth: "We can be gay and Christian."

Along with the governor and most of Oregon's elected officials, many Catholic and Protestant leaders oppose this issue. What will happen to the Gospel witness in Oregon when Evangelical Christians seem to be the only religious group backing this vicious and unjust measure?

Throughout history, when religious leaders get laws passed that impose their morality on the public, it has been disastrous to the church and a crippling blow to the spread of the Gospel. Once you've called me an outcast, I can't hear your good news even if it could change my life. Once I have associated the Gospel with hatred, persecution, and deprivation, how can I be open to its truths again?

I know how difficult and costly it may be for you to say anything about Ballot Measure Nine to your leaders or your congregation; but lives are in the balance and the future of the Evangelical witness in Oregon is at stake. Have you read the ballot measure? Have you considered its consequences to the future of the church in Oregon, let alone to Oregon's gay and lesbian people or their friends and families? What could you say or do in your church to get the matter better understood? Will you at least prayerfully consider, in the privacy of the voting booth, voting no on Nine?

The People of Faith Against Bigotry (503-230-9430) will provide you with a copy of the measure, discussion materials, and the list of your fellow clergy, churches, and denominations who oppose the measure. Know, too, that you may duplicate and share this letter with anyone you wish.

You and I have spent our lives seeking to be true to the Scriptures as we understand them. And though we may disagree on the subject of homosexuality, surely we agree on this: the Bible should not be used to rob any of our fellow Americans of their basic human rights.

Much as we may hesitate to get involved in political issues lest it compromise our witness, political and prophetic issues cannot always be torn apart as the Bible clearly shows. This measure is also a prophetic issue, calling our nation to justice, to mercy, and to truth. When we are silent, we also take a stand. Now, the Gospel is at stake. A single word of wisdom from you could make a momentous difference and even save lives, not just in Oregon but across the nation.

Mel White

c/o Evangelicals Concerned, P.O. Box 4308, Costa Mesa, CA 92628

Letter to Billy Graham
On the Eve of the Antigay
Amendment 9 Vote

(September 5, 1992)

MEL WHITE

Billy Graham
c/o Pacific Northwest Billy Graham Crusade
700 N.E. Multnomah Blvd.
Suite 1040
Portland, Oregon 97214

Dear Billy,

Ten years have passed since we worked together on your book
Approaching Hoofbeats. I remember fondly our times together: walking
the beach or looking through bookstores in Acapulco; interviewing

and editing in the San Francisco Airport Hilton; narrowly missing Queen Elizabeth at Trader Vic's during her California tour; answering the late-night or early-morning phone calls to write or rewrite your speeches to a UN gathering or a World Council of Churches assembly; and sharing those rare, intimate moments when you took time off to talk about your personal feelings and deeply felt dreams.

It made me sad when your phone calls stopped suddenly and without explanation, but I understood. When you were told that I was gay, you (or your advisers) must have thought you had no choice but to end our relationship. And I was still confused enough about my sexual orientation to accept your silence and to disappear unhappily back into my closet.

But so much has happened in this past decade. After thirty years of therapy, including electric shock to "overcome" my homosexuality, and decades of needless guilt and growing despair, I have learned at last to accept my sexual orientation as another of God's gifts and to take my place in the world as a responsible and productive gay Christian. To that end, I am writing you on the eve of your five-day Pacific Northwest Crusade in Portland, Oregon, September 23–27, 1992.

On November 3, just five weeks after the close of your meetings at Portland's Civic Stadium, the voters of Oregon will make their decision about Ballot Measure Nine. If that initiative passes, my gay brothers and sisters in Oregon will suffer a terrible injustice; and the cause of hate, fear, and intolerance will be advanced across the nation.

Ballot Measure Nine lumps homosexuality with pedophilia, sadism, and masochism. It requires the state to set a standard "for Oregon's youth" that discourages homosexuality as "abnormal, wrong, unnatural, and perverse." Gay and lesbian people (or those *perceived* to be gay or lesbian) could be fired from their jobs and evicted from their homes. Public libraries and public broadcasting could be required to remove books or programs that treat homosexuality in a positive or even in a neutral way; doctors, lawyers, accountants, and other professionals who are gay or lesbian (or those *perceived* to be gay or lesbian) could have their state licenses revoked. Harassment and even physical violence against gay and lesbian people (or those *perceived* to be gay or lesbian) would be inadvertently condoned.

I know the people of Portland. I spent seven years (1958-65) living and working among them while earning my BA degree from Portland's Warner Pacific College and my MA from the University of

Portland. During that time I emceed the Saturday-night rallies of Portland Youth for Christ, hosted their weekly television program, produced films and TV specials, created the Alpenrose July 4th Spectacular, and spoke in churches and schools across the state.

In my experience, Oregonians have always been an example to the nation of tolerance and fair play. I'm afraid that those people supporting Ballot Measure Nine have been misled by television preachers (like Pat Robertson) and radio counselors (like Jim Dobson) who use the Bible quite incorrectly to claim that gay people have a choice, that we can "reorient" what was born in us or permanently shaped in our infancy, and that we are even dangerous to the future of "American family values."

In their attempts to rid the world of our "evil influence," the proponents of this bill are claiming that gay people "are responsible for most child molestations"; that gay people "cannot be trusted to teach, pastor, or even serve in the military"; and that gay people's civil rights in jobs and housing should not be protected.

You must know the growing mountain of evidence that demonstrates the exact opposite. There is no scientific data that gay people can be reoriented sexually with any degree of permanent success. Heterosexuals (not homosexuals) are responsible for most child molestation and abuse. Millions of us serve faithfully as teachers, pastors, and priests. Pentagon studies prove irrefutably that gays and lesbians serve their country with skill and honor.

And the authors of those six short biblical passages used to clobber and condemn us knew nothing of sexual orientation. They were fighting pagan idolatry, temple prostitution, and irresponsible sexuality. They didn't know about gays and lesbians living in committed relationships, who lead normal, productive lives, and who cherish and honor their families. Now those same passages are being used to whip up a national frenzy against millions of gay and lesbian Americans who, in spite of the fear and hatred they face each day, live lives that are remarkable for their courage, their creativity, and their commitment.

You know Lyla and my children, Billy. I even have a beautiful granddaughter now. My family love and respect me for my faithfulness and my integrity. And I am just one of the millions of gays and lesbians in this country who love and support their families while dealing realistically with their sexual orientation. We are parents, grandparents, uncles, and aunts. Those who see us as a threat to our own or to other people's children—let alone to family values—are terribly misinformed.

Surely you know how many gays and lesbians work for you in Minneapolis, in Portland, and in every city where you have preached. We help produce your films and television specials. We sing in your crusade choirs. We work backstage on sound, lighting, and security. We usher and we counsel your seekers. We give our time, our money, and our energy to support your causes. We even help you write your books and sermons. Millions of us serve Christ and His church wherever it brings hope and healing to our broken world.

In return, our pastors, our teachers, and our televangelists call us "child molesters" and "perverts." We cannot be ordained to ministry or even serve as volunteers unless we remain in the closet. We are called "faggots" and even clubbed to death by those who hear inflammatory speeches like Pat Buchanan or Pat Robertson gave to the Republican Convention. And now along with our lives, our civil rights are being threatened.

You have always been a man of courage. You stood for racial integration when you were advised to segregate your first crusades. You refused to quit preaching in the Soviet Union when everyone said you were aiding the communist cause. Now, again, will you act with courage on behalf of your gay Christian brothers and sisters who are being persecuted by the very churches they serve?

Last night in a gay Evangelicals Together Bible study, one of our new members told about trying to kill himself by drinking Drāno. All his life he had been told that homosexuality was the "unforgivable" sin. For ten years he had tried valiantly to "overcome" his sexual orientation. "Thank God," he said to us, "I finally found the truth. I can be gay and Christian." All across this country our gay Christian brothers and sisters are suffering in silence, leaving the church in anger and disappointment, and even taking their own lives because too few Christian leaders have the courage to tell that truth: "We can be gay and Christian."

Two thousand years ago, when Jesus saw His children suffering, He spoke this clear warning: "Whoever shall offend one of these little ones which believe in me, it were better for him that a millstone were hanged about his neck, and that he were drowned in the depth of the sea." We know it will cost you to say even one positive word on our behalf, but in the long run the cost of silence will be so much higher for you and for those who trust you to tell the truth, as it certainly will be for us.

You have spent your life and ministry being true to God's Word. Thoughtful students of the Scriptures may disagree on the subject of homosexuality, but surely they do agree on this: the Bible should not be misused to rob anyone of his or her basic human rights.

I know you don't take stands on political issues, but as you know, political and prophetic issues cannot always be torn apart. This is also a prophetic issue calling this nation to justice, to mercy, and to truth. Our lives as gay and lesbian Christians are at stake. Tell them, Billy. A single word of wisdom from you could make a momentous difference and even save lives, not just in Oregon but across the nation. Please, in Jesus' name, won't you help us?

Hopefully,
Mel
September 16, 1992

Letter to Pat Robertson After His "700 Club" Report on the 1993 March on Washington

(May 1, 1993)

MEL WHITE

Pat Robertson, President
Christian Broadcasting Network
700 CBN Center
Virginia Beach, VA 23463

May 1, 1993

Dear Pat,

Late last night, over the telephone, my mother shared her distress at the "700 Club" pictures she had seen reporting on the April 25 gay and lesbian march on Washington, D.C. I could feel her grief and confusion that I had attended the march.

I, too, monitored your program that day. I saw the pictures you showed of a handful of marchers that were carefully calculated to offend your viewers. I taped your false warnings of the alleged "radical gay agenda" and its supposed demands for "special rights" that you falsely claim would "threaten traditional American family values" and "undermine the morals of the nation."

Pat, do you mean to deceive your viewers with these pretend news reports that are replete with half-truth, hyperbole, and lies? Do you mean to bring fear and misunderstanding to my family and to the nation?

I tried to explain the truth to my devastated parents. I tried to help them understand what really happened last Sunday when I met and marched with my gay brothers and lesbian sisters and with our courageous friends and family members who stand with us against the discrimination, suffering, and death caused in great part by your untrue and inflammatory broadcasts, booklets, and mailings.

During the weekend's premarch events, I worshiped on the steps of the Lincoln Monument with at least a thousand other Christian gays and lesbians from our denomination alone. I attended seminars, receptions, and a concert of massed gay bands and choirs. I lobbied my senators to end the military ban and to pass the civil rights bill that would guarantee gays and lesbians the human rights promised them by our Constitution. And I marched proudly with gays and lesbians in local and national government, in business, in the military, in entertainment, in the arts, and in positions of church leadership from across the country.

Whether you believe the National Park count of three hundred thousand marchers or the Mayor's Office estimate of more than 1 million strong, it is amazing that in all that mass of loyal, hardworking, taxpaying American citizens, you had to focus on a minority of our community to support your caricature of gay and lesbian people. How sad that you did not bother to find one gay or lesbian doctor, lawyer, minister, mayor, psychologist, or ghost-writer to photograph or to question about the real issues being raised at this march, the issues of truth, justice, and human rights.

When you hired me in 1985 to ghostwrite your book, *America's Dates With Destiny,* I believed in you and in your ministry. I still remember how excited you were when I discovered the connection between Charles Finney (another lawyer-turned-preacher whom we both admire) and the antislavery and woman's suffrage movements by way of Thomas Weld and Harriet Beecher Stowe.

Do you remember when we wrote these words: "To Finney, Weld, and their associates in this second Great Awakening, discrimination of every kind needed to be overthrown." Or these: "It is tragic that so many of the women and men who stood against sin in the form of slavery and discrimination were discriminated against by the very churches that introduced them to the life and teachings of Jesus."

Now, you must judge your words against gay and lesbian people by your words on pages 140 and 143 of *America's Dates With Destiny*. Like those same white, Christian men who misused the Bible and the pulpit to support slavery and to discriminate against women, you are misusing the Bible against us. Instead of using your powerful presence on television and in print to inform the nation, you are battering your viewers with an endless barrage of disinformation and propaganda that is leading literally to the suffering and death of Christ's little ones.

In 1989, Louis W. Sullivan, the secretary of health and human services under President Bush, downplayed the report on "Gay Male and Lesbian Youth Suicide." According to that study, "gay youth are two to three times more likely to attempt suicide than other young people," and "suicide is the leading cause of death among gay and lesbian youth."

Why will approximately fifteen hundred gay and lesbian young people kill themselves this year, while tens of thousands of others who fail at their suicide attempts will go on living lives of quiet, lonely, closeted desperation? Secretary Sullivan's report makes it clear.

"Gay and lesbian youth," states the Secretary's Task Force on Youth Suicide, "are strongly affected by the negative attitudes and hostile responses of society to homosexuality. The resulting poor self-esteem, depression, and fear can be a fatal blow to a fragile identity. . . . This is especially true for gay adolescents who have internalized a harshly negative image of being bad and wrong from society, religion, family, and peers."

Read the secretary's report, Pat. I would be glad to send you a copy for your information. The data is clear. Over the years, the misinformation that you broadcast leads directly and indirectly to the suffering and death of thousands of this nation's young people. What you are doing has disastrous immediate and long-term consequences, not just for my younger gay brothers and lesbian sisters, but for your own soul.

In all three Gospels, Jesus warns His disciples about what might happen to them if their words or actions lead to the suffering of God's children: "It is better for him that a millstone be placed around his neck and that he be drowned in the depth of the sea."

How many frightened, lonely youth have killed themselves because of what they or their parents have heard on your telecasts or read in your books or mailings? How many American families have been torn apart, how many teenagers have run away or been discarded, how many acts of discrimination or violence have been aimed against gay and lesbian youth because of the homosexual myths and stereotypes that you promote and sustain?

The tragic, trickle-down effects of homophobic rhetoric have been demonstrated over and over again. What you say about homosexuality on the "700 Club" moves with devastating consequences through our homes, our schools, and our churches. The disinformation you distribute appears and reappears in sermons, Sunday school lessons, counseling sessions, and in heartbreaking confrontations between young people, their parents, and their peers.

I know firsthand the kind of fear and self-loathing that young gays and lesbians experience. I discovered my own homosexuality in earliest childhood. I know what it feels like to be president of my youth fellowship, of my Bible club, and of my high school Student body and still feel lost, cut off from God and from my family by my terrible secret.

Finally, after thirty years of "ex-gay" therapy, including electric shock to "overcome" my homosexuality, after decades of needless guilt and growing despair, after my own emotional collapse and suicide attempt, I have learned to accept and even celebrate my sexual orientation as another of God's good gifts and to take my place in the world as a responsible and productive gay Christian man.

It took thirty-five agonizing years; but now at last the truth has set me free. When you and I were researching and writing together, we saw in the lives of Finney, Weld, and Harriet Beecher Stowe how often God's Spirit has to turn people in a whole new direction before they can hear God's voice and become God's instruments of change.

"Stowe was a Connecticut-born Yankee," you wrote in our *Ameri-*

ca's *Dates With Destiny,* "who never lived in the South, but she met and talked at length to many Southern men and women as she prepared her novel. She interviewed slaves and slave owners, abolitionists and antiabolitionists alike. She collected hundreds of case histories of slaves, their mistreatment, their escapes, their recaptures, and their returns. She carefully verified each story and filed them in her memory. Gradually she was transformed by what her investigation uncovered."

Follow Stowe's example, Pat. Talk to gay and lesbian people yourself before you telecast any more images of our community that are calculated to offend your viewers. Listen to the true stories of your Christian brothers and sisters who have tried every possible "exgay cure," who discovered the hard way that there is no real, lasting way to sexual reorientation, who now live in long-term, responsible gay relationships. Hear the stories of discrimination and suffering that we all have experienced before you repeat the lie that we are demanding "special rights." Meet with our leaders before you speak again about our alleged "radical agenda" or its imagined "dangers for America."

Let me help. I will meet with you privately or in public at any time and at any place at my own expense just for the chance to discuss this matter. There is so much fascinating and informative new biblical, scientific, psychological, and sociological data. There are so many true stories—including my own—that could inspire and inform your decision. I have served you faithfully. All I ask in return is a chance to be heard.

In Christ's name,
Dr. Mel White, P.O. Box 35466, Dallas, Texas 75235

Letter to Jim Kennedy
After Another of His Antigay
Fund-raising Letters

(May 26, 1993)

MEL WHITE

Jim Kennedy, Senior Pastor
Coral Ridge Presbyterian Church
5555 N. Federal Highway
Ft. Lauderdale, Florida 33308
Phone: 305-771-8840 Fax: 305-771-2952

Dear Jim,

From that day twenty years ago when I rushed to Ft. Lauderdale to write your "Evangelism Explosion" film, *Like a Mighty Army,* I've tried to be a thoughtful friend to you and to your ministry. When you decided to produce theatrical films, I wrote to warn you of the possible financial consequences of taking such a risk. Now, as an old friend, I must write you once again.

Last week, I saw your TV special warning viewers about the so-called "gay agenda." Your writers repeatedly used half-truth, hyperbole, and lies. Your data about child molestation and gay teachers is totally erroneous. Your two universally discredited "experts" and their claims for reparative therapy are unsupported and dangerously misleading. The young "ex-gays" upon whom you built your case are the same two young men featured in other antigay videos these days. And though there is no doubt that they and the young "ex-lesbian" are sincere, you proved nothing (and you compromised your credibility) by *using* these three innocent, well-meaning kids who have just begun their personal journeys without even considering where their journeys might end. In the whole, your TV special was irresponsible, inflammatory, and deceptive with tragic, long-range consequences for the American family, for the church, and for this nation.

Like hundreds of thousands of your fellow Christian Americans, I spent twenty-five years trying to be an "ex-gay." Even after my conversion experience, I spent tens of thousands of dollars on Christian therapy. Repeatedly, I was counseled, exorcised, electric-shocked, medicated, and prayed for by the saints. Like the young people in your TV special, I began each new day really believing that God had "healed me," when in fact, I was simply refusing to face the facts.

Finally, I realized that my sexual orientation was permanently and purposefully formed in my mother's womb or in my earliest infancy. Because of simplistic, well-meaning, but uninformed teachings on homosexuality like your own, I wasted thirty-five years in guilt, fear, and personal agony. And though there were times I could not feel God's presence, God never left my side. God's Spirit was there always to comfort and to guide me. Now, I have accepted my sexual orientation as a gift from my loving Creator. Finally, as our Savior promised, the truth has set me free to be a productive, responsible, Christian gay man.

Jim, this wave of misinformation and hatred against us must stop. If you can't see what you are doing to hurt others, consider what you are doing to endanger your own soul. In all three Gospels, Jesus warns His disciples about what might happen to them if their words or actions lead to the suffering of God's children: "It is better for him that a millstone be placed around his neck and that he be drowned in the depth of the sea."

TV specials like the one you've just produced lead directly and indirectly to violence against gay people and to depression, self-hatred, and suicide for sensitive, young gay and lesbian Christians who are victims of this avalanche of hatred from Christian TV personalities like yourself. Read Matthew 23 again. Hear Jesus condemning the Pharisees who heap unbearable burdens on the backs of the innocent ones. "Snakes!" he calls them. "Sons of vipers. How shall you escape the judgment of hell?"

I don't want to question your motives. I believe you are a sincere man who wants to do right, but I have discussed your current financial problems with members of your staff and congregation and at least one member of your board. I am convinced that you produced this misleading TV special (and that you created your silly, misleading questionnaire) primarily to raise money and to build your mailing list. There is nothing more pharisaic than to increase another's pain and grief simply for financial gain.

If you are really sincere about helping gay people, you would spend serious time studying and considering the data that supports a more thoughtful, loving approach to gay people and their families. You would not build an entire television special around false propaganda, one largely discredited psychologist, and three young, untested "ex-gays." You would have at least considered new data from biblical scholarship and pastoral care, from psychological and psychiatric studies, from Christian gays and lesbians, their families and friends.

Gay and lesbian Americans have become the victims of a shrill, homophobic media and print campaign conducted by religious broadcasters that leads directly to our suffering and death. Please, Jim, before you add your voice again to the current flood of hatred and misinformation against us, talk to me. I will come to Florida at my own expense just for the chance to share the other side of this story before more lives are lost and more souls, including your own, are put in jeopardy.

Sincerely,
Mel White, Dean of the Cathedral
May 26, 1993

Cathedral of Hope (UFMCC), P.O. Box 35466 Dallas, Texas 75235
Phone: 214-351-1901   Fax: 214-351-6099

Letter to John Paul II
World Youth Day, 1993

MEL WHITE

To: His Holiness John Paul II
   The Vatican
August 10, 1993

Your Esteemed Holiness:

   We represent the largest church in America with a primary ministry to gay and lesbian people. We have more than 6,000 communicants on our rolls and 1,200 active members in our congregation in Dallas, Texas. And our national organization, the Universal Fellowship of

Metropolitan Community Churches, is expanding rapidly across North America and around the globe.

We grow because hundreds of thousands of gay and lesbian Christians who are despised and rejected by the Catholic and Protestant churches of their childhood have no where else to go. Approximately forty percent of our own members are former Roman Catholic Christians who find themselves without a spiritual home because of your current policies discriminating against gay and lesbian people.

Even as you celebrate World Youth Day, you are rejecting hundreds of thousands of your best and brightest young people. Because you are unwilling to deal forthrightly with the new biblical, pastoral, psychological and scientific data about homosexuality, you are advocating an anti-gay policy that leads to the suffering and death of God's children in your care.

In an angry warning to His own disciples, Jesus was very clear about what should happen to religious leaders whose false teachings lead to the suffering of God's children: "It is better that a millstone be placed about your neck and that you be drowned in the sea . . ."

Please, sir, reconsider these tragic policies based on ancient ignorance and fear. If you love us sinners but hate our sins as you say, then meet with us, reconsider the data, discuss the options, and pray with us for the healing of God's church and the reconciliation of all believers.

You are the shepherd of a great and growing flock. Jesus said, "The good shepherd leaves the ninety and nine who are safely in the fold and risks his life to rescue one lost sheep." We aren't lost. We haven't strayed. Our shepherd has chased us from the flock.

On this World Youth Day, show the kind of courage you have shown so many times in the past. Open your arms to all of God's children including gay and lesbian believers who would worship and witness with you.

> In the name of Christ and for His Kingdom's sake,
> Mel White, Dean of the Cathedral

Cathedral of Hope, 5910 Cedar Springs Road, Dallas, Texas 75235

Author's Notes, References, and Resources

For more information on the biblical passages misused to condemn gay men and lesbians:

Boswell, John. *Christianity, Social Tolerance, and Homosexuality: Gay People in Western Europe from the Beginning of the Christian Era to the Fourteenth Century.* Chicago: University of Chicago Press, 1980.
(Winner of the 1981 American Book Award for History).

Mollenkott, Virginia Ramey, Scanzoni, Letha. *Is the Homosexual My Neighbor?* San Francisco: HarperCollins, 1978.

For more information on the history of our current negative attitudes about masturbation and homosexuality:

Kosnik, Anthony, ed. *Human Sexuality: New Directions in American Catholic Thought.* New York: Paulist Press, 1977.

To better understand the suffering of European gay men under the Nazi Third Reich:

Burleigh, Michael, and Wolfgang Wippermann. *The Racial State: Germany 1933-1945.* London: Cambridge University Press, 1991.

Plant, Richard. *The Pink Triangle: The Nazi War Against Homosexuals.* New York: Henry Holt & Co., 1986.

To better understand the connection between antigay religious rhetoric and the current surge of violence against gays and lesbians:

Comstock, Gary David. *Violence Against Lesbians and Gay Men*. New York: Columbia University Press, 1991.

De Cecco, John P. *Bashers, Baiters & Bigots: Homophobia in American Society*. New York: Harrington Park Press, 1985.

Greene, Bette. *The Drowning of Stephan Jones*. New York: Bantam Books, 1991.

For up-to-date discussions of gay and lesbian activism:

Duberman, Martin. *Stonewall*. New York: Dutton, 1993.

Goss, Robert. *Jesus Acted Up: A Gay and Lesbian Manifesto*. San Francisco: HarperCollins, 1993.

Signorile, Michelangelo. *Queer In America,* New York: Random House, 1993.

For a dramatic, case-by-case history of discrimination against gays and lesbians in the armed services:

Shilts, Randy. *Conduct Unbecoming: Gays & Lesbians in the U.S. Military*. New York: St. Martin's Press, 1993.

For more information on the politics of the religious right:

Diamond, Sara, *Spiritual Warfare: The Politics of the Christian Right*. Boston: South End Press, 1989.

A Few Ideas to Help You
and Your Community

KEEP THE RELIGIOUS RIGHT
FROM DOING MORE WRONG

1. Know who they are and what they are saying. Tune them in!

2. Begin to collect their books, their magazines, their direct-mail pieces. Find the passages that are most offensive. Put them on display.

3. Begin to videotape their television harangues, their radio sermons, and talk shows. Make the tapes available to your friends. Create listener guides.

4. Start your own version of a local "to prevent a gay/lesbian" holocaust museum. Demonstrate the similarity between Hitler's Third Reich and the current tactics of the religious right.

5. Help your gay and lesbian friends see that their parents and friends are also brainwash victims of antigay rhetoric. Teach them how to respond.

6. For example, if you have young "lesbigay" friends or students, before holidays or vacations, roleplay the inevitable encounters with family and friends. Get people prepared for those difficult home visits.

7. Encourage people not to argue or talk back, but to stick to their limits. "Mom, you know I love you, but I just won't talk about that."

8. Once we listen closely to the sources of the homophobic propaganda that our parents and friends quote back at us, we are better prepared to smile, change the conversation, or walk away and not be damaged in the process.

9. After vacations or holidays, get your young friends together to share their war stories, to congratulate or to comfort one another.

10. Begin immediately to build networks of support inside and outside the "lesbigay" communities. Isolation will lead to our undoing. Find mainline pastors, priests, rabbis, politicians, who support us against the rhetorical right. Invite them to visit, to share, to lunch.

11. Organize your new coalitions to call radio and television stations quoting the offenders, suggesting they be taken off the air. Follow up with public or even legal pressure when the inflammatory rhetoric continues. Write letters to the editors against the columnists of the religious right.

12. Create a list of the common words and phrases used by the religious right to mislead and misinform. For example: *special rights, gay agenda, sexual preference, gay lifestyle, ex-gay.* Define and discuss these words/phrases with your friends. Help them understand and combat these words in their daily conversations with friends and coworkers.

13. Find your most eloquent spokespersons and create a speaker bureau, offering talks, panels, and discussions on the rhetoric of the religious right to luncheon clubs, mainline churches, schools.

14. Use their antigay videotapes (e.g. *The Gay Agenda*) to illustrate the hate-mongering methods of the religious right. The more our non-gay/lesbian friends and neighbors hear of the extremist right, the more they will understand our plight and support

our cause. "That's going too far" is a major, positive statement for a person on the fence.

15. Commend TV and radio programs/stations that take on the religious right or oppose their causes. Support sponsors who don't give in to their blackmail. Praise politicians who dare to stand against them. Organize against the antigay ballot measures. Provide voter registration at church.

16. Don't shout back with oversimplifications, half-truths, or lies even if they support our point. Tell the truth!

17. And above all, don't give in to the barrage of misinformation, hyperbole, half-truths, and lies. Believe in our cause. It is just. Truth will win the war even though some of us will be wounded and even killed in the battle. Love your enemies. It is still the best weapon we have against the religious right and those who believe their lies.

18. Order *Fight the Right,* an action kit by the National Gay & Lesbian Task Force (110 pages, $10) packed with effective ideas for understanding and confronting the religious right, from NGLTF, 1734 Fourteenth St. NW, Washington, DC 20009. Or, *Challenging the Christian Right—The Activists Handbook* (290 pages, $20) from the Institute for First Amendment Studies, PO Box 589, Great Barrington, MA 01230 (413-274-3786). Get on both organizations' mailing lists. They are doing justice!

Gay/Lesbian Religious Organizations

Affirm (United Church of Canada)
    PO Box 62, Station H, Toronto, Ontario M4C 5H7, Canada
Affirmation/Mormons
    (213) 255-7251
Affirmation/United Methodist
    (708) 475-0499
American Baptists Concerned
    (415) 465-8652
American Friends Service Committee—Lesbian and Gay Program
    (Quaker) (503) 230-9427
Axios—Eastern & Orthodox Christian Gay Men & Women
    (212) 989-6211

Brethren/Mennonite Council for Lesbian and Gay Concerns (BMC)
    (202) 462-2595

Catholic Coalition for Gay Civil Rights
    (718) 629-2927
Christian Scientist
    (415) 485-1881
Common Bond (former Jehovah's Witnesses and Mormons)
    Ellwood, PA 16117

Dignity (Catholic)
   (800) 877-8797

Evangelicals Concerned, Dr. Ralph Blair
   (212) 517-3171
Evangelicals Together (West Coast region)
   (213) 656-8570

Friends for Lesbian/Gay Concerns (Quakers)
   (215) 234-8424

GLAD (Disciples of Christ/Christian Churches)
   (206) 725-7001

Honesty (Southern Baptist)
   (502) 893-0783

Integrity (Episcopal)
   (201) 868-2485

Lambda Christian Fellowship
   (310) 970-1326
Lutherans Concerned/North America, Inc.
   (919) 387-0824

National Gay Pentecostal Alliance
   (518) 372-6001

Presbyterians for Lesbian/Gay Concerns
   (908) 249-1016

Seventh-Day Adventist Kinship
   (213) 876-2076 (west)
   (617) 436-5950 (east)

United Church Coalition, Lesbian/Gay Concerns (United Church of
   Christ) (614) 593-7301
Universal Fellowship of Metropolitan Community Churches
   (UFMCC) (213) 464-5100

World Congress of Gay & Lesbian Jewish Organizations
Washington, DC 20036

Zen Center for Gay and Lesbian Community
(213) 461-5042

All Saints Episcopal Church, 132 N. Euclid, Pasadena, CA 91101
(818) 796-1172

Lesbian/Gay Political and Cultural Organizations

Contact your local chapter or:

Act-Up: AIDS Coalition to Unleash Power, (212) 564-AIDS.
Act-Up NY, 135 W. Twenty-ninth St., Tenth Floor, NY, NY 10001.

DQ: Digital Queers (computer professionals), 5584 Castro St., Suite 150, San Francisco, CA 94114, (415) 826-0500.

GALA Choruses, Inc. Gay and Lesbian Choruses of America, 1617 E. Twenty-second Ave., Denver, CO 80205, (303) 832-1526.

Gay Games & Cultural Festival, 19 W. Twenty-first St., Suite 1202, NY, NY 10010.

GLAAD: Gay and Lesbian Alliance Against Defamation, Inc.
Call local chapter or GLADD/New York, 80 Varick St., Suite 3E, NY, NY 10013, (212) 966-1700.

Human Rights Campaign Fund, 1012 Fourteenth Street, NW, Suite 607, Washington, DC 20005, (202) 628-4160.

Lambda Legal Defense and Education Fund, Inc. 666 Broadway, NY, NY 10012, (212) 995-8585.

Names Project Foundation, 2362 Market St., San Francisco, CA 94114.

National Gay and Lesbian Task Force, 1734 Fourteenth St., NW, Washington, DC 20009, (202) 332-6483.

National Lesbian and Gay Journalists Association, PO Box 423048, San Francisco, CA 94142, (415) 905-4690.

P-FLAG, Parents, Families, and Friends of Lesbians and Gays, 1012 Fourteenth St., N.W., #700, Washington, DC 20005, (202) 638-4200.

Project 10, c/o Dr. Virginia Uribe, Fairfax High School, 7850 Melrose Ave., Los Angeles, CA 90046, (213) 651-5200.

Victory Fund, 1012 Fourteenth St., N.W., Suite 707, Washington, DC 20005, (202) 842-8679.

Dedication

My sincere and enthusiastic thanks to all 20,500 P-FLAG (Parents, Families, and Friends of Lesbians and Gays) members serving our community through chapters in fifty states, Canada, and ten other nations. Whoever you are, whatever your sexual orientation, get to know your friends and neighbors at P-FLAG. Their personal and small group support system and their creative, easy-to-understand books, tapes, and pamphlets are saving lives, healing wounded souls and mending broken families.

DIRECTORY:

NATIONAL HEADQUARTERS:
Parents, Families and Friends of Lesbians and Gays
1012 14th St. N.W. #700
Washngton, DC 20005
202-638-4200

PACIFIC NORTHWEST: Alaska, Idaho, Montana, Oregon Washington, and Western Canada
Candace Steele
83 N. Wightman St.
Ashland, OR 97520
503-482-4017

MID-PACIFIC: Northern California, Nevada, and Utah
Samuel Thoron
3045 Pacific Ave.
San Francisco, CA 94115
415-921-6902

SOUTHERN PACIFIC: Southern California, Arizona, and Hawaii
Adele Start
P.O. Box 24565
Los Angeles, CA 90024
213-472-8952

MOUNTAINS: Colorado, New Mexico, Oklahoma, Kansas, and Wyoming
Nancy McDonald
P.O. Box 52800
Tulsa, OK 74152
918-749-4901

GREAT PLAINS: Iowa, Minnesota, Missouri, Nebraska, North Dakota, South Dakota, and Central Canada
Jean Durgin–Clinchard
P.O. Box 4374
Lincoln, NE 68504
402-435-4688

CENTRAL: Illinois, Indiana, Kentucky, Michigan, and Wisconsin
Marie Jenkins
P.O. Box 5141
Louisville, KY 40255
502-454-5635

SOUTHERN: Alabama, Arkansas, Louisiana, Mississippi, and Texas
Sandra Moore
P.O. Box 48387
Fort Worth, TX 76148
817-498-4855

NORTH ATLANTIC: Pennsylvania, New Jersey, and New York
Jackie Schulze
301 Chestnut St. #1104
Harrisburg, PA 17101
717-238-2376

NORTEAST: Connecticut, Maine, Massachusetts, New Hampshire, Rhode Island, Vermont, and Eastern Canada
Jean Genasci
P.O. Box 55
South Hadley, MA 01075-0055
413-532-4883

MID-ATLANTIC: Delaware, District of Columbia, Maryland, Virginia, West Virginia, and Ohio
Beverly Southerland
P.O. Box 28009
Washington, DC 20038
703-768-0411

SOUTHEAST: Florida, Georgia, North Carolina, South Carolina, Tennessee, and Puerto Rico
Joyce Rankin
P.O. Box 722
Dallas, NC 28034
704-922-9273

The Cathedral of Hope

For a complete list of lesbian/gay/bisexual resources, goods, and services (books, video and audiotapes, gifts, Christian supplies):

Sources of Hope
c/o The Cathedral of Hope
PO Box 35466
Dallas, TX 75235
(214) 351-1901
(214) 351-6099 (fax)

For information about the Cathedral of Hope, about the Cathedral's TV and radio ministries, about forming a Circle of Hope in your area, or about the Truth in Love campaign:

The Cathedral of Hope
PO Box 35466
Dallas, TX 75235
(214) 351-1901
(214) 351-6099 (fax)

For information about the University Fellowship of Metropolitan Community Churches or a congregation in your area:

UFMCC
5300 Santa Monica Blvd.
Suite 304
Los Angeles, CA 90029
(213) 464-5100

For personal correspondence:

Dr. Mel White,
Dean of the Cathedral
P.O. Box 35466
Dallas, TX 75235

Special Thanks

To Lyla, who loved me, believed in me and defended me, even when she was feeling so much grief and pain herself.

To my children, Erinn and Michael, for loving and trusting me, and for never once looking embarrassed or ashamed.

To my parents, Carl and Faythe, and to Lyla's mother, Marjorie, who watched with fear and grief, but never stopped caring.

To our siblings, Marshall and Bunny, Sharon and Grant, and to their children, who supported us at every difficult stage.

To my partner, Gary Nixon, who brings me comfort and strength by his very presence.

To Richard Baltzell, whose wisdom as a friend and skills as an editor helped sustain me from the beginning; to Philip and Janet Yancey, who stayed on as my friends and confidants in spite of everything; to Ken Martin and Tom Cole, Marguerite Shuster, Jay Jarman, Kerry Sieh and Tom Malloy, Dan Stohler, Walt and Fran Becker, Elsa Yolas Legesse, Chuck Gee and others of you who proved to be my friends for the long haul; to Thomas Montgomery, Casey Taylor, Jonathan Potts, Bob Alexander, Gary Cooper, Marty James, and so many other good friends who have died. I miss you!

To George Regas, and the people of All Saints Episcopal in Pasadena, California; to Ralph Blair and the men and women of Evangelicals Concerned, especially those old friends in Pasadena and Laguna Beach; to Troy Perry, and the clergy and laity of the Universal Fellowship of Metropolitan Community Churches; to Chris Glaser,

George Lynch, and to my first lesbian and gay friends at West Hollywood Presbyterian and M.C.C. in the Valley; to D. B., D. C., D. S., S. S., P. G., O. O., S. B., and S. Z.; to Lemar Rodgers and our Truth in Love campaign volunteers; and especially to Michael Piazza, Senior Pastor, and the staff and people of the Cathedral of Hope in Dallas, our new home.

To my agent, Alan Nevins; to my friends at Simon & Schuster, especially Chuck Adams, Senior Trade Editor; and to all of you who made helpful suggestions about the style and content of this book as it was being birthed.

To everyone who brought light into my dark closet and set my feet on the road to freedom, I am grateful. With your help, I found my way into the light, and one day soon, with the help of millions of thoughtful and caring Americans like you, we will win this battle against bigotry and fear, and learn to love one another as Jesus commanded us.